Ethnographic Writing

Edited by Bob Jeffrey & Lisa Russell

E & E
PUBLISHING

© 2018 E&E Publishing

First edition published by E&E Publishing, New Cottage, Painswick, Stroud, Gloucestershire, GL6 6UA

ISBN: 978-0-9931085-7-0

Printed and bound in the United Kingdom by
4edge Ltd, 7a Eldon Way Industrial Estate, Hockley, Essex, SS5 4AD.

E&E Publishing

We publish educational ethnographies between 20-80,000 words of which this is our eighth.

The implications of 'New Populism' on Education
Edited by Yalız Akbaba and Bob Jeffrey (2017)

'Doing Education' Between Monolingual Norms and Multilingual Realities An Ethnography of Multilingualism in Early Childhood Education and Care
Claudia Seele (2016)

Performativity in Education: An international collection of ethnographic research on learners' experiences
Edited by Annette Rasmussen, Jan Gustafsson and Bob Jeffrey (2014)

The primary school in testing times
Bob Jeffrey (2014)

Testing times in English primary schools 1992-2012: The effects of a performative culture on teachers' and pupils' relations and identities
Bob Jeffrey (2013) (E-Book)

Performativity in UK Education: Ethnographic cases of its effects, agency and reconstructions
Edited by Bob Jeffrey and Geoff Troman (2012)

Bullied into it: Bullying, power, and the conduct of conduct
Paul Horton (2011)

Understanding Pupil Resistance – Integrating Gender, Ethnicity and Class: An educational ethnography
Lisa Russell (2011)

Ethnography and Education Book Series – Tufnell Press

The postmodern professional: Contemporary learning practices, dilemmas and perspectives
Edited by Karen Borgnakke, Marianne Dovemark and Sofia Marques da Silva, (2017)

Identity and social interaction in a multi-ethnic classroom
Ruth Barley (2014)

Learning care lessons: Literacy, love, care and solidarity
Maggie Feeley (2014)

Learner biographies and learning cultures: Identity and apprenticeship in England and Germany
Michaela Brockmann (2013)

Young people's influence and democratic education: Ethnographic studies in upper secondary schools
Edited by Elisabet Ohrn, Lisbeth Lundahl and Dennis Beach (2011)

Ritual and Identity: The staging and performing of rituals in the lives of young people
Christoph Wulf et al. (2010)

How to do Educational Ethnography
Edited by Geoffrey Walford (2008)

Performing English with a postcolonial accent: Ethnographic narratives from Mexico
Angeles Clemente and Michael J. Higgins (2008)

Education and the Commodity Problem: Ethnographic Investigations of Creativity and performativity in Swedish Schools
Dennis Beach and Marianne Dovemark (2007)

Creative Learning Practices: European Experiences
Edited by Bob Jeffrey (2007)

Researching Education Policy: Ethnographic Experiences
Geoff Troman, Bob Jeffrey and Dennis Beach (2006)

Table of Contents

---

1. Karen Barad (2007; 2012) uses this term to describe reading for differences that matter in their fine details.

Introduction

Writing is fundamental to the ethnographer, it plays a major role through the collection and development of fieldnotes; reflective and reflexive memos and diaries; to re-present contexts for readers and to create analytical contributions for knowledge via dissemination. However, the uses, purposes and practices of writing are imbued with problematic aspects concerning: philosophy – modes of interpretation, writer values and perspectives; epistemology – validity of analysis and representation; the role of the self as a research instrument and the researcher's relationships to the context and the people within them. A further complication is the question of what defines 'writing', whether drawings, pictures and multi-modal re-presentations can be considered as constituting ethnographic writing.

This series collates eleven articles that have been gathered from across The Ethnography and Education global network, the collection brings together various ethnographers' experiences and reflective practices regarding what is ethnographic writing and how we do it. The book is thus relevant to anyone engaged in Ethnography in any discipline because the articles deal with many common issues and practices including engagement with members of the research site; ethical issues of ethnographic writing; ethnographer self-awareness; performative writing; new materialist approaches and the role of ethnographic writing. There is a significant literature on the varied aspects of fieldnotes, the writing of ethnographic texts and the re-presentations of ethnographic research. Indeed, much of this literature is referenced in this collection and conveyed in the first section that includes a literature review (see Hammersley-1) evaluating the past and current thinking regarding ethnography and writing, so a review of relevant literature is not required in this Introduction.

The articles are divided into three sections: **Writing and fieldnotes, Fieldwork writing practices** and **Researcher relationships with responders and researcher colleagues**. Each section contains new and possibly controversial perspectives concerning writing and ethnography and it is hoped readers will find something useful, as well as issues which they would wish to debate with colleagues.

The first section 'Writing and Fieldnotes', includes Hammersley's review of literature focused on ethnographic writing (Hammersley-1). This brief guide lists some of the literature from 1977 to 2015, includes an annotated bibliography, and provides a useful introduction that outlines the types of discussion available about writing and ethnography. The same author then turns to the more practical aspect of the process of writing itself and identifies some key aspects that need to be taken into account in the course of writing research reports.

Delamont takes this section further by comparing the nature of fieldnotes for anthropologists to later social science ethnographers and notes the differences in attitude to them; the former being publicly reflective about them in a continuous stream of reviews and the latter less interested overall in examining fieldnotes' relations to the self. She suggests that Jackson's theorizing of the liminal and mediating functions of fieldnotes from the anthropological field should be considered by ethnographers as a useful tool. She then goes on to explore how perceiving the status of fieldnotes as 'boundary objects' and 'trading zones' developed by Susan Leigh Star would be useful in educational ethnography.

Borgnakke appears to take a 'left field' alternative perspective concerning the role of fieldnotes and her reflections of them differ considerably from those of Jackson and Star in the Delamont article which acts as a useful counter for academic debate in this area. Borgnakke describes initial fieldnotes taken in the research context as 'observation protocols/diaries', which mainly include chronological text-collection - the mapping of the day, but also containing the necessary facts and information of time/place/activity/number of participants. She calls this data 'cardinal texts' and the moment of collection as a 'cardinal point'. This data collection is examined in detail with examples from the field, including relevant matrices and she then moves onto to explicate the third characteristic 'cardinal writing' an analytical challenge for 'the fieldworker', 'the analyst' and 'the writer'.

The second section describes further alternative **Fieldwork writing practices** focusing on representation, multi modal approaches (Thomson, Wieland) and ethnographic writing as persuasive rhetoric (Jeffrey).

Thomson reviews the troubled issue of 'representation', again harking back to the anthropologists and she examines how they took up the notion of representation and why, and then considers what kind of trouble the concept is now facing. After an extensive investigation of the problems of subjectivity and representation she argues that in the UK, not only is the study of education institutionally and organisationally detached from anthropology, but ethnography is generally not part of essential methods courses taken by social science masters and doctoral students. She suggests that we need to re-engage with the anthropological tradition and focus on questions of text genre, the researcher self in the text, participant responses and the nature of knowledge and knowledge production provides some leads that we educators might follow. Similarly, she suggests that writing research itself also offers matters for educational ethnographers to explore, areas which move well beyond the notion of representation to considerations of what writing does in the world and for the world. This article is, according to the author, a text-based think-piece, to raise issues that educational writers might consider when thinking about the nature of the ethnographic texts that they want to write.

This debate about the nature of representation in ethnographic writing leads neatly to the article by Jeffrey. He is in no doubt, following Anderson, that written fieldnotes of the research context can include texts that are and persuasive, as long as the whole research methodology is steeped in a social science approach that satisfies academic demands of validity. He argues that his writing in the field was based on literary forms, persuasive rhetoric, metaphors and empathetic expressions as he documented in detail the lives of the people he researched. Unlike Borgnakke he did not collect chronological fieldnotes but evocative descriptions. He argues that the credibility, plausibility and validity attached to his work, was not only due to analytical insights, but also to the literary forms he used in representations of people's lives. His argument is that if the evocations appear to the reader to reflect a familiar (subtle) reality then the writing can be considered valid and authentic. He then explores how a literary approach underpins five types of writing: fieldnotes, memos and main narratives; memos; main texts and whole narratives.

The article by Wieland also challenges social science ethnographic practices in education research by suggesting that researchers should pay more attention to a range of modes of data collection, as Thompson proposes above. In her research, Wieland includes textual production as well as collages of photos and drawings with the aim of extending and refining the analytical scope of her ethnographic study and writing. She argues that writing has its limitations as do the others, but if used as different sensory, medial and spatial modes of thinking, this entanglement of different modes of interpretation significantly enhances the research process. Multi-sensory and multi-modal aspects are used as an analytical tool that leads to a deeper or thicker form of analysis. The author includes a number of visual and sonic artefacts alongside written examples, which become an integral part of the research outcome. She suggests that these research results, which include textual, visual and auditory accounts, should be regarded as aesthetic products or artefacts of responsive research and can be understood as a form of new knowledge for the research community.

The last section focuses back to the anthropological issue raised by Delamont, that of reflecting on the **Relationship between fieldnote writer, responder and co-researchers**.

Milstein, Clemente and Guerrero argue that Ethnographers can gain greater insights into 'what's going here' if after taking initial fieldnotes they engage the people upon whom they are focusing in conversation and review collaboratively their notes with them. They argue that this approach is sometimes ignored if young people are being researched as researchers might consider them too immature to take part in this exercise. They provide two illustrations, the first with younger children and an older group and provide details of how they let themselves, the researchers, 'be taught by the children'. They show how they used drawings, writing and included conversations about the children's and the researchers' representations the ethnographers learnt about the responder represented themselves and how their lives. The authors claim that the incorporation of children as collaborators in the processes of writing fieldnotes, questions and transforms the adult ethnographers' interpretations.

Russell continues this theme by arguing that Ethnographers should be aware of how fieldwork research and ethnographic writing constructs and (re)produces relationships, day-to-day experiences, cultures, participants and the researchers' identities. She suggests that all writing is a political act and that that all too often research methods texts remain relatively hushed about how fieldnotes are taken and how they are then used and often morphed for dissemination and publication purposes. In this article participants are viewed as active agents who are knowledgeable about wider hegemonic inequalities and are capable of (re)producing inequalities themselves. The author argues that children and young people generate multiple voices which are negotiated within and sometimes beyond the field and it is the ethnographer's responsibility to be aware of these power imbalances, to actively try and manage them and to listen carefully to how marginalised groups such as children and young people articulate their positions. The article raises questions regarding the effects of allowing participants to view, share and contribute to fieldnotes and the implications this has in terms of validity. How the day-to-day activities, participants and ethnographers' identities are represented and (co)constructed in publications are also considered.

Parker-Webster and Raggl bring us back to the issues raised by Delamont concerning the anthropological interest in reflecting continually on the use of written fieldnotes. Parker-Webster follows another theme in the collection, that of managing a wider set of data. She argues that fieldwork is no longer limited to in-person visits to geographic locations of study as it is now extended beyond the physical site through the use of technology. Classrooms and lunchrooms located within the larger school building may well be supplemented by outdoor classroom spaces of playgrounds, sports fields, and school garden plots coexisting with online classrooms. Online websites may provide spaces for asynchronous class activities, such as online discussion boards or provide a collaborative writing space for students to post class assignments. Such blended classrooms may also incorporate other physical locations outside of the school building, which are "visited" in real time through synchronous online video conferencing spaces. As such, the educational ethnographer can now find herself moving within and across offline and online field(s) along with her participants in the course of the school day (Parker Webster and Silva 2013). However, she goes further and argues that ethnographic data collection activities can be compared with and enhanced by participant scientific data collection to ascertain overlaps and similarities and the writing format of both is a common activity. The research itself takes place in educational sites where students, teachers and scientists conduct scientific inquiry within multiple spaces and the similarities between the participants' research activities and the ethnographic researcher are explored in detail and a matrix is developed. She uses a very useful concept of 'diffractive methodology" as explained by Barad (2007) and identifies and investigates the 'entanglements' of data collection and analysis to problematise the activity.

Raggl identifies some of the issues concerning the writing of fieldnotes in the field. She gives some examples from her own experience of the problematic nature of writing and its effect on her and those in the research context. She then argues that developing one's writing of fieldnotes can be enhanced by sharing fieldnotes with academic colleagues. She shows how she came to understand that writing fieldnotes is a craft and that sharing and comparing fieldnotes with others can help to develop this skilful practice and that fieldnotes can be lived differently. She takes us back to Delamont's argument that educational ethnography needs to adopt a similar approach to that of anthropology by arguing that the sharing of fieldnotes is an attempt to overcome the 'lonesome' activity of carrying out fieldwork; seeing it much more as a joint activity.

We hope that the readers of this collection will find much that is interesting and enlightening, but also that it stimulates debate and discussion concerning the problematic activity of ethnographic writing.

SECTION ONE

Writing & Fieldnotes

Ethnographic writing: a brief guide to the literature[2]

Martyn Hammersley

At one time very little attention was given to the character of ethnographic writing. Minimal advice was offered to students about this aspect of research, and virtually no analytic attention was devoted to how ethnographers formulate their accounts of the social world. The assumption was that 'writing up' research is relatively straightforward, a matter of general writing skills, with analysis being the separate and more challenging part of the research process. In the 1980s, this situation changed dramatically (see Atkinson, 2012). Crucial here, to some degree, was a revival of interest in the ancient discipline of rhetoric (Dixon, 1971; Vickers, 1988 and 1990; Barilli, 1989). But even more significant was the influence of structuralism and post-structuralism (on which see, for instance, Dews, 1987; Gutting, 2001, 2011), the emergence of semiotics (Cobley, 2010; Chandler, 2017), as well as the influence of constructionism more generally (Burr, 2015; Weinberg, 2014). As a result, much greater attention came to be given to the study of texts, and this included those produced by historians, natural scientists and social scientists (see, for instance, White, 1973 and 1978; McCloskey, 1983 and 1985; Nelson, et al 1987; Simons, 1988; Halliday and Martin, 1996; Martin and Veel 1998; Levine, 2011).

As part of this, there was a growth of interest not just in the monographs and articles produced by ethnographic work but also in the writing that takes place during its course, notably in fieldnotes. Some of this interest took the form of discussions of the practical aspects of how to write ethnographic or qualitative accounts (Becker, 1986; Wolcott, 1990/2009; Richardson, 1990b; Emerson *et al.* 1995/2011; Woods, 2006; Gullion 2016), but there was also literature of a more theoretical kind: concerned with the rhetorical devices that ethnographers deploy, the presuppositions on which these are based, the functions they serve, and so on.[3] Much of this occurred within anthropology; ethnomethodology and Science and Technology Studies were also significant contexts. A key text at this time was Clifford and Marcus's *Writing Culture* (Clifford and Marcus, 1986); though there had been significant work analysing ethnographic and other social scientific texts before this (Brown, 1977; Marcus and Cushman, 1982; Atkinson, 1983; Edmondson, 1984). This book prompted a flurry of writing

---

2. This chapter is a revised and updated version of a piece published as Social Research Update, Issue 5, in March 1993. This publication is hosted by the Department of Sociology, University of Surrey, Guildford GU2 7XH, England. It is available online at: http://sru.soc.surrey.ac.uk/index.html

3. These two types of literature are not completely distinct, but there is a significant difference in predominant orientation.

about ethnographic writing in the late 1980s and early 1990s, including most notably the books by Geertz, (1988), van Maanen, (1988), Atkinson, (1990 and 1992), Sanjek, (1990), and Behar and Gordon, (1995).

The interest in ethnographic rhetoric was often associated with criticism of conventional forms of anthropological and sociological writing, on philosophical and political grounds: they were charged with spuriously claiming the authority of science for a neo-colonialist, Western, white, and/or male worldview. Analysis focused on how this purported authority is constituted in and through the discursive strategies employed. A closely related theme was how ethnographic writing shared many of the same tropes and patterns as fiction and travel writing. These criticisms prompted the development of 'experimental' new forms of ethnographic work (Richardson, 1994). Examples of this new writing included: Crapanzano, 1980; Shostak, 1981; Dwyer, 1982; Kreiger, 1983; Mulkay, 1985; Dorst, 1989; Rose, 1989; and Ashmore, 1989. However, it would be wrong to imply that a consensus underlay this new trend. Nor was it received uncritically (see Gordon, 1988; Sangren, 1988; Caplan, 1988/89; Mascia-Lees, et al. 1989; Polier and Roseberry, 1989; Roth, 1989; Spencer, 1989; Hammersley, 1993, 1995: ch5).

This concern with the presuppositions and functions, politics and poetics, of ethnographic writing did not, initially, have much influence in the field of educational research, though see de Castell and Walker's (1991) rhetorical analysis of Shirley Brice Heath's *Ways with Words*. Furthermore, from the mid-1990s onwards, interest in the character of ethnographic writing waned somewhat. However, in the present century, there have been signs of a revival of interest, notably in the appearance of a new edition of van Maanen's *Tales of the Field* (2011) and of Sanjek's book on fieldnotes (Sanjek and Tratner, 2015), edited volumes by Waterston and Vesperi (2011), Starn (2015) Wulff (2016), and various other contributions, such as Tjora, 2006, Denzin, 2013, and Richardson and St Pierre, 2018. There were also contributions within particular fields, including education (see Bagley 2009a; Walford, 2009a, White, 2009, VanSlyke-Briggs, , Sparkes, 2009, Sikes, 2012, Coles and Thomson, 2016, Hohti, 2016,) and the study of organisations (see Fox, 1996, Humphreys and Watson, 2009, Schwartz-Shea and Yanow, 2009, Mahadevan, 2012). Some 'confessional tales' (in van Maanen's terms) about writing have also appeared, for example Stanley (2015). And there have been further developments in the presentation of ethnographic work in the form of novels, drama, dance, and poetry (Pfohl, 1992; Bagley, 2009b; Phipps and Saunders, 2009; Bagley and Castro-Salazar, 2012; Holmes, 2012; Conquergood, 2013; Leavy, 2015; Elliott and Culhane, 2017). There has even been an experimental introduction to ethnography written as a play in seven acts (Pachirat, 2018). Finally, we should note the growth in interest of autoethnography, much of which relies on literary forms (see, for instance,

Ellis, 2004; Reed-Danahay, 1997, Holman Jones et al. 2013, Bochner, 2016; see also Delamont, 2010).[4]

In the remainder of this chapter I pick out a number of key texts that discuss the theory and practice of ethnographic writing, giving brief outlines of their content. The bibliography includes all references plus additional relevant items.

Ashmore, M. (1989)

This book, based on Ashmore's PhD thesis, is a sustained attempt to exemplify and elaborate the concept of reflexivity as it had arisen in Science and Technology Studies in the 1980s (see also Woolgar, 1988). It does this through deploying a variety of literary forms. For example, the initial overview of the chapters is produced as a purported entry in an 'unfinished encyclopaedia'. The literature review takes the form of a lecture ('given, perhaps, by the author, perhaps to undergraduate students') on 'What is the sociology of scientific knowledge?' in which the lecturer is heckled by some of the authors he is discussing who suddenly appear at the back of the lecture hall. And the 'conclusion' is a fictional account of the then yet-to-happen viva of Ashmore the PhD candidate.

Atkinson, P. (1990)

The author is primarily concerned with displaying the textual strategies used in traditional kinds of ethnographic writing. He examines: the sorts of descriptions that ethnographers provide, and how these rely on background knowledge on the part of readers; the role of titles and subtitles; the use of data extracts in the text, notably as one way that multiple voices are introduced; the structure of narratives recounting the biography of research projects or the course of events in some setting; the construction of characters and their relation to social types; the way in which ethnographic texts are structured by assumptions about gender; and the uses of irony.

Atkinson, P. (1992)

The central theme here is the tension between the complexity of social life and the rhetorical forms available to ethnographers for representing it. Atkinson considers the way in which the 'fields' ethnographers study are textually constructed, the writing of fieldnotes and transcription of audio-recordings, the various genres of ethnography, and some of the experimental textual strategies then being explored.

Brown, R.H. (1977)

An early but still illuminating analysis of the rhetorical/poetic strategies used by sociologists in their writing. Brown adopts a perspective he terms 'cognitive

---

4. Many relevant articles dealing with writing in the context of qualitative research generally are brought together in Atkinson and Delamont 2008.

aesthetics' in which both the humanities and the sciences are presented as concerned with 'making paradigms through which experience becomes intelligible'. He argues that choice among paradigms is not based on judgments of truth or falsity but on taste; though he insists that there are canons of taste. In the remainder of the book he seeks to document sociologists' use of various paradigms, for example their adoption of different points of view on the phenomena they describe.

Clifford, J. (1988)

A collection of mostly previously published articles by a key figure in the study of ethnographic writing in anthropology. Of particular interest is the article 'On ethnographic authority'. This examines the realism of conventional anthropological ethnography; and criticises it for hiding the process by which accounts are produced, and for defining the reality of the people studied from a Western viewpoint which is disguised as objective. The constructed and negotiated character of ethnographic research and writing is emphasised, along with its political context and role. Clifford advocates collaborative ethnography and texts that are multi-vocal and open-ended.

Clifford, J. and Marcus, G. (eds) (1986)

A very influential collection of articles dealing with various aspects of ethnography as text. Clifford's introduction is particularly useful. The chapters by Asad and Rabinow offer important qualifications, while that by Tyler exemplifies the 'postmodernist turn'. (See also Marcus and Fischer, 1986.)

Geertz, C. (1988)

Some of the concern with ethnographic writing arose out of the symbolic or interpretive anthropology of which Geertz is a major exponent. In this book he examines the contrasting rhetorical styles used by several prominent anthropologists: Levi-Strauss, Evans-Pritchard, Malinowski and Benedict.

Denzin, N.K. (1992)

In the context of a dispute about the accuracy of Whyte's *Street Corner Society*, Denzin questions the possibility of representation and the functions that 'representational' accounts perform.

Ghodsee, K. 2016

This book addresses many practical issues that arise in ethnographic writing, from word choice and the structure of chapters through to how to combine theory with ethnographic details. As the subtitle 'writing ethnographies that everyone can read' indicates, the book is concerned with making ethnographic writing accessible and appealing to non-academic audiences. Examples are provided from what the author, an anthropologist, takes to be model ethnographies. The book includes a bibliography listing other useful writing guides and what are deemed to be exemplary ethnographic studies in terms of readability and interest.

Gordon, D. (1988)
This is a critical review of Clifford and Marcus's *Writing Culture*, from a feminist perspective. Gordon argues that the new form of anthropology that this volume represents still marginalises women and feminism. And she questions the distinction between conventional and 'experimental' ethnography, denying that this is as significant as that between feminist and non-feminist work. She looks at what feminist anthropologists can learn from analyses of ethnographic rhetoric.

van Maanen, J. (1988; second edition 2011)
van Maanen identifies three broad types of ethnographic writing and the conventions that govern them. Examples of the first style – realist tales – involve the almost complete absence of the author from the text, scenes and events being described 'as they are'. Mundane details are provided about the phenomena described (of a kind that would only be available on the basis of first-hand observation), and quotations from participants are introduced to show that the author knows whereof he or she writes. In 'confessional tales' the ethnographer is centre-stage: what is told is the story of the research itself. Often such accounts take the form of modest and unassuming reports of the problems and struggles of the fieldworker, usually with a happy ending, though they can take a more heroic turn. Finally, there are what van Maanen calls 'impressionist tales'. In these, literary or even poetic effect is primary, allowing the author to exaggerate in order to make a point. It is suggested that impressionist tales may represent the contemporary world more effectively than realist accounts, and that narrative ingenuity on the part of ethnographers should be encouraged. The new edition contains a prologue, and an epilogue tracing developments in ethnography since the first edition was published. In the course of this the author outlines three further types of 'tale': structural tales, post-structural tales, and advocacy tales, though he does not document these in detail.

Marcus, G. and Cushman, D. (1982)
This identifies the dominant genre in anthropology as ethnographic realism, and lists its characteristic conventions, as well as examining the textual strategies that ethnographers use to establish their authority within this genre. At the same time the authors look at variations in rhetoric as much as commonalities. A persistent theme in their discussion is how ethnographers present particular places, events, people etc. as representing cultural wholes. Marcus and Cushman

also discuss experimental deviations from the realist pattern and look at how textual authority is achieved despite these deviations.

Narayan (2012)
This is a book that is primarily about writing ethnography, but draws heavily on Chekhov as a model, and some other literary sources. The primary focus, however, is not Chekhov's plays or his poetry but a non-fiction account he wrote of Sakhalin Island, a Russian penal colony. The focus of the book concerns how 'empirical details combined with literary flair can bring readers face to face with distant, different lives, enlarging a sense of human responsibility'.

Roth, P. A. (1989)
This article looks at the epistemological significance attributed to the literary devices used by ethnographers. In particular, the focus is on the argument that traditional ethnographic accounts conceal the author and therefore obscure her or his role in their construction. Roth claims that explicit self-reflection no more guarantees authenticity than does a pose of detachment. Finally, he challenges what he regards as the confusion of epistemological and political representativeness. Following the article there are responses from Clifford, Tyler and others, plus a reply by Roth.

Starn (ed.) 2015
This collection of essays was produced to mark the 25th anniversary of the publication of *Writing Culture* (Clifford and Marcus 1985). It includes essays by Clifford and Marcus, and by a range of other anthropologists, reflecting on its character, its reception, and its legacy; in particular, on the questions it raised about reflexivity and representation. These discussions take place, of course, against the background of considerable change in anthropology since *Writing Culture* was published: in the nature and focus of this discipline, in the theoretical influences upon and within it, and (not least) in the world it studies and that shapes it. The focus in most of the essays is on what lessons can be learned from this classic text for the pursuit of anthropological ethnography today.

Tyler, S. (1985)
Tyler argues that despite their appearance as representations of a world that has come to be known directly by the ethnographer, ethnographies work through reference and allusion to other texts. Furthermore, they draw on tropes and story forms that are common currency in Western culture. He also questions the legitimacy of dialogical presentation; suggesting that, like realist accounts, it too involves a pretence of representation. Instead he recommends an allegorical, post-modernist ethnography that evokes rather than represents.

Waterston and Vesperi (eds) (2009)
This is a collection of chapters about a wide variety of aspects of ethnographic writing, from stylistic considerations through to the notion of anthropology as a form of literature and to issues concerning politics and impact. Most of the authors are anthropologists, but there are also contributions from other disciplines and from outside the academy.

Webster, S. (1986)
This article considers ethnographic realism and criticisms of it from the point of view of Critical Theory. Various interpretations of the concept of realism are identified. Webster challenges some writers in the field for adopting an idealist position, and for not showing how the study of rhetoric can further a radical reorientation of ethnography. He argues that rather than ethnographic realism being an explicit application of fictional realist rhetoric, it represents an implicit adoption of some of the latter's techniques so as to mark ethnography off from literature and to present it as scientific. He considers the possibility of using the resources of literary realism for critical purposes, but rejects both this and formalistic experimentation in favour of ethnographic writing that self-consciously locates itself within its socio-historical situation.

Bibliography

Ashmore, M. (1989) *The Reflexive Thesis*, Chicago, University of Chicago Press.

Atkinson, P. (1983) 'Writing ethnography' in H.J.Helle (ed.) *Kultur und Institution*, Berlin, Duncker und Humblot.

Atkinson, P. (1990) *The Ethnographic Imagination: textual construction of reali*, London, Routledge.

Atkinson, P. (1992) *Understanding Ethnographic Texts*, Newbury Park, Sage.

Atkinson, P. (2012) 'The literary and rhetorical turn', in Delamont, S. (ed.) *Handbook of Qualitative Research in Education*, Cheltenham, Edward Elgar.

Atkinson, P. A. and Delamont, S. (eds) (2008) *Representing Ethnography: Reading, Writing and Rhetoric in Qualitative Research*, Four Volumes, Thousand Oaks CA, Sage.

Bagley, C. (2009a) 'Shifting boundaries in ethnographic methodology', *Ethnography and Education*, 4 (3), pp.251-254, DOI: 10.1080/17457820903170051

Bagley, C. (2009b) 'The ethnographer as impresario–joker in the (re) presentation of educational research as performance art: towards a performance ethic', *Ethnography and Education*, 4 (3), pp.283-300, DOI: 10.1080/17457820903170101

Bagley, C. and Castro-Salazar, R. (2012) Dance: making movement meaningful', in Delamont, S. (ed.) *Handbook of Qualitative Research in Education*, Cheltenham, Edward Elgar.

Baker, S. (1990) 'Reflection, doubt, and the place of rhetoric in postmodern social theory', *Sociological Theory*, 8 (2), pp. 232-45.

Barilli, R. (1989) *Rhetoric*, Minneapolis, University of Minnesota Press.

Becker, H.S. (1986) *Writing for Social Scientists*, Chicago, University of Chicago Press.

Behar, R. and Gordon, D. (Eds). (1995). *Women Writing Culture*. Berkeley: University of California Press.

Bochner, A. (2016) *Evocative Autoethnography: Writing lives and telling stories*, London, Routledge.

Brettell, C.B. (ed.) (1996) *When They Read What We Write: The Politics of Ethnography*. Westport CT: Bergin and Garvey.

Boon, J.A. (1982) *Other Tribes, Other Scribes*, Cambridge, Cambridge University Press.

Boon, J.A. (1983) 'Functionalists write too: Frazer, Malinowski and the semiotics of the monograph', *Semiotica*, 46 (2-4) pp. 131-49.

Brodkey, L. (1987) 'Writing Critical Ethnographic Narratives', *Anthropology and Education Quarterly*, 18 (2), pp. 67-76.

Brown, R.H. (1977) *A Poetic for Sociology*, New York, Cambridge University

Press. Second edition, Chicago, University of Chicago Press, 1989.

Brown, R.H. (1987) *Society as Text: essays on rhetoric, reason and society*, Chicago, University of Chicago Press.

Brown, R.H. (1989) *Social Science as Civic Discourse*, Chicago, University of Chicago Press.

Brown, R.H. (1990) 'Rhetoric, textuality, and the postmodern turn in sociological theory', *Sociological Theory*, 8 (2), pp. 188-97.

Burr, V. (2015) *Social Constructionism*, Third edition, London, Routledge.

Caplan, P. (1988/89) 'Engendering knowledge: the politics of ethnography', *Anthropology Today*, 4 (5-6), pp. 8-12 and 14-17.

Carrithers, M. (1988) 'The anthropologist as author: Geertz's Works and Lives', *Anthropology Today*, 5 (4), pp. 19-22.

Chandler, D. (2017) *Semiotics: the basics*, Third edition, London, Routledge.

Clifford, J. (1988) *The Predicament of Culture*, Cambridge, Mass., Harvard University Press.

Clifford, J. and Marcus, G. (1986) *Writing Culture: the poetics and politics of ethnography*, Berkeley, University of California Press.

Cobley, P. (2010) *The Routledge Guide to Semiotics*, London, Routledge.

Conquergood, D. (2013) *Cultural Struggles: Performance, Ethnography, Praxis*. Edited and introduced by E.P. Johnson. Ann Arbor: University of Michigan Press.

Crapanzano, V. (1980) *Tuhami: portrait of a Moroccan*, Chicago, University of Chicago Press.

Coles, R. and Thomson, P. (2016) 'Beyond records and representations: Inbetween writing in educational ethnography', *Ethnography and Education*, 11 (3), pp. 253-266, DOI:10.1080/17457823.2015.1085324

De Castell, S., and Walker, T. (1991) 'Identity, metamorphosis and ethnographic research: What kind of a story is *Ways With Words*?' *Anthropology and Education Quarterly, 22* (1), pp. 3-20.

Delamont, S. (2010) 'The only honest thing', *Ethnography and Education*, 4 (1) , pp.51-64.

Denzin, N.K. (1992) 'Whose Cornerville is it anyway?', *Journal of Contemporary Ethnography*, 21 (1), pp. 120-35.

Denzin, N.K. (2013) 'Writing and/as Analysis or Performing the World', in Flick, U. (ed.) *The SAGE Handbook of Qualitative Data Analysis*, London, Sage.

Dews, P. (1987) *Logics of Disintegration*, London, Verso.

Dixon, P. (1971) *Rhetoric*, London, Methuen.

Dorst, J.D. (1989) *The Written Suburb: an ethnographic dilemma*, Philadelphia, University of Pennsylvania Press.

Duneier, M. and Back, L. (2006) 'Voices from the sidewalk: Ethnography and writing race', *Ethnic and Racial Studies*, 29 (3), pp.543-565.

Dwyer, K. (1982) *Moroccan Dialogues*, Baltimore, Johns Hopkins University Press.

Edmondson, R. (1984) *Rhetoric in Sociology*, London, Macmillan.

Elliott, D. and Culhane, D. (eds) (2017) *A Different Kind of Ethnography: Imaginative Practices and Creative Methodologies*, Toronto, University of Toronto Press.

Ellis, C. (2004) *The Ethnographic I,* Walnut Creek, CA, Press.

Emerson, R. M., Fretz, R. and Shaw, L. (1995) *Writing Ethnographic Fieldnotes*, First edition, Chicago, University of Chicago Press. Second edition 2011.

Fox, S. (1996) 'Viral writing: Deconstruction, disorganization and ethnomethodology', *Scandinavian Journal of Management*, 12 (1), pp.89-108 (DOI 10.1016/0956-5221(95)00043-7)

Geertz, C. (1988) *Works and Lives: the anthropologist as author*, Stanford, Stanford University Press.

Ghodsee, K. (2016) *From Notes to Narrative: Writing ethnographies that everyone can read*, Chicago, University of Chicago Press.

Gordon, D. (1988) 'Writing culture, writing feminism: the poetics and politics of experimental ethnography', *Inscriptions*, 3 (4), 7-24.

Gullion, J. S. (2016) *Writing Ethnography*, Rotterdam, Sense Publishers.

Gutting, G. (2001) *French Philosophy in the Twentieth Century*, University Press.

Gutting, G. (2011) *Thinking the Impossible: French philosophy since 1960*, Oxford, Oxford University Press.

Halliday, M.A.K. and Martin, J.R (eds) (1996) *Writing Science: Literacy and Discursive Power*, London, The Falmer Press.

Hammersley, M. (1993) 'The rhetorical turn in ethnography', *Social Science Information*, 32 (1), pp. 23-37.

Hammersley, M. (1995) *The Politics of Social Research*, London, Sage.

Hohti, R. (2016) 'Children writing ethnography: children's perspectives and nomadic thinking in researching school classrooms', *Ethnography and Education*, 11 (1), pp.74-90, DOI:10.1080/17457823.2015.1040428

Holman Jones, S., Adams, T., and Ellis, C. (eds) (2013) *Handbook of Autoethnography*, Walnut Creek CA, Left Coast Press

Holmes, R. (2012) 'Performing findings: tales of the theatrical self', in Delamont, S. (ed.) *Handbook of Qualitative Research in Education*, Cheltenham, Edward Elgar.

Humphreys, M. and Watson, T. (2009) 'Ethnographic practices: From "writing-up ethnographic research" to "writing ethnography"' in Ybema, S., Yanow, D., Wels, H., and Kamsteeg, F. (eds) *Organizational Ethnography: Studying the Complexity of Everyday Life in organizations*, London, Sage.

Jackson, J.E. (1990) 'Déjà : the liminal qualities of anthropological fieldnotes', *Journal of Contemporary Ethnography*, 19, pp.8-43.

Kirby, V. (1991) 'Comment on Mascia-Lees, Sharpe and Cohen', *Signs*, 16, 2, pp394-408.

Krieger, S. (1979) 'Research and the construction of a text', in N.K. Denzin (ed.) *Studies in Symbolic Interactionism*, vol. 2, Greenwich, Connecticut, JAI Press.

Krieger, S. (1983) *The Mirror Dance: identity in a women's community*, Philadelphia, University of Pennsylvania Press.

Leavy, P. (2015) *Method Meets Art: Arts-Based Research Practice*, Second edition, New York, The Guilford Press.

Levine, G. (2011) *Darwin the Writer*, Oxford, Oxford University Press.

van Maanen, J. (1988) *Tales of the Field*, Chicago, Chicago University Press.

Van Maanen, J. (2011). *Tales of the Field*. Second edition. Chicago: University of Chicago Press.

McCloskey, D.N. (1983) 'The rhetoric of economics', *Journal of Economic Literature*, 21, pp.481-517.

McCloskey, D.N. (1985) *The Rhetoric of Economics*, Madison, University of Wisconsin Press.

Mahadevan, J. (2012) 'Translating nodes of power through reflexive ethnographic writing', *Journal of Organizational Ethnography*, 1 (1), pp.119-131. https://doi.org/10.1108/20466741211220714

Marcus, G. (1980) 'Rhetoric and the ethnographic genre in anthropological research', *Current Anthropology*, 21, pp.507-10.

Marcus, G. (1985) 'A timely rereading of Naven: Gregory Bateson as oracular essayist', *Representations*, 12, pp.66-82.

Marcus, G. and Cushman, D. (1982) 'Ethnography as text', *Annual Review of Sociology*, 11, pp.25-69.

Marcus, G. and Fischer, M. (1986) *Anthropology as Cultural Critique: an experimental moment in the human sciences,*Chicago, University of Chicago Press.

Martin, J.R. and Veel, R. (eds) (1998) *Reading Science: Critical and Functional Perspectives on Discourses of Science*, London, Routledge.

Mascia-Lees, F.E., Sharpe, P., and Cohen, C.B. (1989) 'The postmodernist turn in anthropology: cautions from a feminist perspective', *Signs*, 15 (11), pp.7-33.

Mulkay, M. (1985) *The World and the Word*, London: Allen and Unwin.

Narayan, K. (2012) *Alive in the Writing: Crafting Ethnography in the Company of Chekhov*. Chicago: University of Chicago Press.

Nelson, J.S., Megill, A. and McCloskey, D.N. (eds.) (1987) *The Rhetoric of the Human Sciences*, Madison, University of Wisconsin Press.

Pachirat, T. (2018) *Among Wolves: Ethnography and the immersive study of power*, London, Routledge.

Peters, J.D. (1990) 'Rhetoric's revival, positivism's persistence: social science, clear communication, and the public space', *Sociological Theory*, 8 (2), pp.224-31.

Pfohl, S. (1992) *Death at the Parasite Café*, New York, St Martin's Press.

Phipps, A. and Saunders, L. (2009) 'The sound of violets: the ethnographic potency of poetry?', *Ethnography and Education*, 4 (3), pp.357-387, DOI:10.1080/17457820903170168

Polier, N. and Roseberry, W. (1989) 'Tristes tropes: post-modern anthropologists encounter the other and discover themselves', *Economy and Society*, 18, 2, pp245-64.

Reed-Danahay, D. (1997) *Auto/Ethnography: Rewriting the Self and the Social*, London, Bloomsbury.

Richardson, L. (1990a) 'Narrative and sociology', *Journal of Contemporary Ethnography*, 19, pp.116-35.

Richardson, L. (1990b) *Writing Strategies: reaching diverse audiences*, Newbury Park, Sage.

Richardson, L. (1992) 'Trash on the Corner: ethics and technography', *Journal of Contemporary Ethnography*, 21 (1), pp.103-119.

Richardson, L. (1993) 'How come prose? The writing of social problems', in J.A. Holstein and G. Miller (eds.) *Reconsidering social constructionism*, New York: Aldine de Gruyter.

Richardson, L. (1994) 'Writing: a method of inquiry', in Denzin, N. and Lincoln, Y. (eds) *Handbook of Qualitative Research*, Thousand Oaks CA, Sage.

Richardson, L. and St Pierre, E. (2018) 'Writing: a method of inquiry', in Denzin, N. and Lincoln, Y. (eds) *Handbook of Qualitative Research*, Fifth edition, Thousand Oaks CA, Sage.

Rose, D. (1989) *Patterns of American Culture: ethnography and estrangement*, Philadelphia, University of Pennsylvania Press.

Roth, P.A. (1989) 'Ethnography without tears', *Current Anthropology*, 30 (5), pp.555-69.

Sangren, P. S. (1988) 'Rhetoric and the authority of ethnography: "postmodernismÓ and the social reproduction of texts', *Current Anthropology*, 29, pp.405-35.

Sanjek, P. (ed.) (1990) *Fieldnotes: the making of anthropology*, Ithaca NY, Cornell University Press.

Sanjek, R. and Tratner, S. (eds) (2015) *eFieldnotes: The Makings of Anthropology in the Digital World*, Philadelphia PA, University of Pennsylvania Press.

Schwartz-Shea, P. and Yanow, D. (2009) 'Reading and writing as method: In search of trustworthy texts', in Ybema, S., Yanow, D., Wels, H., and Kamsteeg, F. (eds) *Organizational Ethnography: Studying the Complexity of Everyday Life in organizations*, London, Sage.

Shostak, M. (1981) *Nisa: the life and words of an !kung woman*, Cambridge, Mass., Harvard University Press.

Sikes, P. (2012) 'The literary turn: fiction and poetry', in Delamont, S. (ed.)

Handbook of Qualitative Research in Education, Cheltenham, Edward Elgar.

Simons, H.W. (ed.) (1988) *Rhetoric in the Human Sciences*, London, Sage.

Smaling, A. (2002) 'The Argumentative Quality of the Qualitative Research Report' *International Journal of Qualitative Method*, 1 (3), pp.62-9.

Sparkes, A. C. (2009) 'Novel ethnographic representations and the dilemmas of judgement', *Ethnography and Education*, 4, 3, pp.301-319, DOI: 10.1080/17457820903170119

Spencer, J. (1989) 'Anthropology as a kind of writing', Man, 24 (1), pp.145-64.

Stoddart, K. (1986) 'The presentation of everyday life: some textual strategies for "adequate ethnography"', *Urban Life*, 15 (1), pp.103-121.

Stanley, P. (2015) 'the PhD Journey(s): An Autoethnography of Zine-Writing, Angst, Embodiment, and Backpacker Travels', *Journal of Contemporary Ethnography*, 44 (2), pp.143-168

Starn, O. (ed.) (2015) *Writing Culture and the Life of Anthropology*, Durham, NC, Duke University Press.

Strathern, M. (1987) 'Out of context: the persuasive fictions of anthropology', *Current Anthropology*, 28, pp.251-81.

Tedlock, D. (1979) 'Analogical tradition and the emergence of a dialogical anthropology', *Journal of Anthropological Research*, 35, pp387-400.

Tedlock, D. (1983) *The Spoken Word and the Work of Interpretation*, Philadelphia, University of Pennsylvania Press.

Tyler, S.A. (1985) 'Ethnography, intertextuality and the end of description', *American Journal of Semiotics*, 3 (4), pp.83-98.

Tedlock, D. (1987) *The Unspeakable: discourse, dialogue and rhetoric in the postmodern world*, Madison, University of Wisconsin Press.

Tjora, A. (2006) 'Writing small discoveries: an exploration of fresh observers' observations', *Qualitative Research*, 6 (4), pp.429–451.DOI: 10.1177/1468794106068012

VanSlyke-Briggs, K. (2009) 'Consider ethnofiction', *Ethnography and Education*, 4 (3), pp.335-345, DOI: 10.1080/17457820903170143

Vickers, B. (1988) *In Defence of Rhetoric*, Oxford, Oxford University Press.

Vickers, B. (1990) 'The recovery of rhetoric: Petrarch, Erasmus and Perelman', *History of the Human Sciences*, 3 (3), pp.415-441.

Walford, G. (2009a) 'The practice of writing ethnographic fieldnotes', *Ethnography and Education*, 4 (2), pp.117-130, DOI: 10.1080/17457820902972713

Walford, G. (2009b) 'For ethnography', *Ethnography and Education*, 4 (3), pp.271-282, DOI: 10.1080/17457820903170093

Waterston, A. and Vesperi, M.D. (eds) (2009) *Anthropology off the Shelf: Anthropologists on Writing*. Chichester: Wiley-Blackwell.

Watson, G. (1987) 'Make me reflexive, but not yet: strategies for managing essential reflexivity in ethnographic discourse', *Journal of Anthropological Research*, 43, pp.29-41.

Webster, S. (1982) 'Dialogue and fiction in ethnography', *Dialectical Anthropology*, 7, 2, pp91-114.

Webster, S. (1983) 'Ethnography as storytelling', *Dialectical Anthropology*, 8 (3), pp.185-205.

Webster, S. (1986) 'Realism and reification in the ethnographic genre', *Critique of Anthropology*, VI (1), pp.39-62.

Weinberg, D. (2014) *Contemporary Social Constructionism*, Philadelphia PA, Temple University Press.

White, M. L. (2009) 'Ethnography 2.0: writing with digital video', *Ethnography and Education*, 4 (3), pp.389-414, DOI: 10.1080/17457820903170176

White, H. (1973) *Metahistory: the historical imagination in nineteenth century Europe*, Baltimore, Johns Hopkins University Press.

White, H. (1978) *Tropics of Discourse: essays in cultural criticism*, Baltimore, Johns Hopkins University Press.

Wolcott, H. (2009) *Writing up Qualitative Research*, Third edition, Thousand Oaks CA, Sage.

Wolf, M. (1992) *A Thrice Told Tale: feminism, postmodernism and ethnographic responsibility*, Stanford, Stanford University Press.

Woods, P. (2006) *Successful Writing for Qualitative Researchers*, Second edition, London, Routledge.

Woods, P., Jeffrey, B., Troman, G., Boyle, M., and Cocklin, B. (1998) 'Team and Technology in Writing up Research', *British Educational Research Journal*, 24 (5), pp. 573-592

Woolgar, S. (ed.) (1988) *Knowledge and Reflexivity*, London, Sage.

Wulff, H. (ed.) (2016) *The Anthropologist as Writer: Genres and Contexts in the Twenty-First Century*. Oxford: Berghahn.

On the practical matter of writing

Martyn Hammersley

The reference to practicality in my title is intended to mark off what I have to say here from the literature that is concerned with what might be called the theoretical aspects of ethnographic writing: in particular, with critical analysis of rhetorical strategies and of the philosophical and political assumptions which, it is claimed, are built into them (see Chapter 1). The relationship between theory and practice is no less problematic in ethnography than it is in other areas. The issues raised, and arguments presented, in the theoretical literature about writing are important and have implications for practice. However, there is the danger that giving them a great deal of attention can lead to paralysis, or at least to getting no writing done except for writing about writing. As with other good things, one can have too much reflexivity. Given the differential status sometimes accorded to the theoretical and the practical, it is worth emphasising here the importance of the practical aspects of writing, and these are my focus (there have been several books on this too, for references see Chapter 1).

When people talk of 'writing up' their research, this seems to suggest a brief and straightforward activity, and one that only takes place when all the data have been collected and analysed. It may be like this in some kinds of research, but often it is not; and this is especially true in ethnography. Certainly, I have never found 'writing up' quick or easy. And the reason for this, or so I like to think, is that writing is also thinking: an important part of the data analysis is done in the course of writing research reports. And, for this reason, writing should be done throughout the research process. Of course, in a sense it inevitably is: for instance, producing fieldnotes and transcribing audio or video recordings. But writing analytic notes, potential drafts of sections of the final report, etc. should also be attempted from early on. Doing this can provide useful clarification of the focus of the research and of the direction in which it needs to go; but, also, getting started on the writing early means that one has considerable resources available when, towards the end, writing becomes the main task: it avoids having to start from scratch.

So, a general point that is worth making is that writing, or at least good writing, takes a considerable amount of time and effort; partly because it cannot be forced, partly because even when it is going well it goes slowly. One hears stories of people dictating articles or even books as they fly from one conference to another. There may be people who are capable of this, but I've never met them (nor am I sure I want to!). For most of us, writing is a painfully slow and uncertain business; so that one of the most important virtues for any writer is perseverance.

For the sake of simplicity, most of my discussion will relate to writing a relatively short research report, rather than a book or thesis; though I will consider the added complications of longer reports very briefly at the end. Also, before I begin, a word of caution. Different people have different ideas about what is good writing, and also about how to go about producing it. What is presented here necessarily reflects my own views and experience. It may not suit everyone, but I hope that some will find it useful.

The practical problems I will discuss can be grouped, roughly, under three stages in the process of writing: getting started; structuring and formulating the text; and correcting and polishing. There is, of course, no very sharp distinction between these three stages. Each blurs into the next. Nevertheless, they provide a rough framework.

Stage 1: Getting started

What is to be written *about* is sometimes a matter of choice, sometimes not; and this can make a difference to how one gets going. Having little or no choice regarding one's topic can arise in a number of ways. First of all, the research focus itself may have been part of a brief that one was given; for example, by a funding agency. But, even if the research problem was freely chosen, the theme of the paper to be written may be constrained. One may have been commissioned to write on a particular topic, or be writing a paper that has to fit into a particular slot in a book that someone else is editing. Contrary to what might be expected, it is sometimes easier to write to someone else's topic than to write to a self-chosen one. And, even where there is external constraint, there will usually be some leeway. Of course, if at all possible, it is necessary to avoid setting out on pieces of writing that address topics in which one has little interest, or where one does not have a reasonable grasp of the issues, or where the data provide little grounding. Writing is difficult enough, without stacking the odds against its successful completion.

As with all other activities, the trajectory of each writing project can vary a great deal. On some occasions it is possible to have a clear sense of what to say right at the beginning, this providing a structure that can be followed, thereby getting through the first two stages of writing I will discuss in no time at all. For most of us, most of the time, though, the trajectory is likely to be much more problematic; with false starts, uncertainties and even false endings.

There are no failsafe recipes for solving the problems that arise in this first stage, where the task is to try to clarify what it is one wants to say. Writing *something* is certainly one requirement, whether this is an attempt at a plan, at the drafting (and re-drafting) of an opening paragraph or of a paragraph that will go somewhere else in the as-yet-only-anticipated product, or an attempt at an abstract of the not-yet-written paper. There are no rules about where to concentrate effort at the beginning. As in climbing, one tries to find a footing, testing out each step in the conviction that gradual progress can be made. There may be times when nothing seems to work and very little gets written; but this does not mean that nothing has been gained. There is a substantial subconscious element to writing, and it is not unusual to find that after an apparently fruitless period things improve, as if fallow time had been a necessary preparation.

In whatever is written at this stage, it is important not to be overly concerned with getting the words exactly right; this can be left until later. The aim is usually to begin to map out the overall shape of what you want to say. However shoddy the writing, it may nevertheless do this quite effectively. Of course, if you find that the words flow well, make the most of it. There are all too few times when this happens, in my experience, so none should be squandered.

There will almost certainly be obvious gaps in what is produced at this stage, which will need to be filled in later; and others may emerge during the course of further re-drafting. These may require extra data analysis, reading, or thought; and trying to deal with them at this initial stage is probably not advisable. But if you have ideas about how they could be filled write these down for subsequent use. At this stage, the task is to get as much of the piece outlined and filled in as can be done reasonably quickly.

There are various argumentative structures that can be used in writing up ethnographic research. Challenging a popular, or recently presented, point of view is one, tracing the course of events in a setting is another, outlining the contrasting perspectives of different people is a third, but there are others. Familiarity with publications in the area in which you are working, and some thought about how they are structured, can help here.

A key issue one needs to keep in mind at this point is the intended audience. Of course, you can never control who will read your work, but you will need *some* idea about the target audience and their characteristics, in terms of what they are already likely to know, and what they will be interested in. After all, the aim is to deliver some news to them: to tell them something they don't already know and that is also of interest. The nature of this will hinge on the kind of story you are planning to tell.

Let me emphasise, though, that news does not have to be completely unprecedented or spell-binding. As in the mass media, news may involve updating on a previous story. Indeed, usually, this is precisely what is involved with research report writing: one is contributing to a developing story on a particular theme. Given this, it is usually necessary to begin by reminding the audience, or bringing them up to date, about previous news related to that theme, as a platform to launch your own message. This is one function of the review of the existing literature that usually forms part of a proposed report, paper, or article.

When some sort of structure has been mapped out, and at least the early parts of it written, we are into the second phase.

Stage 2: Structuring and formulating the text

One of the most distressing features of the task of writing is that progress is not assured. Not only may one find it difficult to get started, but, occasionally, having mapped out a structure and written substantial parts of it, the disconcerting discovery is made that it doesn't work and one is thrown back into Stage One. While it is disappointing when this happens, to say the least, the situation is not always as bad as it seems. It may appear as if everything is falling apart, but often what looked like a major obstacle turns out to be a minor one that can easily be circumvented. Sometimes it *is* a major problem, but resolving it may solve other problems as well; though it can also sometimes create new difficulties! As already mentioned, what is required at this stage is persistence, and a sustained confidence that problems can be resolved.

Leaving what you have written and coming back to it in a few days, or a few weeks, can sometimes work the little miracle that is required to suggest a solution to your problem. Of course, there is a danger that one may never come back to it. Many writers have drawers full of unfinished papers or projected but incomplete books. This is to be avoided if at all possible; but I have to admit that I have accumulated considerable debris of this kind, over the years. Yet, on several occasions, I have returned to a half-written paper some considerable time after it was started and have managed to complete it; though, of course, this has involved updating references to the relevant literature.

But let us assume that all is reasonably well and that you now have a structure which seems to work, and that you have started to write some parts of it. The task from here on is to make this structure as tight and compelling for the reader (and for you) as possible. This is a matter of ensuring that the points which make up the structure are in the right order, that everything is included that is necessary, and that not much is there that is not absolutely essential. Gaps in an argument can be troublesome for a reader, affecting their understanding of what you are trying to say. They can also undermine the persuasiveness of your report. Equally, digressions can be diverting, with the result that readers may never pick up the threads of your argument again; and this is especially so when the relevance of the digression to the main part of the piece is obscure. Of course, one is always reluctant to cut material out (especially if it seems to be the best section of all). The consoling thought, however, is that digressions can be the seeds of other writing projects, so that excluding them is not necessarily a loss. They may flourish much better in a larger pot of their own.

At this stage, as in the previous one, there are no recipes that guarantee success, but the problems are usually more straightforward than they were earlier (though not always). What I mean by this is that, whereas the first stage requires some element of creativity, this second one is more a matter of craft and graft. This is not to say that it is easy. That writing *is* a craft cannot be repeated too often: it involves problem-solving that can be very hard work indeed. Certainly, this is so if it is going to be done well – unless one has exceptional writing skills (and few who think they have these do!).

So, this stage is likely to be a long haul. Don't give up on it, though. Once you've got a structure, and you think that it's basically sound, you're more than half way there. If it's not exactly down hill after this, at least you're no longer having to climb, or the incline is not as steep as it was in the first phase. (Of course, sometimes, we sprint up the initially steep path only to find that the stamina for the longer more gently inclined part of the journey is what we lack. All that can be done then is to keep reminding ourselves how lucky we were to get so high so quickly – and to make the most of it by pressing on, but with plenty of breaks for recuperation.)

One useful trick at this stage, and even earlier when you are trying to create the argumentative structure of the paper, is to try to summarise your argument in note form: as a series of main points, with subsidiary points under them. Sometimes just putting these down on paper as a list immediately points up problems of sequence, omission or inclusion. And identifying these can make the writing easier. Moreover, this is a technique that can be used over and over again as the draft develops, every time a problem arises, gradually ironing each one out. Closely related to this is the usefulness of headings. These not only help a reader to understand the structure, they will also facilitate your own understanding of what you're writing, what should go where, etc. Of course, it is also possible to use the 'Outline' and 'Table of Contents' facilities in *Word* for much the same purpose – some people find these useful, though it may be that not everyone will.

Here again, in what you write you will need to think about your audience, in terms of what they will and will not need to be told. Equally, you must think about which of the points you are making will require the most effort to persuade the audience of their importance and/or validity. This has implications for how much detail needs to be provided, for how much (and what kind) of evidence is required (whether this consists of references to or quotations from the literature, or the provision of primary evidence from your own research).

In the previous section I noted that there may be gaps in the initial draft that you recognised but did not feel able to fill when writing it. It is at this second stage that these need to be worked on. This may well involve going off to read a body of literature or to do further analysis of one's data. Both reading and analysis are usually easier when one knows quite specifically what one is doing them *for* (which is not always the case in earlier stages of the research). But, of course, it is necessary to be careful that one does not come back simply with what one wanted to find. Discovering that a gap cannot be filled, or cannot be filled in the way that was assumed, is not uncommon (and ought not to be uncommon). It is one of the reasons that it is sometimes necessary to go back to the beginning to reorganise the whole structure in order to avoid a problem that has been discovered. Sometimes, this may result in a draft being abandoned, but that should be a last resort. More usually, it results in a much better product. Indeed, it can lead to important discoveries and thereby to a dramatic improvement in the newsworthiness, as well as the validity, of what one has to say.

A feature of this second stage is that some bits that one had already written get cut out because they no longer seem to be essential, or even relevant. I usually put the material which I exclude in a 'rem' (remainders) section at the end of the draft, in case I want to retrieve any of it later, which I often do. One of the slightly disturbing things that can happen when one has produced a coherent and effective draft is that a glance through the remainders section reveals a variety of previously excluded bits that can now be put back in at various places. The result of this is apparently to move backwards away from completion: one goes from a draft that looked lean and mean to one that is cluttered by all sorts of inserts which have not yet been properly worked in and that may even cause problems for the structure. However, this is often a process which improves the final version considerably; even though, after reflection, some of the material retrieved and re-inserted in the text eventually finds its way back into the remainders section at the end!

Stage 3: Correcting and polishing

This final stage is the easiest bit, but it won't necessarily feel like that, and it can go on for some time (unless you have a very tight deadline). Certainly, time needs to be allowed for correcting and polishing if what you write is to be of the best quality you can manage. Here we are still on the look-out for problems with the structure, but for the most part it's a matter of reformulating sections already written to make them more effective, adding bits of detail and evidence here and there to fill out the argument, moving paragraphs or sentences from one place to another so that they find their most effective position, etc. This can seem tedious. Indeed, this could be the stage at which it is most difficult to maintain your motivation to carry on. However, you need to remind yourself that you have come too far to abandon the trip; not to put in the final effort is to waste all the hard work you have already spent on the paper. Here it's worth revisiting your original thoughts about who the piece is for and what they know and will find of interest. This may lead to revised judgements about what needs to be included or excluded; or even about who your intended audience is. It may also help you with formulating what you have to say in the most accessible manner for that audience.

Finding the right words is not just a matter of persuasive communication, of course. The meanings of the words you use carry implications for the phenomena you are writing about. Becker stresses this point, advising careful thought about the terms in which we choose to describe and explain social phenomena (see Becker, H. S. (1986) *Writing for Social Scientists*, Chicago, University of Chicago Press.). Even the decision between what seem at face value to be synonyms can sometimes involve choosing between significantly different characterisations of those phenomena. This is because words that are similar in denotation can involve different connotations. Sometimes they will involve different metaphors or analogies, and it is worth thinking about how well these apply, and in what respects.

At this stage, try to get the grammar and spelling as sound as possible. Use a spelling dictionary and/or a spell checker: it's worth the effort. But don't become obsessed with worry about whether you have made grammatical or spelling errors. The bottom line is intelligibility. Poor grammar can sometimes get in the way of this, spelling less often (though spelling errors can have a negative effect on audience reception). Also, take reassurance from the fact that however many times you read it through and check it there will always be at least one typographical error remaining. This is the nearest thing we have to a universal law! (There are at least two published papers of mine where egregrious errors slipped through the net: the one I remember with most pain is spelling the name of Virginia Woolf wrongly; and what makes it worse is that it was in an article about writing! No, I'm not going to give you the reference!)

In this third phase, you will need to read through what you have written several times, thinking about exactly what you are trying to say and judging whether it comes across effectively. Over time this judgement becomes largely subconscious: you will know when a paragraph works and when it does not. (This does not mean to say that the next time you read it your judgement will be the same, or that if you make an alteration you will not alter it back to how it was next time around. But most of the time your judgements will concur.) Over the course of the many readings and corrections, you will make less and less alterations until these are only sparsely distributed through the text. You are now nearly finished; except that, if at all possible, you should get someone else to read what you have written, and (of course) what they say may force you to revise it in various respects.

Beggars can't be choosers in recruiting readers for your work. Ideally, though, you need someone who could be (or can pretend to be) a surrogate member of your intended audience. Make what use you can of their comments. Don't dismiss them out of hand, however threatening to your sense of your own competence they may be. At the same time, don't assume that what they say is always sound. Sometimes other people's comments relate to a rather different paper from the one you have written, one that they feel they would have been more interested in reading. Also, some of their suggestions may not be workable. By this point you will know what you have written better than anyone else, so you have a good basis for judgement about what is and is not useful. Rely on that judgement, while always being prepared to reconsider the decisions you have made at some future date.

Finally, you need to let go. When you've read through your piece many times, and the alterations are down to minor punctuation and changes of words here and there, make this your last reading and send it off to wherever it is going. However, before you do so, it is worth just checking those parts that you have corrected in the final version to make sure that you have not unwittingly introduced some new error, for example by mis-keying. Of course, if your paper is to be published you can look forward to having to read it again, perhaps several times, to deal with the reviewers' comments and editor's queries and/ or to check the proofs; and you will still be able to make minor (but not major) alterations then.

Above all, remember that what you have written does not have to be the last word you will ever write on this topic. You can always write a different, and perhaps better, paper later. Treating it as your last word is likely to lead to your never completing it.

Addendum

I have assumed that the task is to write a relatively short report, say an essay or an article for a journal. Where the aim is to write a chapter of a thesis or book the same problems arise, but the task is more complex. Here what needs to be got straight is not just the internal structure of the chapter itself but also that of the whole thesis or book. The chapter must fit into this. But the structure of the chapter must also make sense in its own terms. In any writing, one is simultaneously working at several different levels of organisation: from the words to be used, up through the structure of sentences or paragraphs and the ordering of these, to the arrangement of different sections, and then perhaps to the chapter headings and overall organisation of a thesis or book. And the problems at one level cannot be sorted out on their own, they have implications for the others. Rather like a Rubik's cube, one is constantly making adjustments which have consequences for the other levels of organisation. Eventually, though, order starts to prevail at all levels. And, changing the metaphor, when that happens you know you're on your way out of the maze, even though there may still be quite a way to go.

Fieldnotes and the Ethnographic Self

Sara Delamont

Fieldnotes, and the accompanying 'out of the field' reflections, are foundational to ethnography. Anthropologists, have, since 1990, published some reflections on their fieldnotes (Sanjek, 1990; Jackson, 1990) and given interviews about them (Okely, 2012). Other social sciences including education, which have strong ethnographic traditions have been less engaged with the issues raised by anthropologists about their uneasy relationships with their own fieldnotes, such as privacy and shame. Anthropologists have reflected on why fieldnotes are guarded and kept private, and on their strongly held belief that the fieldnotes of others must be better than theirs. Jackson's theorising of the liminal and mediating functions of fieldnotes have not been widely deployed or disseminated in educational ethnography. This chapter draws on the anthropological writing, and on the ideas of boundary objects and trading zones developed in Science and Technology Studies by Susan Leigh Star (2010, to explore the status of fieldnotes in educational ethnography.

Introduction

> I don't generally show my working observational pads to people; they couldn't read the writing anyway. I have had people say "Right let's have a look at them?" Some have tried to grab them in staffrooms, so I am aware of that. (Walford 2009: 124)

This is a quote from an interview Geoffrey Walford did with Bob Jeffrey, mostly about the latter's work on the 'effects of inspection on primary schools' in England. The quote is part of the data Walford (2009) reports in an unusual piece of research about the ethnography of education. Not a participant observation project in a university or a school, but an investigation of how other researchers who had studied teaching and learning had conducted their projects. He interviewed four educational ethnographers (Paul Connolly, Sara Delamont, Bob Jeffrey and Lois Weis) about the *minutiae* of their fieldwork recording processes. Walford asked about what was recorded, how it was recorded, and what happened to the fieldnotes once the scholar was back in the office. Walford's study is still a rare project despite the steady rise of ethnography in educational research since the 1960s, and the self-scrutiny of anthropologists and interactionist sociologists about their fieldnotes since the 1980s. The level of detail Walford collected from his four informants about fieldnotes is unusual. Walford hoped that his paper would be 'just a start to a wider discussion of the role of fieldnotes in ethnography' (2009: 127) but in the decade since its publication no other empirical papers on the topic have been published. This chapter is one continuation of that discussion involving two of the ethnographers from Walford's original project. This theoretical discussion is authored by Delamont, herself one of Walford's interviewees, written specifically for this volume edited by another of Walford's key informants, Bob Jeffrey who is quoted above.

This is not an autobiographical or 'confessional' chapter, like many of the published reflections on fieldwork which have provided a useful and an entertaining resource for doctoral students and fellow authors. For over thirty years educational researchers have written about their methods and practices, and published those accounts in edited books such as Burgess (1985a and 1985b), Walford (1994) and Bennett de Marrais (1998). Most of those 'confessional' or autobiographical papers say little or nothing data collection at the level of specificity that Walford's project addressed. He asked about the size and shape of notebooks, decisions about which lessons to avoid and which to observe, where the ethnographer spent the lunch break, how fieldnotes were subsequently coded, and other *minutiae* of everyday research life both in the school and back in the university or athome. This chapter does not recapitulate Walford's work, nor is it a confessional, and is not a practical chapter about the techniques of data collection (see Delamont, 2016, Chapter Four for such advice) but an exploration of how to think about fieldnotes.

The structure of the chapter is as follows: I explain what fieldnotes are, and some of the debates around their collection and deployment, outline the history and consequences of the rhetorical or literary turn, and then suggest some theoretical concepts which could enhance educational researchers' discussions of fieldnotes. It sets out to use the material published by anthropologists and some sociologists to explore their thinking about fieldnotes and suggests some ways to theorise about the status of fieldnotes in educational ethnography. In anthropology the main literature is a collection of papers edited by Roger Sanjek (1990) in which anthropologists reflected on their fieldnotes, an article by Jackson (1990a, 1990b) reporting a study of anthropologists' thinking about their fieldnotes, and a set of interviews conducted by Okely (2012) with anthropologists on their careers which paid detailed attention to their research practices. In interactionist sociology there is a practical volume by Emerson *et al.* (2011) which offers advice on how to write fieldnotes and use them to develop ideas drawing on the experience of its authors.

This chapter draws on two conceptual models which can be deployed to theorise fieldnotes in educational ethnography. Neither has been used to focus on fieldnotes in educational ethnography, and the two concepts come from different disciplines and have not been compared and contrasted in educational research. One theoretical perspective is used by Jackson, the anthropologist, which is the idea of a liminal object: one used in, and symbolising, a liminal state. The other is a concept developed by Susan Leigh Star a scholar from the field of STS (Science and Technology Studies) the 'boundary object': a powerful theoretical tool with which to explore what we know about fieldnotes in educational ethnography.

Fieldnotes

Emerson *et al.* (2011: *xvi*) argued that 'ethnographers have failed to closely examine the processes of writing fieldnotes' and suggested that in everyday practice sociological ethnographers write them in different ways which should be openly discussed and the efficacy of each should be debated. They contrast those observers who mix observations and other 'facts' with their 'own thoughts and reactions' and those who keep these separate, separating the 'fieldnotes' from 'a diary or journal'. In other words, Emerson and his co-authors conclude, it is important to discover and explore the reality of ethnographic practice: namely that experienced ethnographers vary a good deal in how and when they actually write. A second distinction made by Emerson and his colleagues is between those who 'work up' their notes as soon as possible, and those who do not. Some investigators aim to make abbreviated notes *in situ*, and to turn these into a longer, more elaborated and explicit report as soon as possible. Others aim to leave their notes relatively untouched while they focus on thinking about wider issues rather than focusing on their recording of *minutiae* of everyday life in their chosen setting. Emerson and his colleagues argue for 'making explicit the assumptions and commitments they hold about the nature of ethnography as a set of practical research and writing activities (p. *xvii*). In that spirit, I have illustrated some of the practicalities with my own practices.

Taking fieldnotes, and writing them up, is hard work. Gaye Tuchman told Shulamit Reinharz that:

> Participant observation is a method for the young. When one is in one's 20s or 30s it may be possible to observe for 10 to 16 hours a day and then type notes before sleeping. Later in life such long hours pose problems. (Reinharz, 2011: 185)

Tuchman assumes here that everyone records their fieldwork in the first mode: 'write up detailed notes as soon as possible': and does not suggest that practices could change to accommodate the researcher's own aging. As an ethnographer who is still doing fieldwork regularly at the age of 71, this is a telling observation. It is not the actual observation, but the writing up which is increasingly hard work. My current research is on how two martial arts are taught in the UK: African-Brazilian capoeira and French kickboxing (called *Savate*). The classes take place in the evenings and there are also weekend events. I make my initial notes in the settings, in reporter's notebooks, in an illegible self-devised set of abbreviations, and then write up a much longer and more detailed account in A4 notebooks as soon as possible, because the longer the gap is, the less likely I am to be able to read what I wrote *in situ.*

My notes are focused on what I see, hear, smell, touch and taste (if there is food or drink). Because the focus is on how these two martial arts are taught, the notes are primarily about the instructor's strategies and how the students respond to their classes. This does not mean that I ignore my 'ethnographic self' (Coffey, 1999) or theory, but I prefer to record thinking about those issues by producing a separate on-going account. I think it is vital to keep a diary or journal about the on-going reflections of the researcher, and to record the developing ideas about theory, the literature, and the focus of the next stages of the fieldwork. Being unenthusiastic about autoethnography (Delamont, 2009). I keep a rigorous division between the A4 notebooks with 'the data' and the 'Out of the Field diary' which is kept in A5 spiral notebooks. The capoeira and savate data are recorded in separate series of notebooks, but one 'diary' is kept for both projects. The reason for that is purposive: the savate fieldwork was conceived as a strategy to force me to treat capoeira as anthropologically strange rather than as a second empirical project conducted alongside the capoeira study. I had been studying capoeira for six years in 2009 and feared I was losing my sense of strangeness, and ought to find a contrastive fieldsite, to follow my own precepts about fighting familiarity (Delamont, 1981, 2005, 2012, 2016). One diary would, I decided, facilitate the constant comparisons that I expected I would be making. It is easy to defend that separation, less understandable is my use of handwriting only. I did not type in the early years of my career and I do not use any IT now, so I keep all my fieldnotes and reflections in handwriting. In an increasingly technological world, where mobile phones and laptops are widely used by informants and researchers, that makes me an anachronism (an exhausted anachronism).

In this century, two technological changes mean that fieldnotes do not have to be handwritten, as they had been for a century. Alongside ethnographers who do write are others who take a laptop or tablet into the field and wordprocess their notes, while others have adopted speaking their 'notes' into a device that uses word recognition software. The availability of relatively cheap and portable devices to the ethnographer has been paralleled by the ubiquity of similar devices in the hands of everyone else in the setting. A modern phone, which can collect data in several different modes; visual, audio, and text, can revolutionise fieldwork. I do not have a mobile phone, but, unless the research is going to take place where carrying a smart phone could endanger the investigator, it is the 'obvious' choice for most people today.

Most of the advisory books, such as Emerson *et al.* (2011), predate those technologies, and focus on writing. Those books which offer advice on doing ethnography in online settings, in contrast, stress that an advantage of online studies is that the data *are* collected digitally, and so do not have to be processed as a separate stage of the data collection. (Boellstorff, Nardi, Pearce and Taylor, 2012). All the ethnographers studied by Walford (2009), by Jackson (1990a, 1990b) and by Okely (2012) had done their main projects before those technologies were widely available and had worked with handwritten notes that were subsequently typed or wordprocessed. It is likely that the new technologies will have changed some things, but not others, but we do not yet have new investigations to compare with those of the 1990s. New researchers especially ethnographers working today would probably focus more on using devices and safeguarding the data from hacking and IT faults than their predecessors. The technology is unlikely to change the privacy and even secrecy around fieldnotes, and the debates about fieldnotes as texts that need academic analysis and discussion. The rest of the chapter focuses on such a discussion, and for that some historical context is needed, to provide the background for the anthropological and sociological literature on fieldnotes.

The Crisis of Representation

It is not often that one conference and its subsequent publication as an edited book produces a shock wave through a discipline and its main method. In the 1980s a volume which argued that anthropologists had much to learn from literary criticism, of the postmodern and very theorised kind, about how to write, and how to read, the findings of the discipline caused what sociologists of science and technology call a paradigm shift.

When James Clifford and George Marcus edited the collection of essays called *Writing Culture* in 1986 they produced a new standpoint for, or argument about, ethnographic writing. That collection and their arguments are still controversial thirty years later. Their volume provoked a 'crisis of representation' in cultural and social anthropology. The phrase 'crisis of representation' was used because the initial response from fellow ethnographers was of horror, despair and panic. When the contributors to Clifford and Marcus argued that anthropologists had not deployed their epistemological beliefs about how data should be collected and understood either when they came to read the work of other scholars, or when they wrote their own publications, many felt that the bedrock of the discipline of anthropology was being undermined. If the monograph could not be read as a factual, true, authoritative account, what did that do to the discipline? The four volumes edited by Atkinson and Delamont (2008a) reprint several of the most famous papers which generated and developed the controversy such as Denzin (2002), Flaherty (2002) and Manning (2002) in the USA and Spencer (1989, 2001) in the UK. Collections of essays are still being published responding to Clifford and Marcus's volume, such as Zenker and Kumoll (2010), Waterston and Vesperi (2011), Starn (2015) and Wulff (2016).

Today these "new" forms of thinking about texts, both reading them and writing them, are generally called, much more neutrally, 'The Literary Turn' or 'The Rhetorical Turn' (e.g. Atkinson, 2012). It was this self-conscious reflection on ethnographic texts which led to a set of publications about how fieldnotes are written (Sanjek, 1990) and how transcription is done (Mishler 1991, Hammersley 2012).

The most important criticism of the Clifford and Marcus collection, which has implications for any discussion of fieldnotes in educational ethnography, came from feminists. The chapters in the collection were analyses of classic texts by distinguished male anthropologists such as Malinowski, Evans Pritchard, Firth and Geertz. All the contributors except one, Mary Pratt (1986) who was not herself an anthropologist, were men. That meant, as the feminist critics who wrote together in a collection edited by Behar and Gordon (1995) pointed out, that these choices of great men, and of the authors to discuss them, produced an account of the discipline and its textual genres which was far more homogenous: that is it presented a much more homogeneous history of 'anthropology': than a wider scoping or sampling collection could ever have produced. If Clifford and Marcus had chosen a wider range of the publications of Anglophone anthropologists between 1920 and 1970, they would not have been able to make several of their claims about the textual genre. Their author selections were too similar and were simultaneously therefore unrepresentative of Anglophone anthropology. Behar and Gordon pointed out that many anthropologists who wrote differently from the 'great men' had not been given their correct place in the history of thediscipline and their work had not been analysed at all. Authors such as Ruth Landes and Zora Neal Hurston who wrote very differently from the dominant men, and who incidentally, have much greater relevance for educational ethnographers today than those men, were entirely absent from the book. Educational ethnographers today do not enter their fieldsites from the same standpoints as the foundational fathers of anthropology, or write about their informants in the same ways as they did. (Atkinson and Delamont, 2008b). Against that background we can consider the two theoretical concepts boundary objects and liminality that can help us think more reflexively and productively about our fieldnotes in educational settings.

Boundary Objects

Star and Griesemer (1989) developed the analytic category of boundary objects during research in a regional zoology museum in the USA. Boundary objects are defined as things which exist at the intersections of different social worlds, or subcultures, interact with some degree of shared interests. In the natural history museum the specimens were one example of boundary objects which were of central importance to, but served different functions for, among others the volunteer guides and demonstrators, the taxidermists, the clerical staff, the members of local scientific societies, the curators, the university zoologists, the university administration, a powerful patron and the volunteer and paid 'collectors' (who killed, gathered and sent new specimens to the museum).

Star and Griesemer (1989) defined the boundary object as follows:

> This is an analytic concept of those scientific objects which both inhabit several intersecting social worlds *and* the informational requirements of each of them. Boundary objects are objects which are both plastic enough to adapt to local needs and the constraints of the several parties employing them, yet robust enough to maintain a common identity across sites (p. 393)

They continue their definition stressing that boundary objects are 'strongly structured' when used in any one individual site, but 'weakly structured' in ordinary use. Boundary objects may, they stress, '"be abstract or concrete", and have a common structure which make them recognisable in several worlds, but will have different meanings in each.

As Clarke and Star (2008) argued 'the study of boundary objects can be an important pathway into complicated situations' (p. 121) and fieldnotes are certainly part of a complicated situation. Star (2010) is a subsequent clarification of the concept. The idea has not been widely used in the methods literature or in educational research, but it is productive for thinking about fieldnotes. A parallel example to Star and Griesemer's original museum study is Wylie's (2015) research on palaeontology laboratories, and the different meanings attached to the dinosaur bones that are prepared there. Fieldnotes can be seen afresh by considering them as boundary objects.

The fieldnotes taken by ethnographers in educational settings meet the Star and Griesemer definition of a boundary object. That description and definition could have been written about fieldnotes. They inhabit several intersecting social worlds: typically the field setting(s), the researcher's home, and the university. Fieldnotes satisfy the informational requirements of all of these; the actors in the setting(s) can see the ethnographer writing, the family or flatmates can see the pile of notebooks growing, the university can be shown the hard evidence of the data collection. They are plastic enough; illegible to the actors in the field setting(s), and the people 'at home', yet when written up they are data for the thesis, the report to the funding body and eventually transmitted into publications. If the ethnographer is a doctoral student, they are plastic enough to be talked about in supervisions and other bureaucratic settings. Simultaneously fieldnotes are robust enough to give them a common identity across sites. Walford's four informants could all talk about their fieldnotes for example. Ethnographic fieldnotes are both concrete (there are now 204 reporter's notebooks from my capoeira research in a cabinet in my university office) *and* abstract (my knowledge of capoeira classes in the UK floats free of any specific notebook). The fieldnotes are certainly a pathway into complicated situations such as classrooms, laboratories, lecture theatres, sports halls and gymnasia.

There are strong similarities between the sociological concept of the boundary object, and the anthropological concept of liminality. That idea has been used to characterise traditional anthropological fieldnotes, and in the next section that work is applied to educational ethnography. Then the usefulness of both concepts to help us think productively about fieldnotes is discussed.

Liminality

The term 'liminal' is not widely used in social sciences other than anthropology, although other disciplines such as geography do focus on boundaries and on 'border country'. The research on school transfer (e.g. Delamont and Galton, 1986), which focuses on liminal issues, generally uses the more sociological and prosaic concept of the status passage. For anthropology liminal states are generally dangerous, perilous or potentially polluting in the ways Douglas (1966) wrote about human categorisation systems. Fieldwork in many cultures has revealed that people undergoing changes, such as being initiated into a religion are particularly vulnerable during the transition. Magliocco (2004) did ethnographic research on neopagans in San Francisco, and describes a rite of passage (pp. 117-118) arranged for her, precisely to create and strengthen her self-efficacy beliefs. Magliocco was at the time divorced, desperately homesick for the site and people of her doctoral fieldwork in Sardinia and the "authentic" research she had done there. She had been moving around the USA in a variety of temporary posts for nine years, trying to get a tenure-track appointment. Her closest friends in a small neopagan coven in which she was apprenticed helped her devise a ritual that would change her

> from a stranger to a native, from an outsider to an insider, from a position
> of insecurity and rootlessness to one of security, prosperity and belonging,
> through a series of symbolic transformation. (11)

That was a typical liminal experience.

Jackson, herself an anthropologist, interviewed seventy social scientists who did ethnography, sixty three anthropologists and seven scholars who were not. The anthropologists were all living in the USA, and included both 'obscure' and famous scholars. Her two papers (Jackson 1990a, 1990b) about those interviews are well worth reading by ethnographers from disciplines beyond anthropology.

She reports one informant saying 'I am a fieldnote' (p. 21) and stresses that fieldnotes are simultaneously 'data' and 'me'. That is the anthropologist creates the fieldnotes and the fieldnotes create the anthropologist. The concept of liminality is best understood in the context of studies of rites of passage.

Societies or subcultures which have ceremonies or rituals to mark changes in social status whether public or private, usually called rites of passage, such as weddings, funerals, or initiations into adulthood or secret societies allow an ethnographer not only to learn about the statuses that are changing (from a single person to a married one) but also to be alerted to wider features of that society or culture. Van Gennep (1909, 1961) argued that anthropologists should pay attention to three phases of any rite of passage – the pre-liminal, the liminal, and the post-liminal. Subsequently ethnographers have focused on liminal objects, and Jackson (1990a) explored the ways in which fieldnotes are productively analysed as such. They mediate between the field and the home, between the personal and the academic, between being in control and the feelings of being confused, out of control or inadequate.

Jackson also reports that her informants regarded their fieldnotes as very private and secret, and that was because:

> Fieldnotes can reveal how worthless your work was, the *lacunae*, your linguistic incompetence, you not being made a blood brother, your childish temper' (p. 22)

Many of her informants expressed guilt and inadequacy about their fieldnotes, 'using words like anxious, embarrassing, defensive, depressing' (p. 27). Some of those interviewed even accused her of 'trying to make me feel guilty' (p. 27)

The writing of the fieldnotes, and the tools of the trade are also liminal between the observer and the informants: the researcher is the person with the notebook.

There is also a tension between 'doing' the fieldwork and making the notes: that is watching the actors dancing tango and writing notes or dancing oneself. Anthropologists see fieldnotes as a sacred, mysterious source of their academic authority, in ways that educational researchers *probably* do not. This may be because of the subject matter: anthropologists often study the unfamiliar, exotic and even supernatural for example (Brown's 1991) work on Mama Lola, a Haitian Vodou priestess in New York. Educational researchers have a different task: to make educational settings anthropologically strange (Delamont, Atkinson and Pugsley 2010, Delamont, 2014, 2016).

The work of Jackson enables us to focus on the ethnographer's sense of self, fieldwork roles, and self-critical reflexivity, rather than the notes themselves. Researchers in educational settings, such as school classrooms, playgrounds, staff rooms, and university dormitories and fraternity houses frequently report their liminal status(es). They are an adult among children or adolescents, a non-teacher in the staff room, a lecturer among students (e.g. Moffatt, 1989), the ivory tower intellectual in the 'real' world. All the tensions reported by Jackson's informants are recognisable to educational researchers. A parallel study of a large number of educational ethnographers would be illuminating.

Boundary Objects and Liminality

These two sensitising, or middle order, concepts are useful for what Paul Atkinson (2017) calls *Thinking Ethnographically*: that is moving from data to ideas about them. In this case, I am arguing, they enable us to think creatively about our fieldwork and fieldnotes. Good ethnography depends on critical reflexivity at every stage of the process and these two concepts can help that process. There are two ways in which conceptualising our fieldnotes as boundary objects can support self-critical reflexivity. We can think of our fieldnotes as boundary objects in order first to make problematic, or 'trouble', the borders between fieldsite and home and university and second to focus on how they have different meanings in the several worlds where they are recognisable. Boundary objects are strongly structured in any one site, but weakly structure in ordinary use: working out what that means in practice in an educational ethnography is helpful to clarify what any specific researcher's fieldnotes are 'for'. Of course the concept may also be useful during the fieldwork but that is not the focus here. The concept can also be helpful for understanding how fieldnotes, when used as data in research reports, can be received very differently. In a parallel way, an understanding of liminality and liminal objects can aid the research's reflexivity about fieldnotes. The notes are a liminal object, of course, which is similar to a boundary object, and can be used conceptually in similar ways. The concept of liminality helps the researcher to focus on their precariousness and peril, and how these must appear in the ethnographer's reflexive diary, or equivalent space. Given how hard it is to sustain and maintain critical reflexivity, these two concepts are a valuable aid.

Conclusions

Educational ethnographies are well aware of the consequences of the literary or rhetorical turn for their publications. Journals such as *Qualitative Studies in Education* celebrate new textual genres, and the acceptable styles of writing have changed since 1986. However the practice of taking fieldnotes and what happens to them has not yet been affected by parallel developments. Drawing on two concepts, 'boundary object' and 'liminality', this chapter has proposed a way forward.

Acknowledgements

I am grateful to Mrs R.B. Jones for word processing this chapter.

Bibliography

Atkinson, P.A. (2012) The literary or rhetorical turn, in S. Delamont (ed). *Handbook of Qualitative Research in Education*. Cheltenham: Edward Elgar, 512-20

Atkinson, P.A. (2017) *Thinking Ethnographically*. London: Sage

Atkinson, P.A. and Delamont, S. (eds) (2008a) *Representing Ethnography*. (Four Volumes) London: Sage

Atkinson, P.A. and Delamont, S. (2008b) Editors' introduction|: ethnographic representation and rhetoric. In P.A. Atkinson and S. Delamont (eds) *Representing Ethnography*(Four Volumes), London: Sage

Behar, R. and Gordon, D. (eds) (1995) *Women Writing Culture*. Berkeley, CA: California University Press

Bennett de Marrais, K. (ed.) (1998) *Inside Stories*. Mahwah NJ : Erlbaum.

Boellstorff, T., Nardi, B., Pearce, C. and Taylor, T.L. (2012) *Ethnography and Virtual Worlds*. Princeton: NJ: Princeton University Press

Brown, K. McCarthy, (1991) *Mama Lola*. Berkeley, CA: California University Press

Burgess, R.B. (ed.) (1985a) *Field Methods in the Study of Education*. London: Falmer.

Burgess, R.G. (ed.) (1985b) *Strategies of Educational Research*. London: Falmer.

Clifford, J. and Marcus, G.E. (eds) (1986) *Writing Culture*. Berkeley, CA: California University Press

Clarke, A. and Star, L. (2008) The social framework: A theory/methods package. In E.J. Hackett *et al.* (eds) *The Handbook of Science and Technology Studies*. Cambridge, MA: The MIT Press 113-138

Coffey, A. (1999) *The Ethnographic Self*. London: Sage

Delamont, S. (1981) All too familiar? *Educational Analysis*, 3, (1), 69-84

Delamont, S. (2005) Four great gates. *Research Papers in Education*, 20, (1), 85-100

Delamont, S. (2009) The only honest thing. *Ethnography and Education*, 4, 1, 51-64

Delamont, S. (2012) Leaving Damascus. In S. Delamont (ed) *Handbook of Qualitative Research in Education*, 1-20. Cheltenham: Edward Elgar

Delamont, S. (2016) *Fieldwork in Educational Settings*. (3rdedition) London: Routledge

Delamont, S. (2014) *Key Themes in the Ethnography of Education*. London: Sage

Delamont, S., Atkinson, P. and Pugsley, L. (2010) The concept smacks of magic. *Teaching and Teacher Education*. 26, 1, 3-10

Delamont, S. and Galton, M. (1986) *Inside the Secondary Classroom*. London: Routledge

Denzin, N.K. (2002) Confronting ethnography's crisis of representation. *Journal of Contemporary Ethnography*, 31, 4, 482-489

Douglas, M. (1966) *Purity and Danger*. London: Routledge

Emerson, R.M., Fretz, R.I. and Shaw, L.I. (2011) *Writing Ethnographic Fieldnotes*. Second Edition. Chicago: The University of Chicago Press

Flaherty, M. (2002) The 'crisis' in representation. *Journal of Contemporary Ethnography*, 31, 4, 508-516

Hammersley, M. (2012) Transcription of speech. In S. Delamont (ed) *Handbook of Qualitative Research in Education*, 439-445. Cheltenham: Elgar

Jackson, J.E. (1990a) *Deja entendu*: The liminal qualities of anthropological fieldnotes. *Journal of Contemporary Ethnography*, 19, 1, 8-43

Jackson, J. (1990b) I am a fieldnote: fieldnotes as a symbol of professional identity. In R. Sanjek (ed) *Fieldnotes*. Ithaca, NY: Cornell University Press 3 - 33

Magliocco, S. (2004) *Witching Culture*. Philadelphia: University of Pennsylvania Press.

Manning, P.K. (2002) The sky is not falling. *Journal of Contemporary Ethnography*, 31, 4, 490-498

Mishler, E. (1991) Representing discourse: the rhetoric of transcription. *Journal of Narrative and Life History*, 1, 4, 225-280

Moffatt, M. (1989) *Coming of Age in New Jersey*. New Brunswick NJ: Rutgers University Press.

Okely, J. (2012) *Anthropological Practice*. Oxford: Berg

Reinharz, S. (2011) *Observing the Observer*. New York: Oxford University Press

Sanjek, R. (ed) (1990) *Fieldnotes*. Ithaca, NY: Cornell UP

Spencer, J. (1989) Anthropology as a kind of writing. *Man*, 24, 1, 145-164

Spencer, J. (2001) Ethnography after postmodernism. In P. Atkinson *et al.*) (eds) *Handbook of Ethnography*. London: Sage, 443-452

Star, S.L. (2010) This is not a boundary object. *Science, Technology and Human Values*, 35, 6, 600-617

Star, S.L. and Griesemer, J.R. (1989) Institutional ecology. *Social Studies of Science*, 19, 4, 387-420

Starn, O. (ed) (2015) *Writing Culture and the Life of Authors*. Durham, NC. Duke University Press

Van Gennep, A. (1909) *The Rites of Passage*. English Translation (1961) Chicago: The University of Chicago Press

Walford, G. (2009) The practice of writing ethnographic fieldnotes. *Ethnography and Education*, 4, 2, 117-130

Waterston, A. and Vesperi, M.D. (eds) (2011) *Anthropology off the Shelf*. Chichester: Wiley

Wulff, H. (ed) (2016) *The Anthropologist as Writer*. Oxford: Berghahn

Wylie, C. (2015) 'The artist's piece is already in the stone': Constructing creativity in paleontology laboratories. *Social Studies of Science*, 45, 1, pp 31 - 55

Zenker, O. and Kumoll, K. (eds) *Beyond Writing Culture*. Oxford: Berghahn

Cardinal writing: following the observed process
Karen Borgnakke

In this paper, I refer primarily to ethnographic full-scale studies, long-term fieldwork and large empirical collections. Hereby, I refer to a spectrum of methods and to a diverse data-collection where writing fieldnotes have a central role – being the researcher's cardinal point and hereafter the cardinal text. The continuous sequence of fieldnotes and observations protocols are, as chronological text-collection, process-oriented and it is the field research product, where "all" observed situations are transformed into text and narratives. Therefore, this research text requires description and reflection of 1) how the fieldnotes collection is a part of the research process and 2) how it is used in ethnographic analyses and combined with other documents and the embedded mix of data.

Introduction
With the fieldnote collection as the starting point for ethnographic analysis, the systematic interpretation and writing however is challenged by both the complexity from the observed practical context and by the complex data collection. The challenge is reflected in the methodology literature and was in introductions from the 1980s conceptualized as the need to transform the use of qualitative methods to an analytic strategy keeping the awareness for the holistic approach and for criteria as a matter of 'ecological validity' (Hammersley &Atkinson 1983, Hastrup 1988, Borgnakke 1996, Kvale 1997). Currently the ethnographic approach is further challenged by multi-sited field research and the need to develop a strategy for cross-cases analysis and discourse analysis (Hammersley 2006, 2017, Marcus 2009, Borgnakke 2010, 2017, Eisenhart, 2017). If we still consider the classic fieldnote collection as a cardinal text, as I will argue in this paper, we need further clarification of the analytical task as well as we need to outline perspectives and potentials.

   In the first sections of this paper I will characterize the analytical challenge and task focusing on the characteristic acts and phases shifting in the process of ethnographic research between fieldworks observation and data collection, systematic interpretation and analysis. Next, the analytic writing is oriented towards giving the analytical overview, documenting the important empirical findings, themes and issues and to perform the exemplary close-up-analysis. Hereby the significance of fieldnotes as ethnographic text can be reflected in relation to the explored context and the observed practical process. Against this background the paper finally reflects the renewal of the basic principle for ethnographic holistic and critical approach to practice oriented and research based analysis. Hereby the principle of ecological validity and the reference to what I call authentic complexity will be sharpened.

The analytical challenge between the fieldworker, the analyst and the writer
The analytic challenge is reflected in the above mentioned methodology literature in relation to the overwhelming amount of data and the need for both broad description and in-depth analysis. Involved in this research debate, I stated that the challenge is not only to face the amount of data but to face the complexity of data and the need for analytical strategies coping with the complex. Further I stated the necessity of reflection on the shift from 'collecting data' to 'analysing data' and hereby reflect the shifting position of the ethnographer as 'fieldworker' – 'analyst' and 'writer'. The argumentation is elaborated (see Borgnakke 1996: 243-273) and closely related to my experiences as a fieldworker with intensive day-to-day observations spending months or even years in the field.

Facing the analytical challenges posed both by the richness and the complexity of the ethnographic data a more nuanced description of the analytical task was needed. The analytical task was in the research literature expressed as a matter of a) going beyond the descriptive level, and b) handling the detailed and holistic descriptions in a corresponding analytical/theoretical interpretation (Krarup and Rieper 1981: III-IV).

Similarly, Hammersley and Atkinson described the phase and position in ethnographic research and stressed how the analytical task becomes noticeable, the longer you get into the research process. They also stressed that there were very few explicit reflections of what they call the "writing act" (Hammersley and Atkinson 1983) and similarly understand as a theoretical and analytical interpretation act.

Since then, Hastrup (1988) gave an interesting summary. Not only did the interpretation act take place before, during and after the research process. The ethnographer and the Anthropologist, had to experience and thus 'create': first the ethnographic data, then the text, as noted by Hastrup (1988) as a relation between the experienced and observed LIFE maintained Text and Genre.

Through Hammersley and Atkinson and Hastrup, we approach clarification of the field researcher as "writer" and author of experienced and interpreted life.

The underlining of the importance of the "the writing act " and the "text work" are essential and need to be followed up. Here, the new challenges for ethno-methodology are to create strategies for the systematic analytical framework.

Instead of linking the challenge exclusively to the manufacturing side or to the act of writing, ethnographic analysis shows the necessity of linking the challenge to the analytic act meaning the act where 'the fieldworker' and researcher as 'the analyst' go through the empirical material making the systematic and thematic analysis.

This, the systematic interpretation act is of another nature than the fieldworker participates in while observing and collecting data. The fieldworker acts in the field – the analyst is at her office writing the analysis as a thesis, a book or a '250 pages long analysis giving overviews and close up analysis'.

The ethnographic point and challenge is that the systematic interpretative act is placed after the process of field observations and data-collection. The systematic interpretative act followed by the analytical writing act is symbolically distinct from the chaos and order of the field. The analyst in the interpretation act shall deconstruct and reconstruct (Borgnakke, 1996). And this as a process of systematic analysis and draft writings is a process producing the empirical- analytical overview, making cross case analysis preparing close op analysis.

Conclusions are that there seem to be three coherent aspects at stake:

Firstly, analytical reflection involves differentiation of the spontaneous interpretative acts that have been implicated in field research as well as clarifying the systematic interpretation act, there must be the characteristics of the analysis. Secondly, it involves a reflection of strategies for the actual implementation of the empirical results concentrated as thematic analysis. Thirdly, we have to deal with writing consequences of the choice of analytic strategy.

The systematic interpretation and the analytical challenges posed by the complex data, is reflected in the methodology literature as almost THE challenge. At the same time it is a vivid question challenging the research literature and the classic genres in a spectra from the academic thesis, book to the academic article. For ethnographic writing keeping analytic overview, empiric richness and close up analysis as ambition this means that there is a genre-challenge as well as a connectable ideal-typical text, namely the fieldnote and next the collection of fieldnotes.

Against this background my concluding comments will be: if the above described analytical challenges shall be met the collection of fieldnotes potentially is confirmed as a cardinal text – matching the challenge. Let me elaborate this in the following sections and let me exemplify by referring to my own long-term fieldwork and already done analysis to make sure that the documentary dimensions are in order[6].

The fieldnotes collection regarded as the cardinal text

In my long term field work conducted during the 1980s I followed educational experiments at the Project-based Aalborg University (AUC) in full scale and full time[7]. Based on these experiences I will start claiming as follows: With participatory observation as the most important research instrument, the observation protocol

6. See Borgnakke 1996 vol. 1&2, where both the methodological reflections and the empirical analyses are described in details.
7. AUC 1981-1982 and Open University 1984-86, Borgnakke 19xx

(and hereby the fieldworkers diary) become the most important researcher produced text regarding the ongoing course, the activities and the situations. The significance of the collection of day-to-day reports, the overall text, for full scale studies and for fieldwork investigating practical processes must be emphasized. Firstly, the continuous sequence of protocols and diaries is, as a chronological text collection, close to the process. Secondly, this collection is the fieldworker and the observer's main produced text, it is where "it all" stands. Therefore, this text collection requires both reviews and descriptions of how it is embedded in the research process and how it has been used in the analysis process. Starting with an example from my AUC fieldwork following the educational program and the group of teachers and students in its full length, I will characterize how the series of single fieldnotes was designed and what the collection contains.

In my description (Borgnakke, 1996) referring to a half year day-to-day observation among 50 students, organized in 7 project groups I stressed the same routines as for example mentioned in Hammersley and Atkinson (1983) and recalled later by Delamont (2008) when it comes to observation and fieldnotes referring to the observed situation. But since my research interest was the daily routine and the amount of day-to-day observation was huge I needed to develop a fieldnote routine meeting the challenge by covering the serial of activities, and the serial of participators and speakers in correct order meaning in the order they occurred. This means that every single fieldnote (and the collection in total) is written keeping the observed real chronologic serial order. It also means that the observed activities and actors own words and settings are noted to make sure that the field protocols were a collection of the original sequences, wordings and sayings. Video and tape recordings were used as a recorded/transcribed data collection for close up analyses of the idealtypical situations[8]. Still fieldnotes from the recorded activity were written to make sure that the recording day also was one of the observed day to match the effort to place and replace every situation and activity in the broader context and ongoing process.

The participant observation and the daily writing fieldnotes had attached the most important form of conversation: the continuous conversation with the teachers, the students, individually and in groups. Without these spontaneous conversations before/after a given activity, on the hallways, in the group sums, in the teacher's office, in the secretariat, no meaningful observation.

The spontaneous conversation was maintained in the observation protocols/ diaries and hereby are the important versions of every day conversations and participators comments to the ongoing process embedded in the overall diary material.

---

8. The ideal typological situations: Lecture, Plenary, Project Supervision, Intern/external evaluation are covered with close up analysis in for example Borgnakke 1996, 2005.

All in all, it meant that I already during the process of observation realized the importance of developing the fieldnotes collection as a cardinal and comprised text. Further, I realized the importance of writing fieldnotes maintaining the serial of activities in real chronology, the ongoing interaction and the actors own words. There are several layers in these issues as I elaborated them in reflections of the scientific basis for the fieldworks research methodology (Borgnakke, 1996). But the issues are also a concrete matter for the fieldworker. Let me therefore elaborate below keeping the concrete manner in focus.

To maintain activities in real chronology, ongoing interaction and the original statements

Each observation protocol contains the mapping of the day, but it also contains the necessary facts and information of time/place/activity/number of participants (noted Teachers, Students, Male/Female).

Very fast, I experienced that such notations became a pure reflex and in addition I made rapidly notations of descriptions of the given activity, or the given topic. At the same time however, there is a coding language of the listing, which is exceedingly saturated with important signals about the environment. Further there is an ongoing reference to different forms of texts, study books and materials, institutional documents etc. The observation protocol's "activity" therefore includes attached enclosures of any common written materials for the activity, such as agendas, minutes of meetings, written presentations etc. It also includes architectural sketches over the room, table layouts, participants' locations.

Next, it is essential that each protocol maintains the observed activity as ongoing interaction communication and conversation. Discussion topic, presentation, question/reply sequences, discussion movements (change in presentation question/reply) are maintained by writing the original statements while they are being said.

To maintain original statements, I considered both as important for the continuous observation and as a research virtue. I tried to stay as long as possible from the minutes style.

Stressing the retention of original statements as a virtue, I am referring concrete to 'what is said' and 'what words are written and noted' while the activities and interactions are being observed.

It goes without saying that the observer does not sit bent over the table, cling to the pen and writes and writes, but rather sits like the participants, and repeatedly notes. After I made quick notes about time/place etc. I put a mark or took a new page. From then on, "all words on paper" were the words of the observed participants. As such, and from the mark onwards "no words were mine". On these papers, I only wrote words and sentences that were said until I made a new mark and added for example new scenic details to the protocol.

During pauses, after observations and in the evenings, I wrote minutes, episode descriptions, analyses drafts, and overall considerations, usually 6-10 pages of diary text. However, I left the notes on the observed activity, usually 4 pages, intact as a row of original statements, which I did not mix my own words into.

Since the decision to do so was mine, I added meaning in doing so. But the real meaning, I discovered only after several months of intense observation, as I sat out to read the full collection and row of "the four pages" together. In the meanwhile, the number of pages had grown to about 200 and represent what I called an empirical gold mine about the "original course" and the process.

Despite the fact that I had become eager due to my abilities to make tape recordings almost redundant, I was obviously aware of the "four-page" limitations – and they were of course never meant to stand alone as raw data at any time. On the contrary, along with the collection of "four-pages", I had a massive collection of written materials related to the activities, as well as to selected types of activities, which was recorded and afterwards transcribed.

When I maintained original statements, in the situation, of course, I did not manage to list all the soft words and phrases, nor the full content of the small talk. Let me give an example of what I noted in relation to what I considered as the minor entity of the study, namely a replica in a sequence.

In a protocol from a plenary meeting discussion reaching a level of potential decision making about the student groups procedures for making democratic decisions, a student remark is reproduced as follows:

"(...) Susanne: I think it's stupid to vote. We have to have some arguments on the table first and some discussion, otherwise it's such a flat feeling to vote (...) "

Compared with the original statements the words: "I", "stupid (to) vote", "we", "need arguments on the table", "discussion" and "otherwise" (it's a) "flat feeling", are correctly maintained and reproduced, like words and phrases, noted while being performed and hence it is Susanne's choice of words.

My retention of original statements has for a start of course a staccato-like character, which takes form into a more fluent spoken language in the immediate after-writing but continues with all of the listed original statements kept intact.

The row (= chronology of the discussion sequence) of the listed individual replies is correspondingly correct. This means that movements between teacher-student (and student-student) sequences of discussions are maintained in accordance with the original course. This also means that the fieldnote and next the fieldnote collection can be regarded as 'the narrative text'. This, the narrative text referring to the observed educational processes is emphasized on grounds of what gradually during the fieldwork becomes the field's own language, discourse and names.

In the observation focusing on the students start of the project work the fields notes begins to refer to the project groups by their new names: "The Culture

Radicals", "The Ireland Group", "The Women-Men-Movement Group", "The Anarchist Group," etc., or groups characteristics are given as alleged references for example "The Silent Group 5". Fieldnotes also refer to rooms and locations by their shifting names. For example, the room named: "Lecture room" and "The main group room" was used for a wealth of different activities. In period of time where student directed activities were on the agenda the room was referred to among students as 'our main group room'. When the teachers announced the semester course the same room was referred to as the "Lecture room". By the students, the room was called 'The classroom' or sometimes referred to as 'the teachers room'.

The ethnographic point is, firstly, as described above about the original statements: The words and names in use are not the fieldworkers or the observers, but words and names of the students and the teachers, e.g. the field's and the participants' own words integrated in their everyday language.

This also applies to "The Silent Group 5", a term used among the group members themselves when I talked to them on a project group visit.

The ethnographic point is, secondly, that the series of fieldnotes mirror the observed process and point to for example the problem of 'being silent' at the time of the process when the problem occurs. At the time the group was expected to talk and discuss both in-group and in public, but they couldn't. Furthermore, the ethnographic point is that we get a symbolic, but yet precise reference to what is going on and how the group is getting and going along. We are brought directly into the room where the "Ireland Group" works: The Northern Irish question, or where the "Women/Men's Movement" discusses whether the movements have anything to say about gender-conscious education. We are also brought directly into the 'main group room' facing group meetings directed by the students or a lecture room and a classroom setting directed by a teacher or an external evaluation ruled by examiners. With the latter being references to the institutional arrangement the fieldnotes remind of a main challenge and questions to be answered firstly by the participant observer secondly by the analyst; namely how to maintain all these institutional arrangements and observed situations of formal and non-formal teaching and learning. How do you observe non-formal learning? How do you talk about 'tacit knowledge' and how do you document 'the invisible' interactive patterns showing how the noticed schoolifization is going on? As an experienced fieldworker I know that off course we cannot expect questions/answers to be linguistic satisfied versions of non-formal learning, tacit knowledge or schoolifization. Neither can we expect hidden agendas or contradictions between teacher direction and students' self-direction to be crystal clear in expression. However, I do claim, by experience and documentation (see Borgnakke, 1996), that if we cannot hear the impact of non-formal learning, schoolifization and contradictions between teacher and student direction we can both see it and feel it – in the situation. I also claim that these statements 'what you cannot hear, you maybe can see and feel' (or read) are a part of the strong argument for recalling the classic version of day-to-day observation and to rethink the strength of the day-to-day fieldnotes like diaries. I also confirm that especially the ongoing spontaneous conversations, maintained in the observation protocols/diaries, are important versions and documentations of what teachers and students saw, heard and reflected as problematic or as important issues, seen from the participant perspective. Hereby the involved teachers and students put hidden and contradictory agendas into words and make invisible patterns and strategies visible. Let me give an example from one of my group work observations and analysis of the student's project work process.

Making the student directed agenda visible
The group calling themselves "The Cultural Radicals" and "Rindalism Group", designed the project under the common theme framework "Popular Movements". As the project names of the group tells, they have chosen to make projects about Rindal, Rindalism (a Danish right wing culture critical movement) and art and culture. The group delivers along the way project-pedagogically speaking, quite correct problem formulations. The group ends up handing out the written report and slide show, completing the project semester's most successful evaluation. In that regard the groups written and submitted materials mirrored the project-pedagogical framework, the common theme as well as the official agenda. At the same time, I realized that the group had a more in-official version of their project and interest. This interest was a vivid student self-directed agenda and the group was eager to make it visible for me as the following section from my observations protocol shows.

"(...)
 On the "The Culture Radicals" door there was a sign:
"COME AND GET A COOKIE AND SOME DIXI MUSIC"
I walked by and took the group's new door sign as an invitation and went on a random visit.
Rune, Rolf and Richard are in the project group room. Rune sits at the machine, Rolf with a book in the corner, Richard in the middle of the room on a chair.

Richard: Take a cookie... and next there is music!
Rolf: No, we do not play the music, but you have to see some scores. (Rolf shows me a book, where there are pages with charts, or rather curves that you should play).

I: Is that what you analyze ... I mean modern music to show what Rindalismen reacted to?

Rolf: Yes, but not only music, but also visual art and literature. We are dealing with Rindalism in order to deal with what we want, namely art.

I: If it is Art that interests you, why don't you go straight to it, why go the way about "Rindalism"?

The three in the mouth to each other and with a laugh: Otherwise, it is not related to the common theme. Art is not a popular movement.

(...)

I: Are you in control of the project, you think?

Rune (tastes long on the formulation) in control of the project; in control – laughing – next addressed to me: I rather say that the project is in control of us.

Rolf: We have written a lot, for example some good papers about how Rindalism started, what it meant, etc. And we also ended up with what we were supposed to do, namely a problem formulation.

(...) "

(Cit. Obs.prot. ProGr. Visit. M.pos.)

For the process oriented observation this conversation (and hereafter the fieldnote) was important because the group member gives me the story they will share with me and talk about, but not write about.

Orally and situationally, the group gives its own, almost private, reasons ("We are dealing with Rindalismen to deal with what we want, namely art"). They relate to the official and common requirements that they are familiar with ("Otherwise, it is not under the common theme frame. Art is not a popular movement"). They readily talk about the used texts, where they with an ironic twist refer to the "Quran" and "the Bible", and then promptly demonstratively point to their own important Bible, namely the Art-book.

They clarify yet another important common requirement - and relate to the official project pedagogical cardinal points that they strategic relate to as the requirements ("And we also ended with what we were supposed to do, namely a problem formulation").

What the group "must do", they say, is in sharp contrast to what the group says they "themselves want". But, as stressed in the situation, they do what they must – and what they want.

The Culture Radicals was the group demonstrating the relation (and the contradiction) between the project pedagogical agenda in the teacher directed versions and the student directed version to the point. And when this group goes to the point they make the cardinal point in the practical process visible.

Against this background the ethnographic point is both the official agenda, the teacher directed version and the student directed practice. But I admit that to cover and cope with these examples of practical complexity and different layers in the observed interaction and communication is an ongoing challenge for ethnographic writing, firstly in terms of writing fieldnotes secondly in terms of writing analyses.

The guideline for the analytic description and documentations was in the above case what the students talked about and reflected as important issues. The students' perspective and eager to perform their own ideas is imbedded in their wordings and contradictions between teacher and students' strategies become visible. Hereby the ethnographic analytical interest for strategies is guided to further exploration of the practical process and the cardinal point.

To maintain the process and the cardinal point I prefer to refer to the same principle as mentioned above, namely to maintain interactive patterns and the organized activities by drawing sketches of the room, marking where the students, groups and teachers were placed and with arrows, buns and crosses note the flow of interaction. Hereby, I marked what I called 'the authoritative speech center' and its peripheries.

Writing close-up analyses using fieldnotes and sketches to document the authoritative center and its peripheries

The ethnographic point with the many sketches embedded in the fieldnote collection is similar to the collection of the "four pages": Each sketch was of course an empirical document with a very high degree of detail and saturated with symbolic meaning. But the full collection of sketches was most important. Suddenly, I could see and document the interaction's architectural basic category, e.g. the classroom.

All of my sketches had the "classroom" imbedded in the situation, no matter what situation they were drawn over. Even the one drawn over a project group discussion held on the lawn on a sunny day, had the "classroom" in it. And why is that? Because the sketch showed that the group's supervisor also sat there in the middle of the circle, with a pile of A-4 folders and books in front of him, as though it was a cathedra and he had some extra space around him; because the project group members, like "pupils", were almost half a circle, and because all speech streams had the teacher as a center. Questions came from "teacher" who also received answers, and then held a smaller presentation (the teacher's monologue), which spelled out a question whose answer was "teacher" coordinated.

An important matrix for all these sketches, which I actually signed along in 117 different ways were The Classroom. The Classroom and the interactional pattern could be observed in variations during the course and even in project and student directed settings where students should not act like "teacher/pupil". The illustration below refers to a sketch drawn during observation of a group performance in what I note as an Ending-position – the final evaluation. Just before the official start the parties: teacher and censor, the Ireland-group and the opponent group (students as well) entered the room and placed themselves spontaneous like sketched below. During the evaluation teacher and censor took the leading role, a Male-student from the Ireland group was primarily the speaker of the group (gave answers to teacher and censor). Three female members were almost silent and so were the members of the opponent group. As observer I recognized the interactive pattern though surprised over the strength in the schoolish teacher-student and gender behavior. However, it goes with the story that the evaluation all in all went well also in the students' eyes. The group, i.e. their male chairman, answered the questions correctly and they got a good grade!

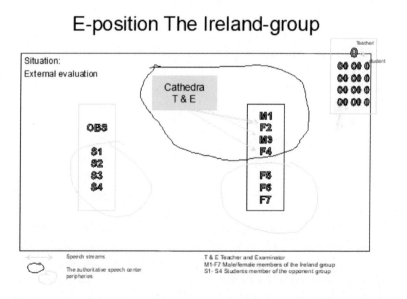

By reproducing the architectural design, I maintained the observed situation in a concrete manner. I also maintained an educational cultural expression. And when the symbolically recreated "Classroom" let the interaction take place in this room's likeness, the association series is also: school life, everyday life, school routine, teacher and student, as well as the sketches at one and the same time referring to the desired alternatives and to routines over classroom-like interaction patterns.

For writing close-up analyse of the classroom-like patterns the important background is of course the observed situation and in addition the continuous conversation with the teachers, the students, individually and in groups. The maintained situation and interactive pattern in the observation protocol are hereby also in function as a day-to-day comment problematizing the "classroom" or marking the authoritative center and its peripheries like a Female/male matter.

Let me illustrate this by going back to the fieldnote maintaining the above described and sketched E-position of the Ireland group's final evaluation.

During the observation there was no doubt about the high degree of teacher direction and therefore no doubt about when the project groups member are given a question to be answered. In addition, there was no doubt that it was primarily the group members who took initial introductory questions to answer questions. But when they answer the questions, they are obviously deceived by what are closed, open or half-open questions.

There is a guessing atmosphere: What does teacher and censor mean and which type of answers is expected? As the section from my fieldnote exemplify below, the teacher calls for something that could look like a specific answer to an important question, but what?

"What was it England really wanted from Ireland?"

"(...)
At a relatively early stage in the interrogation center passages, the teacher asks:
"What was it England really wanted from Ireland?"
The question leaves the group silent. The teacher focuses on the three from the project group, who until now seem to be the ones who answer questions. The teacher concentrates against Ivan, from the start of the evaluation has emerged as the group's first speaker.
Ivan begins to answer, mumbling in front of him, supplemented by Irene, who until now has also heard of those who respond.
In semi-high sentences, they repeat the question separately.
The teacher, in turn, repeats the question, and adds: "You might say that England, the powers, would have power, but what was it they wanted?"
Ivan and Irene, like the assistant respondents, try again, repeating the question, plus the new addendum: "they would have power yes, but... it also had consequences... (/mumbles here a bit unclear for us who are furthest away)
At one point, the teacher eagerly begins to nod, the respondents' voices rise: "... which meant, among other things, that Ireland had to export grains (/Now the teacher is nodding mumbling yes yes go on/)

/) ... even in periods when the Irish people were dead close to hunger. "

Teacher: YES, England would simply have built a grain store! "

(...) "
(Cit. obs. prot. Ireland E. m. pos.)

The characteristic teacher directed pattern for this evaluation, moving from open to closed to guessing and back again, are one reason why discussion in such passages cannot occur. If "England would simply have built a grain store" and that was the answer – then there is hardly anything to discuss.

But at a time when a discussion about the power relations between Ireland/Northern Ireland and England is opened tries one of the three more active group members to be incorporated, thinking high:

"(...)
Irene tries with a reflection on: "that Northern Ireland will not be able to do without financial support or external intervention in the long run. It seems that Ireland can do better financially. They can offer working class people work. But in Northern Ireland, the working class people will always be oppressed ... "
Both teacher and censor look very unexpected. They ask promptly, eager questions: "Working class? - Northern Ireland, economically weakest?

Irene becomes silent. At any rate, she does not respond quickly to the newly asked questions.
Censor continues: "Who is the strongest financially?

Ilse, who has so far said nothing (/might be able to answer the now closed question) begins to answer the questions: "Northern Ireland ... (with censor confirming nods, she continues) because it has received support from England on the way. Censor with direct inquiry back to Irene: "Well, then it must be a contradiction when.... (/Censor interrupted by Irene)
Irene: "What I think is that the Catholics in Northern Ireland can never get work, houses, etc. It will always be a source of turmoil. So without intervention and support from the outside, Northern Ireland cannot manage financially "
/Hereafter, the teacher and the censor, each in their own way, begin to ask more 'real' supplementary questions and give a longer examination of the question. They do not agree with Irene, but they signal acceptance that there might be a problem that gave rise to

reflections and discussion, and consequently not only a contradiction.
(...)
(cit. obs.prot. as above)

For the close-up analytic framework this observations protocol has huge value because of the exact reference to the situation and the maintained sequences of teacher/censor – students' questions/answers/argument. The interactive patterns, the authoritative speech streams, and peripheries are of course transformed to text, but as illustrated above both the content and the dynamic process is still present. For ethnographic analytical writing it means that the observed practical process can be reconstructed and the analysed interactive and in the case teacher-directed communicative process can be documented.

The strength coming from the fieldnotes and the collection of the embedded observations-protocols is the closeness to the situation. Having the collection from the observed evaluations the field researcher as 'the analyst' can reconstruct the process and the S-E-M position and 'the writer' can document the process referring not only to the observed oral evaluation but also to the written material. In the above-illustrated case the Ireland groups 70 pages report on The North-Irish question is incorporated in the observed situation as well as in my material collection.

For research purposes, the value of the material collection is its totality. Within the framework of the explored field, an almost complete archive of the involved texts has been obtained (the students project report and assignments included). The significant value of this archive became clearer when the empirical data collection was completed and the process of doing analyses was started. The archive was a significant reference to the practical processes. The archive was as text-in-context referring to the ongoing process from start to ending positions. Hereby the archive and the collection of fieldnotes and embedded observations protocols refer to what I could regard as the matrice for the ethnographic cardinal writing and process analytical framework (Borgnakke, 1996).

The matrice, following the process from S-M-E position

The huge empirical collection was the participant observations and hereby 'the fieldworker's intention. However, for 'the analyst' and 'the writer' it is a problem. By experience the problem, albeit time-consuming, can be resolved by the principles of systematization (Borgnakke, 1996). Furthermore, the institutional arrangement and the basic components of the education, in advance, arrange - according to the educational logic and structure – even the most comprehensive and chaotic material sets. For ethnographic writing in general – and for what I regard as cardinal writing in specific, it means that any text, and any series of interactive and communicative 'question/reply' course, maintained in the fieldworkers empirical archive, can be replaced and analysed by using either the model of communicative action (sender- message- receiver), the didactical triangle or my model of the basic component referring to "Teacher/student component or the "Academic Subject, Case/Learning Situation" component (Borgnakke, 1996).

This means that the basic model combined with in my case the project pedagogy's own phase model, can bring the huge and somehow chaotic material back in order. Further, the observed process following the observation protocols sequences of cardinal point can be regarded as the matrice for the writing framework. In relation to the important S-, M-, S-positions the matrice can be illustrated as follows:

The observed process

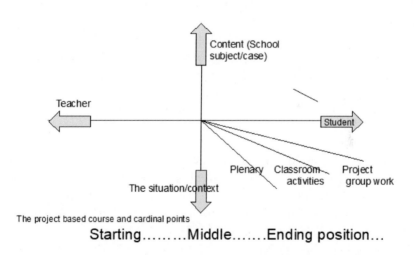

The project based course and cardinal points

Starting.........Middle.......Ending position...

The way in which the institutional arrangement and the process from starting to ending point in itself arranges the activities and materials of field research is maintained in the fieldnotes collection and in the sequence of de embedded observations protocols ("the four pages"). Following these, means that the cardinal writing can follow the course and the involved parties in ongoing action and movement: From plenary activities to project activities, from teacher directed activity and strategies to students directed processes, from one consequential S-, M-, or S-positioned action to another.

I deliberately use the term "in ongoing action" to force the ethnographic writing to match the aim from the process observation, namely in my case: to follow the alternative project organized education and the teaching and learning strategies in daily practices.

Being interested in the progressive alternative meant that I also had a pointed interest for the systematic analysis of the inner work of project pedagogy, the milestone of the process, the interactive patterns etc. For writing the empirical analysis it meant that there were cardinal points where the intensive observation and the material collection were markedly interrelated[9]. As illustrated above with the Ireland group as example both the observation protocols, sketches and the students own project report were in use and therefor documented in the written close up analysis (see Borgnakke, 1996: vol 2:600-620).

In addition to the close-up analyses focusing on the project groups process and performance the fieldnote collection as a cardinal text also made it possible to focus the cardinal writing on the school or educational level where the S-, M- and E-positions are mapped and characterized for tendencies referring to all the groups and parties involved. In analytical sense, it means that the ethnographic writings point of view is clarified as seen from the S, M or E-positions, respectively.

Let me give an example. Based on intensive observation of the entire S-position the new students´ entry into the project-based education and learning environment were mapped and given an ethnographic and analytical overview (Borgnakke, 1985). This overview describes how the new generation, "The New", learn to know the progressive Academia from inside and shows requirements, norms and values, which conversely are quite familiar to the environment and have almost become the obvious for older students and teachers – "The Experienced". Showing the characteristic for the S –position and the relation between "The New" and "The experienced" for the writing process also meant to make use of the broadest spectrum from the archive. Observed Well come activities, materials, the big well come from the university principal, the presentation from the tutor group (a play), the teacher group (an oral performance and a poem) meaning all kinds of oral and written genre are in use (Borgnakke 1984, 1996).

By writing up and by documentation of the variety I gave an overview of firstly the S-position later on the M- and the E-position (Borgnakke 1996 vol 2: part 4 and 5) exemplifying the complicated network of norms, habits, rules and requirements in shifts from teacher directed and student directed strategies and perspectives.

During the year of fieldwork I had to study the nature of the environment – almost become part of it - to then later make myself a stranger in analytical distance.

---

9. In Borgnakke 1996 vol. 2: pp I analyse the process and the cardinal points in detail. The article *Project Work and Learning Processes: Viewed Practically and Analytically* (Borgnakke, 1999) represents a short version.

Basic principles in perspective: ecological validity and authentic practical complexity

Ethnographic and cardinal writing in my version is based on an analytic overview reconstructing the process-oriented observation, the fieldnote collection and the archive. In this sense both empirical findings and materials from S-, M-, E-positions are present as the driver for overall process analysis as for close up analyses of the exemplary situations. In total, the overall analysis refers to fieldwork and empirical data-collections at two one-year programs (Basic BA education at Aalborg University), 6 semesters organized educational programs, approx. 100 teachers and students through 7 project periods. However, the important point is not in the mere numbers, rather that the educational program, the courses and project works have been followed in their real chronology, to a full extent referring to all participants, all groups, all periods and all types of activities. The importance of this is reflected in relation to the principle of representativeness and validity – on the premises of the field and the qualitative methods (Borgnakke, 1996). As stated I suggest that an empirical material collection is regarded as representative and valid, in the sense of high coverage, depth and validity of the course, precisely when it covers the entire course/a whole period, all participants and all types of activities.

When material in my case from long-term fieldwork covers the educational process from S- to E-positions, the internal representativeness and validity is very high. Reflected along with the concept of ecological validity described by Hammersley and Atkinson (1983: 87), I will claim that the cardinal writing strategy and its empirical basis and material collection has ecologically validity in relation to the process, the milestones and the teacher- and student- directed activities and trajectories. The process oriented reflection of ecological validity as a basic principle refers to fieldworks done during the 1980's, but it also provides renewal of the principle in my fieldworks conducted in the 2000s. Related to research in the area of IT & learning, the principle of ecological validity was confirmed but also stressed in connection with a principle referring to what I call the authentic practical complexity.

My fieldwork in upper secondary schools was focused on three IT-school and covers cases the different organizational levels, from leader-, teacher/colleague- to teaching practice level (Borgnakke 2007, 2011b, 2012). Hereby fieldwork and school case material collections referred to the different levels and to the practical complex by being a network of different data types, learning platforms and IT-settings. Observing these settings and classrooms loaded with technology, confirmed the importance of renewing the classic field observations and even the importance of the use of handwriting to get a proper fieldnote! I was also confirmed that the fieldnote collection (with all the relevant links embedded) needed to have the sequence of observations protocol referring directly to the

IT-based learning situations, and to shifts between online and offline activities as they were performed in the moment of action.

Ethnographic analyses of the practical use of technology confirm in a broader sense the daily routines for teaching and learning as a mix of media used in situations you can conceptualize as 'mediated' (Hjarvard 2008) and as a mix of online- and offline situations where the flow of texts and multi-modalities are in use (Borgnakke 2015: 14).

In ethnographic sense that means that you regard the question about IT-based or IT-enhanced learning as situated in practice complexity and therefor reconstruct the IT-use 'correctly', meaning in correct order, in the S-, M-,E process. In analytic sense, it means that you refer to a context specific authentic complexity.

I use the term 'authentic complexity' with a general and a specific reference. In general, I suggest that we conceptualize learning as situated in a scholastic context or in the (work-) practical context. This practical context is in ethnographic terms to be described in authentic complexity as 'an ordinary day' in a school context or as an ordinary day in the clinical practice, as shown in observations of nursing students (Noer 2016). 'An ordinary day' is filled with different professional learning or health care technologies, practical procedures and interaction series involving professionals, students and patients. It is of course also filled with different professional demands and positions and with emotional reactions. But the point is that it doesn't matter what the actors (or the fieldworker) want to describe as embedded in 'An ordinary day', it is still a part of 'the authentic complexity' of the everyday context.

In relation to the on-going case studies in which IT-enhanced settings and e-pedagogical frameworks are investigated it means that ethnographic research is confronted with a field of practice where a mix-media blended strategy integrates both organizational development, education and learning research into a common framework for coping with both innovations and the digital everyday conditions (see special issues Borgnakke et al Seminar.net 2015, Innovation og Uddannelse, 2016). These are the characteristics of the current innovative context, but as Borgnakke (2013) and Hammersley (2006, 2017) also points out, ethnography following processes of development changes in response to (to blend with and follow) developments. This means that developments in its context of investigation become characteristics of ethnography too. To cope and cover following the processes of development challenge the research strategy and the mix between the use of new technology and media in the ethnographic process and using the classic participative observation and spontaneous conversations and material collection. As stressed in this article the classic observation and the classic fieldnotes are still second to none when studying living dynamic processes.

Against this background ethnographic writing following full-scale education based on empirical material having ecological validity and authentic complexity, is a strong concept for showing the practical process, milestones and different strategies. Stressing the Marcus inspired principle of 'following the case' (Marcus, 1995) you can say that the methodological renewal is IT-based, but the research process and phases with observations and interviews is confirmed as based on principles, genres and material collections known from long-term fieldwork.

Bibliography

Borgnakke, K. (1984). En, to, tre, fire... Dette er et basisår! Om social regulering og differentiering på AUCs basisuddannelse. *Gløder - Tidsskrift for Filosofi, Sociologi, Politik*, (7), 99-43.

Borgnakke, K. (1999). Project Work and Learning Processes: Viewed Practically and Analytically. I S. Tøsse (red.), *Corporate and Nonformal Learning: Adult Education Research in Nordic Countries* (s. 159-175). Trondheim: TAPIR Akademisk Forlag.

Borgnakke, K. (1996) Educational field research (vol.1), The methodology of process analysis (vol.2), Danish University Press.

Borgnakke, K. (2005). *Læringsdiskurser og praktikker*. København: Akademisk Forlag.

Borgnakke, K. (2007). *Nye læringsstrategier i de gymnasiale uddannelser: Casestudier i It-klasser og projektarbejde*. Syddansk Universitet: Institut for Filosofi, Pædagogik og Religionsstudier. Gymnasiepædagogik, Bind. 59

Borgnakke, K. (2010) The methodological challenge: To cover a field of practice by mapping the field from macro to mezo to micro levels Paper Higher Education Close Up 5, Lancaster July 2010.

Borgnakke, Karen (2011a). *Et universitet er et sted, der forsker i alt undtagen i sig selv og sin egen virksomhed*. København: Institut for Medier, Erkendelse og Formidling & Institut for Nordiske Studier og Sprog, Københavns Universitet.

Borgnakke, Karen (2011b). Blandt professionelle idealister og pragmatikere – en caseanalyse om professionalisering i gymnasiefeltet. In: Christensen, Gerd & Berthelsen, Eva (red.). *Pædagogiske perspektiver på arbejdsliv*, København: Forlaget Frydenlund.

Borgnakke, K. (2012). Challenges for the Next Generation in Upper Secondary School - Between Literacy, Numeracy, and Technacy. In: Pink, William (ed.). *Schools for Marginalized Youth*. Hampton Press, in print.

Borgnakke, K. (2013). *Etnografiske metoder i uddannelsesforskningen*. Inst. f. medier, erkendelse og formidling, Københavns Universitet.

Borgnakke, K. (2015a). Coming Back to Basic Concepts of the Context. Seminar.net : Media, technology and lifelong learning, 11(1).

Borgnakke, K. (2015). How is learning in class like using a mobile phone? Ethnographic approaches to explore learning in late modern contexts. I A. Czejkowska, J. Hohensinner, & C. Wieser (red.), *Forschende Vermittlung: Gegenstände, Methoden und Ziele fachdidaktischer Unterrichtsforschung* (s. 57-76). Wien: Löcker, Vienna. Arts & Culture & Education, Nr. 10.

Borgnakke, K. (2017). Meta-ethnography and systematic reviews – linked to the evidence movement and caught in a dilemma. *Ethnography and Education*, 12(2), 194-210. DOI: 10.1080/17457823.2016.1253027

Delamont, S. (2008). For lust of knowing – observation in educational ethnography, How to do Educational Ethnography, Walford, G. (ed.) *Ethnography and Education*, Tuffnell Press.

Eisenhart, M. (2017). A matter of scale: multi-scale ethnographic research on education in the United States, *Ethnography and Education*, 12:2, 134-147, DOI: 10.1080/17457823.2016.1257947.

Hammersley & Atkinson. (1983). *Ethnography. Principles in Practice.* London and New York: Routledge.

Hammersley. M. (2006). *Ethnography: problems and prospects,* *Ethnography and Education*, 1:1, 3-14, DOI: 10.1080/17457820500512697

Hammersley, M. (2017). What is ethnography? Can it survive? Should it? *Ethnography and Education*, DOI: 10.1080/17457823.2017.1298458

Hastrup, K. (1988). *Introduction, Hastrup, Ramløv Feltarbejde. Oplevelse og metode i etnografien.* Akademisk Forlag.

Hjarvard, S. (2008). The Mediatization of Society. A Theory of the Media as Agents of Social and Cultural Change. *Nordicom Review* 29(2): 105-134.

Kvale, S. (1997) *Interviews, An introduction to Qualitative Research Interviewing*, London, Sage publications.

Krarup, K. , Rieper, O. (1981). *Forordet til kvalitative metoder. Hvad er kvalitative metoder (What are Qualitative methods?) Kvalitative metoder i Dansk Samfundsforskning, Nyt fra Samfundsvidenskaberne* 50, 2.udg. Copenhagen

Marcus, G. (1995). "Ethnography in / of the World System: The Emergence of Multi-Sited Ethnography." *Annual Review of Anthropology* 24: 95-117.

Marcus, G. (2009). "Multi-sited Ethnography: Notes and Queries" in *Multi-sited Ethnography: Theory, Practice and Locality in Contemporary Research*, edited by MA. Falzon, 181-196. Surrey: Ashgate Publishing.

Nielsen, C.S. (2017). *Professionsstuderende i det interprofessionelle læringslandskab*, thesis, University of Copenhagen.

Noer, V. R. (2016). 'Rigtige sygeplejersker': Uddannelsesetnografiske studier af sygeplejestuderendes studieliv og dannelsesprocesser. København: Københavns Universitet, Det Humanistiske Fakultet.

Seminar.net, Special Issue, Exploring the learning context in shifts between online and offline learning, Borgnakke (ed) Volume 11, issue 1, 2015 http://www.seminar.net/volume-11-issue-1-2015

Section Two

Fieldwork writing practices

Troubling 'writing as representation'

Pat Thomson

Representation. The portrayal of people, things, relationships, ways of being and becoming, events, beliefs – a description that is at best a likeness.

Representation, as a concept, is attributed to a text, be it verbal, visual, aural or multimedia. Representation, as a concept, is used as a textual analytic. A reader might ask of a text understood as a representation – who wrote this text, where and when? How might context, culture and relationships have produced this text? For whom is this text intended? Who or what is not in this text? What might these omissions mean? What are people and things doing, how are they relating, who is saying what? What might this mean? In other words, what kind of representation is this and how does this matter and to whom? Representation, as a concept, is also used by writers themselves to speak about their own text. It is commonplace for instance to read ethnographic writing that refers to representation and/or its underpinning onto-epistemology/ies. A representation is not the real thing. It is a copy, and an inexact one.

For social scientists, the term representation often acts as a synecdoche for an onto-epistemological stance: a stand-in/stand-on concept that signals the writer's positioning. Inserted in a text, the word representation means a complex set of interrelated understandings - there is a material reality but research is a process of interpreting it, making sense from it; sense-making is always culturally located, it is particular, partial and situated; the texts and the ideas that are expressed in them are always approximations and thus have omissions, emphases and idiosyncrasies associated with their construction; objectivity is achieved through scholarly consensus and the application of rigorous approaches to inquiry (Haraway, 1988; Harding, 1993; Lather, 1991). A representation is always discursively produced, a product of its time and place (Hall, 1997). The use of the word representation is a health warning to a reader that the text must be read with some caution, the reader must understand its limitations.

However, there might be more to writing than representation. In this chapter, I examine the ways in which the discipline of anthropology took up the notion of representation and why, and then consider what kind of trouble the concept is now experiencing. I add additional concerns through briefly considering writing research. My intention in the chapter, a text-based think-piece, is to raise issues that educational writers might consider when thinking about the nature of the ethnographic texts that they want to write.

Anthropology and writing as representation: Two interventions

In *The interpretation of cultures* (1973) Clifford Geertz elaborated the notion of culture as a social and semiotic system. His book can be seen as a signal of the wider 'linguistic turn' in the humanities, a disruptive move which had anthropologists giving up on finding 'law-like' processes in societies and instead, embracing their hermeneutic positioning. Geertz' argument focused primarily on the difficulties of 'seeing', understanding and then communicating about a specific social context and its inhabitants. A focus on the social and semiotic, he suggested, required the anthropologist to interpret, and to use "thick description" in order to convey something of the complexities of the places and peoples being researched.

Geertz' next book, entitled *Works and lives: The anthropologist as author* (Geertz, 1988) developed an argument about anthropological texts and their 'authors', a term which invokes a literary rather than a scientific tradition. Geertz reasoned that anthropology could not claim to present objective truth as experience was mediated via the person of the researcher. His examinations of historical texts led him to conclude that both the anthropologist and the 'truth' that they conveyed were produced through a particular style of writing. The use of a shared vocabulary and writing in the third person in a matter of fact style, piling up fact after fact, conveyed a false sense of authenticity and scientificity. Geertz proposed moving away from writing that had the surface appearance of a scientific treatise towards writing which recognised the differences between material reality and its representations.

Much of the early concern about Geertz' work arose from the implications of the move to recognise representation. His work was worrying either because of his relativist epistemological stance and/or his lack of attention to the important role of scholarly communities; both omissions seemed to lead to the promotion of an un-systematic approach to knowledge production. Carrithers (1988) for instance saw that Geertz' account missed seeing ethnography as a principled discipline in which scholarly standards prevailed. Ethnographic writing did not have the "plausibility or inner harmony of realist fiction" he suggested, but must adhere to things which are verifiable: texts must have "fidelity to what has been experienced and learnt" (p. 22).

Geertz himself, reflecting on his career (2002) agreed with the need for fidelity and disciplinary standards on rigour, but pointed to the difficulties that the discipline had in coming to agreement. He noted the fragmentation of anthropology into anthropologies. What was lacking, he reflected, "was any means of ordering the field, of providing an "encompassing paradigm" (p. 10). This was not due to deficiencies within the discipline, he suggested, rather it was a product of larger changes in society and in the academy; the end of the twentieth century was a time of conflict more generally, not just in anthropology. Change had

> ...produced both an intensification of polemical combat and, in some quarters anyway, angst and malaise. Not only did there appear a series

of trumped up "wars" between imaginary combatants over artificial issues (materialists vs. idealists, universalists vs. relativists, scientists vs. humanists, realists vs. subjectivists), but a generalized and oddly self-lacerating skepticism about the anthropological enterprise as such – about representing The Other or, worse yet, purporting to speak for him (sic) (p.11)

Internal anthropological debates were not simply about writing, according to Geertz, nor even about how writing did the ontological and epistemological work of representation. They were rooted in matters of ethical-political consequence. Research in societies which had been subject to colonialism and commercial exploitation by a discipline which had itself been part of the colonial project, he noted, inevitably produced high levels of reflexivity. It was not surprising that there were multiple points of view in tension about what to research, where and how to write about it (Geertz, 1996).

Just before Geertz' book on authoring ethnography, James Clifford and George Marcus published *Writing culture. The politics and poetics of ethnography* (Clifford and Marcus, 1986). They too focused on the dual problem of researching 'the other', as well as writing about them. Clifford and Marcus were concerned with the ethnographer's cultural/historical/institutional/contextual lens and how this shaped their work in field and office. Making texts from relationships and events was not a neutral practice, they argued. Clifford and Marcus were particularly concerned with the traditional exteriority of the ethnographic gaze, and visualised positioning - the anthropologist-as-viewer. Writing in the introduction to the edited collection, Clifford noted that

(t)he predominant metaphors in anthropological research have been participant-observation, data collection, and cultural description, all of which presuppose a standpoint outside – looking at, objectifying, or, somewhat closer, "reading," a given reality. (Clifford 1988: p. 11)

Clifford problematised this approach. The researcher was always inside, he stated. Their presence changed what happened. So, to construct a representation that was about neutrality and lack of influence was inaccurate. It was a representation of a type of knowledge production, not of the actual ethnographic inquiry itself. Mobilising the notion that cultures are relational, negotiated and intersubjective, Clifford proposed that

Polyvocality was restrained and orchestrated in traditional ethnographies by giving to one voice a pervasive authorial function and to others the role of sources, "informants," to be quoted or paraphrased. Once dialogism and polyphony are recognized as modes of textual production, monophonic authority is questioned, revealed to be characteristic of a science that has claimed to *represent* cultures. (Clifford 1988: p. 15)

Clifford and Marcus' edited collection focused on written representations where contributors took more literary approaches - metaphor, narrative, figuration and polyvocality - to the writing. This move to the literary was not to suggest that ethnographies were fictional per se, but that they had given up the quest for unachievable 'fact'. These more literary texts indicated that ethnographers were self-conscious about their writing, and the knowledge work that writing accomplished.

Challenging representation
Anthropologists continued to debate the linguistic representational turn and seminal moments. Writing not long after Clifford, Marcus and Geertz, Michael Taussig in *Mimesis and alterity* (1993), argued that understandings that knowledge and texts were social constructions and representations had been "converted into a conclusion" – e.g. "sex is a construction". It appeared, he asserted, that it was sufficient to acknowledge that what was thought and said was socially framed. Nothing more was required.

> The brilliance of the pronouncement was blinding. Nobody was asking what's the next step? What do we do with this insight? To adopt Hegel, the beginnings of knowledge were made to pass for actual knowledge. (p. xvi)

Taussig proposed that the discipline needed to continue to work on what the understanding of representation actually meant for research and for writing. Other anthropologists agreed.

It is now possible to discern some distinct trends in anthropological responses to the linguistic turn, some of which do, as Taussig suggests, try to find ways beyond representation. The trends include but are not limited to:

Writing centred ethnography/ies
In the forty or so years since anthropologists took serious account of representation and writing, they have engaged in various textual experiments. Taking their cue from Clifford and Marcus, anthologies of ethnographic writing attest to widespread and ongoing experimentation with genre, narrative, humour, paratexts and description (Van Maanen, 1995; Wulff, 2016). Fiction is blended with the more obviously factual (Ghodsee, 2011) and some writers explicitly engage in dialogue with fiction (e.g. Narayan, 2012 in conversation with Chekov). The journal *Cultural Anthropology* has collaborated with the literary journal *American Short Fiction* to

explore the affiliations across and blurred boundaries between fiction, ethnography and criticism (see https://culanth.org/curated_collections/5-literature-writing-and-anthropology). While social realism still dominates the field, despite textual experimentation, there is a trend to non-realist narratives (see for example Taussig, 1997 and his use of magic realism).

Critical analysis of the 'I' who writes
Almost every aspect of the craft of ethnographic writing has been and is deconstructed, including the ethnographic self (e.g. Reed-Danahay, 2005 on Bourdieu). There are highly personal ethnographic accounts which address the researcher's emotional commitments to the people with whom they research (Behar, 1996), and their mixed feelings about field work experiences and memories (Collins and Gallinat, 2011). Bouchetoux (2014) for instance spends a chapter of his monograph on 'uninhibited methods' discussing guilt and shame, emotional states that he argues are built into the discipline.

> Reflexivity is a strategic device through which anthropologists cope with their guilt regarding integration. Integration is both lacking (as reflected in boredom and loneliness in the field and disappointing descriptions) and intrusive (as reflected in spying and camouflage games in the field and disappointing reciprocity). … relationships cannot be sincere enough and respectful enough to make the idealism of populist ethnography come true. (p. 12)

According to Bouchetoux, being reflexive means writing about emotional dilemmas and difficulties, not presenting a sanitised representation of experience. While there is a clear danger of such writing lapsing into solipsism, leading to self-indulgent confessionals, there is a time and place for uncomfortable writing, he asserts. Bouchetoux proposes writing which addresses the structurally produced embodied difficulties that the ethnographer encounters. Bouchetoux illustrates his point with a discussion about the repulsion he felt while researching in an advertising agency, he not only recoiled from the practises of advertising and the staff but also from himself as a participant. We might think, in educational ethnography, of a parallel in the contentious description of the intimate relationship between Harry Wolcott and the 'sneaky kid' (Wolcott, 2002).

Concerns about participants' responses
Anxieties about the question of the consequences of representation have not been resolved. The ethical and political dimensions involved in writing about others remains a primary concern. The understandings that texts are not mimetic – but situated interpretations of people, events, customs, rituals, conversations, things

and their meanings – continues to cause trouble. Anthropologists do not agree on who should have the last word about a text, as the edited collection *When they read what we write* (Brettell, 1996) illustrates. Should participants have the right to veto what they do not agree with? Is the researcher's partial exteriority and their defamilarised understandings better than those of others in the research, or more worthy of publication? Such questions are not easily resolved.

Participatory research practices can provide a process through which some representational differences can be negotiated (Lassiter, 2005). But such collaborations requite serious commitment to process and time. And why should 'participants' engage at in this way? What benefits come to them, as opposed to the researcher? These questions can be particularly tricky in situations where researchers have historically been complicit in unethical practices in relation to ownership of knowledges (Dei, Hall, & Rosenberg, 2000). The ongoing implications of anthropological imbrication in colonial collecting, cataloguing and naming practices (Bennett, 1995) are far from settled. But even if ethnographers work in situations where appropriation of knowledge and single authorship have been less fraught, the ethical question of the power-knowledge relationships embedded in ethnographic practice, and in the production of writing about the research, remains. Such questions are now almost always integral to any ethnographic research.

Written representations are self-aware of their complicit and/or contradictory positioning. Is it sufficient to simply acknowledge this?

Explorations of ethnographic 'knowledge'
Anthropologists and ethnographers in other disciplines have been folded further into debates about knowledge. The body has returned as a site of knowing, and knowledge making (Conquergood, 2013). Acknowledgment of the sensual, the visual and the haptic which constitute an important part of 'being there' for researcher and participants (Pink, 2006, 2009) is increasingly common. Anthropology has not been exempt from the turn to 'affect'. How these non-word-based knowledges are made into text has supported further experimentation with film, poetry, performance, and multi-modal text. These are sometimes seen as questions of method – how best to research, rather than as questions of representation. As Elliott and Dara, (2017), from the aptly named Centre for Imaginative Ethnography in Toronto, explain

> While anthropologists have conventionally considered the artistic *products* created by research subjects as objects of study, many contemporary anthropologists and artists are turning their attention to creative methodologies, to articulating ethnography and artistic practices in the process of research, and to ethnographic knowledge co-creation. (p. 7)

Sometimes, the focus shifts slightly to the question of knowledge domains and interdisciplinarity. The affordances of multimedia have allowed various digital anthropological experiments with different forms of knowledge (see for instance Philip Vannini's 'Innovative ethnographies' series for Routledge which incorporate print and digital texts, https://www.routledge.com/Innovative-Ethnographies/book-series/INNOVETHNO).

Contemporary artists have identified common interests with anthropologists and have produced collaborative anthologies, events and exhibitions which explore visual, ethical and textual knowledge practices (Laine, 2018; Schneider and Wright, 2010). Taking a cue from contemporary art, some anthropologists suggest that ethnographic writing might do well to focus more on unknowing (Fisher and Fortnum, 2014), than presenting a representation that fabricates completeness. As Pandian and Mclean put it, writing might become

> …a means of marking and maintaining an openness to events, surprises, and contingencies, to a reality that is as much a source of questions and provocations as of answers (Pandian and McLean 2017: p. 4).

The linguistic turn and the elevation of language is now placed under considerable duress by feminist, postcolonial, new materialist and queer research traditions taking a post-representational turn. While accepting that cultural linguistic and symbolic forms exist and are worthy of research, a non-representational approach sees these as second-order interventions (Massumi, 2002). The idea of representation offers a static and permanently structured view of the world and posits a hierarchical view in which language is more important than anything else. The notion of representation ignores the ways in which words and things coexist, collide, move and combine and detach from each other. Representation is a-temporal. According to Maggie Maclure (2013), language must therefore be

> …deposed from its god-like centrality in the construction and regulation of wordly affairs, to become one element in a manifold of forces and intensities that are moving, connecting and diverging, (p. 660)

Abandoning representation is a move which eschews the conventions of social science writing, with its certitude of argument and firm conclusions and implications (Somerville, 2007). Post representational researchers find Deleuzian notions of emergence and assemblage helpful when wrestling with how to deal with continually moving and shifting things and people. Taussig (2012) for example, sees writing as an emergence, where meaning is not, and cannot, be fixed. This notion shifts the researcher's focus from 'what the writing is, to what the writing does' (Deleuze 1995: p. 21) – how problems are coming into being, the entanglings and becomings of ethnographers and their tools and materials.

Explorations of ethnographic knowledge production

The craft of ethnography continues to be explored. The ubiquitous practise of fieldnotes (Sanjek, 1990) and thick description (Freeman, 2014) are defamiliarized. Methods are expanded (Bakke and Peterson, 2017). Tim Ingold, for instance, has argued strongly for an anthropology which focuses on doing, observing, rather than observation. He argues against a focus on writing and proposes a graphic anthropology which participates in action and activity through watching and drawing. This is an ethnographic practice akin to that of Michael Taussig, whose *I swear I saw this. Drawings in fieldwork notebooks, namely, my own* reveals a mix of observings, meditations and open-ended musings. Andrew Causey (2017) has developed a visual pedagogy for ethnographers – a set of etudes, or exercises, which use drawing as a means of sharpening what ethnographers can 'see'. Causey's approach focuses attention on perception, focus, peripheral vision, and the important difference between looking, where "images float across the visual terrain without direct engagement", and seeing, which "brings the visible into being" (p. 12).

George Marcus has been keen to move on from simply acknowledging representation. Reflecting on *Writing cultures*, he suggested that "the visions and tropes of the '90s have become plans, designs, and technologies for giving form to fieldwork in the present" (Marcus 20:12 p. 432). These equate to laboratories, he proposes, which take place in 'the field', but just as often in experiments at home

> ...ethnographic experimentations (that) are active, animated, open-ended, multileveled, and transitive in authorings, genres, publics, commons, and internal relations, monitoring the shifting conditions of producing ethnographic research today. (p. 438)

Together with 'dynamic archives', Marcus also advocates studios, labs and para-sites, in which researching practices are subject to ongoing dialogic analysis, and projects alongside projects. Marcus advocates the deliberate creation of arenas for the continued problematisation of the practices of anthropological knowledge production and representation – from the inception of projects to their completion (see for example the work of Paul Rabinow, 2008; Rabinow, 2011; Rabinow, Marcus, Faubion, & Rees, 2008).

The role of theory, and its relationship to methods is now well and truly open for debate and development (Boyer, Faubion, & Marcus, 2015). A collection of "new compositions of matter" curated by Faubion and Marcus, offers

...three doubled or split dimensions: audits (listening, accounting), projects (promissory logics, transitional objects), and the active value-added work of interpretations – cultural encounters (Fischer 2009: p. 3)

This listing of conceptual concerns is a long way from a more singular focus on representation.

Anthropology also continues to address what ethnography is and its relationship to anthropology. Tim Ingold for instance argues that anthropology (and one might read other disciplines that have adopted ethnographic methods) has too long conflated its purpose with its practice. Anthropology and ethnography are not the same thing, he suggests. According to Ingold, anthropology is concerned with critically understanding the world. Ethnography on the other hand, is directed to the description of "the lives of people other than ourselves, with an accuracy and sensitivity honed by detailed observation and first-hand experience." (Ingold 2008: p. 21). Ingold argues that while ethnography is the signature methodology of anthropology, its goal is documentation, while anthropology is geared to the production of "acceptable generalisations" (p.21). The two are not so neatly separated however, as anthropologists use ethnography/ies in order to generate the "stuff" from which they make judgments about social life-processes, always in motion, never fixed (p. 23).

Many, but not all of anthropology's concerns about representation have been taken into educational ethnography. However, before I conclude with a few provocations about what educational ethnographers might take from anthropological thinking about post representation, I briefly consider what writing research might have to offer.

Writing research and ethnography

Writing itself has been subject to the ethnographic gaze – for instance how historical fiction might be subject to ethnographic research (Cohen, 2013). Writing researchers have explored the ways in which academic writing is produced via 'textographies' (Swales, 1998). Ethnographic methodology is a hallmark of New Literacy Studies (NLS) (Street, 1995). Often anthropologically *and* linguistically trained, NLS researchers offer a social and situated view of literate practices (Ivanic, Hamilton, & Barton, 1999) – for example producing studies of 'textual worlds' (Barton and Papen, 2010), reading practices (Boyarin, 1993), local literacies (Barton and Hamilton, 1998), and children's linguistic practices (Heath, 1983).

But while writing research has taken up ethnography, most ethnographers have been less enthusiastic about mobilising writing research. In this section of the chapter I consider one threshold concept in writing research that might have implications for the ways in which ethnographers approach the task of text production.

I mobilise the notion of a threshold concept in relation to writing. The idea of threshold concepts is situated in research on the pedagogies of higher education disciplines (Land, Meyer, & Flanagan, 2016; Meyer and Land, 2012). A threshold concept is a conceptual gateway – passing through the gate means that things that seemed previously mysterious, nonsensical and incomprehensible become clear. A threshold concept is something that is held in common by a disciplinary community. A threshold concept often brings apparently disparate disciplinary ideas and arguments together. The threshold concept provides a language and a history of ideas, but also offers possibilities for building new knowledges; threshold concepts create a working space of possibility, perhaps for new forms of ethnography and ethnographic writing… perhaps for moving beyond thinking about representation to consider what else might be thought and written.

Writing is performative

The idea that writing has the capacity to do something in the world is usually attributed to Kenneth Burke (1966) who wrote about symbols and action. Burke saw writing as symbolic action; writing is both produced by and produces social action. Burke's argument has been taken up as a foundation for various traditions of language, linguistics and writing research.

It is generally accepted by writing researchers that writing is understood as social because

1. the text is oriented to a reader. The writer has a reader in mind and wants to communicate something to them.
2. there are social conventions about writing. Writing is not produced in a vacuum. It is subject to relational, disciplinary and institutional rules.
3. writing is undertaken in particular contexts and with particular resources and tools. The writing is also shaped by larger social/cultural/political relationships (Adler-Kassner and Wardle, 2015)
4. the reader is recognised as having agency. The meaning of any text is not necessarily what is intended by the writer, the text is reconstructed by the reader – reading is understood as rewriting in literary reception theory (Holub, 1984). The text demands, the reader responds. Writ more abstractly, writing makes something happen in the world, usually via the interpretations and actions of readers.

These understandings underpin the notion that writing is performative – it does things in the world. One sense in which writing is performative is epistemic. Writing both produces and reproduces ways of knowing and thinking. This is where writing research connects with anthropology's concerns about the nature of anthropological writing. Anthropological writing (re)produces the discipline, just as Geertz suggested. But there are other senses in which writing can be seen as performative.

It is easy to see how written legal judgments for instance constitute a social action – as a result of being written, legal documents cause something to be done. A house is sold. A fund is administered in particular way with particular consequences and benefits. A person is imprisoned. The same kind of social action results from written marriage or birth certificate. As a result of these texts, a particular status is afforded for which there are consequences. The penalties of not having appropriate 'papers' for instance are severe for refugees, whereas mobile people have relevant passports and visas which produce entitlements and benefits.

From the social action/performative perspective it is not too difficult to see how the writing that students do in assignments also accomplish work. Assignments are normally discussed as a representation of student learning, as a kind of 'stand in' or approximation of something much bigger – learning in its entirety. However, a test or assignment can also be understood as a bid for something to happen The assignment requires a response from the teacher. The assignment writer wants the teacher to offer the reward of marks, approval and qualifications. In order for this to happen, the assignment writer has to present themselves in the text as a good/bad student. Assignment writing is this not only productive of benefits but also of a particular identity. In just the same way, academic writing produces particular kinds of scholarly identities which are more or less acceptable to the discourse communities in which they are located, or seek to join. Academic writing produces academic reputation and rewards.

If we see texts as performative, then we do not see them as static, but as having an ongoing life in the world. The life of a text might be short-lived or have far-reaching consequences. And performative texts do not act alone, they are socially produced *and* socially performative. Writing can thus be understood as possessed of a kind of agency, the kind that is recognised in actor network theory (Latour, 2007) for instance. Through an ANT lens, a text can direct other network agents to a particular activity. A text can be enrolled in numerous networks as it is mutable – infinitely translatable by readers and users, as Derrida (1978) argues.

If we accept writing as performative, rather than as simply a representation, then we are able to ask what is the work that ethnographic writing does. Rather than analyse the text for its representational choices, or use the epistemological waiver that the text is representational, we might ask: What networks or assemblages does this writing join? Is this ethnographic text primarily concerned, like a student assignment, to gain approval from ethnographer's line managers? To accrue citations that are useful to university audit regimes?

To provide material useful for reproducing the discipline via teaching? How does this ethnographic text provide benefit for those people and things that participated in it? Can this ethnographic writing escape its dominant social framings?

The artist Hito Steyerl argues that the performative power of texts is also changing. He suggests that the mutability of any text has been expanded by social media.

> Social media makes the shift from representation to participation very clear: people participate in the launch and life span of images, and indeed their life span, spread and potential is *defined* by participation. (http://dismagazine.com/disillusioned-2/62143/hito-steyerl-politics-of-post-representation/)

It is not the maker's intention that is most important in thinking about a performative text, nor even its original referent, it is the ways in which a text is made and endlessly remade that must now be accounted for. This perspective coalesces with the increasing interest in the reception of texts within anthropology, and with calls for a public anthropology. Public anthropology actively solicits diverse responses to an ongoing project and this interlocution becomes an integral part of its development. Dialogic space is where anthropologists engage with pressing questions of public concern (http://www.publicanthropology.org/public-anthropology/).

Educational ethnographic writing conversations

I have suggested that questions about representation writing proliferate, particularly in the home discipline of anthropology. But the conversation is now very alive in other disciplines, for instance in geography, where non-representational theory, as it is called there, is seen as a way of thinking. Geographers interested in the non-representational attend to the flows of everyday life, to the beings and becomings that precede human subjectivity, to the body, sensation and its co-evolution with things. Like their counterparts in anthropology, non-representational geographers adopt a kind of experimentalism and a refusal to arrive at a fixed answer or static representation (e.g. Lorimer, 2005; Thrift, 2007).

Education however has not yet seen the same interest in these debates. The field of education intersects with other social science and humanities disciplines and sometimes there are shared conversations in journals and conferences. Sociologists in education for instance are well connected with the larger sociological community. But perhaps because of the ethnography/anthropology distinction that Ingold points to, there is not such an overlap between anthropology and education ethnographers. This varies by country of course, and there is a strong tradition of educational anthropology in North America. However, in the UK where I am now situated, not only is education institutionally and organisationally detached from anthropology, ethnography is generally not part of essential methods courses taken by social science masters and doctoral students. Ethnography is more often offered as an elective 'master class' for those who are interested.

The consequence of the isolation of education from most other social sciences in general and anthropology in particular is that onto-epistemological and ethical questions that arise from ethnography and its textual practices are as not widely known. Within educational journals, outside those concerned directly with ethnography, there are few papers published which use ethnographic methods of any kind (see for example my survey of methods used in educational leadership and management journals, Thomson, 2017). And when ethnographic method is elaborated in these journals it often uses the kinds of exteriorised methods language to describe process, while nodding to representation as its epistemology. The ongoing conversations in qualitative methods journals are a notable exception to this rule.

There are signs that this situation is changing, and this book is perhaps part of a move towards using the lens of writing and text to raise questions about the wider purposes and practices of ethnography. We have much to learn from anthropology in this endeavour, as I hope to have demonstrated. Anthropology's continued focus on questions of text genre, the researcher self in the text, participant responses and the nature of knowledge and knowledge production provides some leads that we educators might follow. We might also follow Ingold's thinking and ask what kind of education we are bringing into being through our ethnography and writing. Similarly, writing research itself also offers areas for educational ethnographers to explore, areas which move well beyond the notion of representation to considerations of what writing does in the world and for the world. How, we might perhaps ask ourselves following writing researchers, is this educational ethnographic writing for, rather than about, education?

Troubling representation does mean getting out of our comfort zones. It might mean a stronger focus on reflexive forms of experimentation as well as different kinds of texts. There is a huge potential for educational ethnographers to move away from representation, an unmoving proxy for the educational worlds we inhabit. As Michael Taussig (2006) puts it, this means ethnographic writing that lives in and transports us and readers to the river...

To step into the river means to immerse oneself in the beingness of the world, which is messy, as well as ride the incandescent wave of instability and contradiction whereby the rule is both followed and broken, which is even messier. (p.v.)

This is performative and productive writing which both recognises the material reality being produced for and by readers, and also acknowledges its simultaneous duplicities, its masquerade.

Bibliography

Adler-Kassner, L., & Wardle, E. (Eds.). (2015) *Naming what we know. Threshold concepts of writing studies.* Logan, UH: Utah University Press.

Bakke, G., & Peterson, M. (Eds.). (2017) *Between matter and method. Encounters in anthropology and art.* London: Bloomsbury.

Barton, D., & Hamilton, M. (1998) *Local literacies. Reading and writing in one community.* London & New York: Routledge.

Barton, D., & Papen, U. (Eds.). (2010) *The anthropology of writing. Understanding textually mediated worlds.* London: Continuum.

Behar, R. (1996) *The vulnerable observer. Anthropology that breaks your heart* Boston: Beacon Press.

Bennett, T. (1995) *The birth of the museum.* London: Routledge.

Bouchetoux, F. (2014) *Writing anthropology. A call for uninhibited methods.* London: Palgrave.

Boyarin, J. (Ed.). (1993) *The ethnography of reading.* Berkele: University of California Press.

Boyer, D., Faubion, D., & Marcus, G. (Eds.). (2015). *Theory can be more than it used to be. Learning anthropology's method in a time of transition.* Cornell: Cornell University Press.

Brettell, C. B. (Ed.). (1996) *When they read what we write. The politics of ethnography.* New York: Praeger.

Burke, K. (1966) *Language as symbolic action.* Berkely: University of Califorina Press.

Carrithers, M. (1988) The anthropologist as author: Geertiz' 'Work and lives". *Anthropology Today*, 4(4), pp. 19-22.

Causey, A. (2017) *Drawn to see: Drawing as an ethnographic method* Toronto: University of Toronto Press.

Clifford, J. (1988) Introduction: Partial truths. In J. Clifford & G. Marcus (Eds.), *Writing culture. The politics and poetics of ethnography* (pp. 1-26). Los Angeles: University of California Press.

Clifford, J., & Marcus, G. (1986) *Writing culture: The politics and poetics of ethnography.* Los Angeles: University of California Press.

Cohen, M. (Ed.). (2013) *Novel approaches to anthopology: Contributions fo literary anthropology.* New York: Lexington Books.

Collins, P., & Gallinat, A. (Eds.). (2011) *The ethnographic self as resource: writing, memory and experience into ethnography.* Bergahn Books.

Conquergood, D. (2013) *Cultural struggles. Performance, ethnography, praxis.* Ann Arbor, MI: University of MIchigan Press.

Dei, G. S., Hall, B. L., & Rosenberg, D. G. (Eds.). (2000) *Indigenous knowledges in global contexts.* Toronto: University of Toronto Press.

Deleuze, G. (1995) *Negotiations 1972-1990* (J. Joughin, Trans.) New York: Columbia University Press.

Derrida, J. (1978) *Writing and difference* (A. Bass, Trans.) (1995 ed.) London: Routledge.

Elliott, D., & Dara, C. (Eds.). (2017). *A different kind of ethnography: Imaginative practces and creative methodologies.* Toronto: University of Toronto Press.

Fischer, M. (2009) Foreword: Renewable ethnography. In J. D. Faubion & G. Marcus (Eds.), *Fieldwork is not what is used to be. Learning anthropology's method in a time of transition.* Cornell: Cornell University Press.

Fisher, E., & Fortnum, R. (2014) *On not knowing. How artists think.* London: Black Dog Publishing.

Freeman, M. (2014). The hermeneutical aesthetics of thick description. *Qualitative Inquiry,* 20(6), pp. 827-833. doi:10.1177/1077800414530267

Geertz, C. (1973) *The interpretation of cultures* New York: Basic Books.

Geertz, C. (1988) *Works and lives. The anthropologist as author* (1994 ed.) Stanford, California: Stanford University Press.

Geertz, C. (1996) *After the fact: two countries, four decades, one anthropologist* Boston, MA: Harvard University Press.

Geertz, C. (2002) An inconstant profession: The anthropological life in interesting times. *Annual Review of Anthropology,* 31, pp. 1-19.

Ghodsee, K. (2011) *Lost in translation: Ethnographies of everyday life after Communism* Durham: Duke University Press.

Hall, S. (Ed.). (1997) *Representation. Cultural representations and signifying practices.* London: Sage.

Haraway, D. (1988) Situated knowledges: The science question in feminism and the privilege of partial perspective. *Feminist Studies,* 14(3), pp. 575-599.

Harding, S. (1993) Rethinking standpoint epistemology: What is "strong objectivity"? In L. Alcoff & E. Potter (Eds.), *Feminist epistemologies* (pp. 49-82). New York: Routledge.

Heath, S. B. (1983) *Ways with words: Language, life and work in communities and classrooms.* New York: Cambridge.

Holub, R. (1984) *Reception theory. A critical introduction* London: Methuen.

Ingold, T. (2008) Anthropology is not ethnography. *British Academy Review* (11), pp. 21-23.

Ivanic, R., Hamilton, M., & Barton, D. (1999). *Situated literacies: theorising reading and writing in context* London: Routledge.

Laine, A. (2018) *Practicing art and anthropology. A trandisciplinary journey* London: Bloomsbury.

Land, R., Meyer, J., & Flanagan, M. (Eds.). (2016) *Threshold concepts in practice.* New York: Sense Publishers.

Lassiter, L. E. (2005) *The Chicago guide to collaborative ethnography* Chicago: University of Chicago Press.

Lather, P. (1991) *Feminist research: with/against* Geelong: Deakin University Press.

Latour, B. (2007) *Reassembling the social. An inroduction to Actor Network Theory* Oxford: Oxford University Press.

Lorimer, H. (2005) Cultural geography: the busyness of being 'more-than-representational'. *Progress in Human Geography*, 1(29), pp. 83-94.

Maclure, M. (2013) Researching without representation? Language and materiality in post-qualitative methodology. *International Journal of Qualitative Studies in Education*, 26(6), pp. 658-667.

Marcus, G. (2012) The legacies of Writing Culture and the near future of the ethnographic form: A sketch. *Cultural Anthropology*, 27(3), pp. 427-445.

Massumi, B. (2002) *Parables for the virtual: Movement, affect, sensation* (B. Massumi, Trans.) Durham NC: Duke University Press.

Meyer, J., & Land, R. (Eds.). (2012) *Threshold concepts and transformational learning.* New York: Sense Publishers.

Narayan, K. (2012) *Alive in the writing. Crafting ethnography in the company of Chekov* Chicago: The University of Chicago Press.

Pandian, A., & McLean, S. (2017) Prologue. In A. Pandian & S. McLean (Eds.), *Crumpled paper boat. Experiments in ethnographic writing* Durham: Duke University Press.

Pink, S. (2006) *The future of visual anthropology. Engaging the senses* London: Routledge.

Pink, S. (2009) *Doing sensory ethnography* Thousand Oaks: Sage.

Rabinow, P. (2008) *Marking time. On the anthropology of the contemporary* Princeton: Princeton University Press.

Rabinow, P. (2011) *The accompaniment: Assembling the contemporary* Chicago: The University of Chicago Press.

Rabinow, P., Marcus, G., Faubion, J. D., & Rees, T. (2008) *Designs for an anthropology of the contemporary* Durham: Duke University Press.

Reed-Danahay, D. (2005) *Locating Bourdieu* Bloomington, ID: Indiana University Press.

Sanjek, R. (Ed.). (1990) *Fieldnotes. The making of anthropology.* Washington DC: Cornell University Press.

Schneider, A., & Wright, C. (Eds.). (2010) *Between art and ethnography. Contemporary ethnographic practice.* London: Bloomsbury.

Somerville, M. (2007) Postmodern emergence. *International Journal of Qualitative Studies in Education*, 20(2), pp. 225-243.

Street, B. V. (1995) *Social literacies. Critical approaches to literacyk in development* London: Routledge.

Swales, J. (1998) *Other floors, other voices: A textography of a small university building* New York: Routledge.

Taussig, M. (1993) *Mimesis and alterity. A particuar history of the senses*: London.

Taussig, M. (1997) *The magic of the state* New York: Routledge.

Taussig, M. (2006) *Walter Benjamin's grave* Chicago: University of Chicago Press.

Taussig, M. (2012) I'm so angry I made a sign. *Critical Inquiry*, 39(1), pp. 56-88.

Thomson, P. (2017) A little more madness in our methods? A snapshot of how the educational leadership. management and administration field conducts research. *Journal of Educational Administration and History*, 49(3), pp. 215-230.

Thrift, N. (2007) *Non-representational theory: Space, politics, affect* London: Routledge.

Van Maanen, J. (Ed.). (1995) *Representation in ethnography*. Thousand Oaks: Sage.

Wolcott, H. (2002) *Sneaky kid and its aftermath. Ethics and intimacy in fieldwork* Walnut Creek, Lanham, New York, Oxford: Rowman & LIttlefield.

Wulff, H. (Ed.). (2016) *The anthropologist as writer: genres and contexts in the twenty first century.* New York: Bergahn Books.

Responsive research: Sensory, medial and spatial modes of thinking as an analytical tool in fieldwork

Janna Wieland

Introduction

In this paper, I use multimodality as an analytical tool to describe the different sensorial, medial and performative modes of doing ethnographic research and writing. As a cultural anthropologist with a spatial sociological perspective, especially one on social space, I am conducting ethnographic research in postmigrant theatre productions, incorporating and engaging with different media such as photographs, notes, memos, drawings and sound recordings, exploring the different interpretative modes and the interplay of these media in ethnographic research. This exploration is also related to the intersecting discourses and methodologies of *New Materialism, Spatial Theory* and *Sensory Ethnography* that are crucial to the research project this paper is based on called 'Transcultural Practices in Postmigrant Theatre and in School'.[10]

A main challenge in ethnographic research and analysis is discovering something that was not previously expressed in (spoken) language. As sociologist Stefan Hirschauer (2001) argues, one problem of ethnographic writing is to grasp the voiceless, inexpressible, auditive and indescribable (Hirschauer, 2001: 429). As Clifford Geertz writes, the main goal of the ethnographer's work is to grasp and to analyse a variety of complex and often superimposed and interwoven structures of imagination that are somehow unordered, hidden and alien (Geertz, 1999: 10). Referring to Bruno Latour, this 'fluidity of the social' (Latour, 2007: 133) contains situations that take place 'in between', in which cultural forms of human behaviour are articulated and pointed out as fundamental cultural meanings (Geertz, 1999: 10). These cultural meanings are, speaking with Deleuze and Guattari, represented in socio-material assemblages – which in turn are in constant change, and bundle in the process, recursively assembling and re-conceptualizing (Deleuze and Guattari, 2005).

I ask how can these fluid assemblages, in which meaning and knowledge are articulated through different modes, be researched and analysed through my own multi-sensory perception in the field? How can cultural meaning and the production of knowledge – which take place on a multisensory and multi-modal level, that includes both the spoken, the heard, the seen, and the sensed – be explored? How can the spatial-social aspect with its different modes,

---

10. The research project is funded by the 'Federal Ministry of Education and Research' (BMBF) at Leuphana University Lüneburg/Germany. Project leader is Prof. Dr. Birgit Althans.

its complexity, its layers, its bundling and its composition of socio-material assemblages be explored – without simplifying it?

My aim is to identify (cultural) meaning in situations of transcultural education and formation in the research field, that takes place in a fluid and multisensory space. Doing a 'responsive research' (Althans et al., 2016), I as an ethnographic researcher, have to react in response to these sensorial, medial and performative modes that generate meaning with my own research modalities. The multi-modal sensations produced in the field could be analysed through multimodality – as an analytical response to reflect sensorial modes of experiences in a multi-layered research field – as one logic of revealing cultural meaning as 'aesthetic products' or 'artifacts' (Althans et al., 2016).

In the 'responsive research' project mentioned above, we work with the theoretical-methodological approaches of *New Materialism* and *Material Feminism* as a framework. As part of this framework 'responsive research' has the aspiration to gain new insights through a mutual exchange of science and practice (see Althans et al., 2016). The concept of *Material Feminism* gives me the opportunity to reflect on (and diffract, see Barad 2007) my own research practice and modes, and thus responding to the research field. Working with different sensory, medial and spatial modes brought me reconstructively to the term multimodality as a tool for analysis and interpretation. In the following part I engage with multimodality as an analytical tool and ethnography at the intersection of sensory and material approaches, and how these approaches and concepts together can be productive in reflecting on ethnographic research, and writing, performing and/or illustrating processes that creates aesthetic products as an outcome.

Multimodality and ethnography
At the intersection of sensory and material approaches

Multimodality is becoming more involved in ethnographic research methods. Besides Gunther Kress there are authors such as Carey Jewitt, Jeff Bezemer or Kay O'Halloran who have introduced the term multimodality in the context of (ethnographic) research. *Qualitative Research* (2011) produced a special issue on multi-modal research as part of a relatively recent increase of multimodality in ethnographic research, with the introduction: 'Multimodality and ethnography: working at the intersection' (Dicks et al., 2011: 227). In *Qualitative Research* the author Gunther Kress writes on the topic of multimodality and ethnography as a partnership in research. However, Kress emphasizes that in a changing world, differently and fluidly constituted spatial environments need co-constituted and co-evolved disciplines that can handle the changes and questions mirrored in existing disciplines (Kress, 2011: 239).

Carey Jewitt edited the *Routledge Handbook of Multimodal Analysis* (2014), in which different positions and definitions of multimodality are discussed. David Howes brings anthropology and multimodality in connection with the conjugation of the senses (Howes 2014: 323). Jeff Bezemer states that similar to multimodality, ethnography also draws attention to a range of cultural and social resources, which are perpetually used by people in daily life (Bezemer et al., 2018). In Bezemer's words:

> 'This leads to analysis of a variety of data sets, including visual data (e.g. buildings, drawings, photographs, video recordings); and verbal data (e.g. fieldnotes, policy documents, audio recordings, transcripts). Indeed, in both approaches –ethnography and multimodality – the aim is to produce "thick", "semiotic", and "microscopic" (Geertz, 1973) descriptions of cultural practice.' (Bezemer et al., 2018: para. 1)

In order to elaborate on the use of multi-modal strategies in my fieldwork, I will draw from the discourse of multimodality and subsequently define, how I understand 'mode' as an analytical tool. To follow Gunther Kress's (2014) definition, a mode is a 'socially shaped and culturally given resource for making meaning' (Kress 2014: 60). Examples of modes used in cultural and aesthetic forms of expression are writing, layout, music, gesture, speech, image and others (Kress, 2014: 60). Modes in ethnographic research are seen, from Kress' perspective, as a result of social shaping. Based on their interests, a community creates resources to perform knowledge. This kind of resource appears differently depending on the kind of community and their interests and needs for communication and negotiation of meaning. For example, font types or article genres may for one group represent essential modes of meaning, for another group the modes may be less in written forms and more audio-visual, for instance (Kress, 2011: 247).

A main point of Kress' definition of multimodality is that all the resources for making meaning are seen as equal in their ability to contribute meaning – 'language' is just one among these resources – to a diverse and complex entity, for example a text (Kress, 2011: 242). Referring to Jewitt, she points out that there are different opinions on the potential of these resources. Some authors argue that the differences between, for example, speech and image are too large to handle within one setting or framework. She maintains – a position I approve reflecting my own ethnographic writing – that 'notwithstanding the differences it is still possible, at a more general level, to establish common principles of meaning making' (Jewitt et al., 2016: 4). Furthermore, Jewitt argues that of course each mode has its specific constraints and offers distinct possibilities of co-occurrence and interplay of diverse means. Though different resources produce or give different meanings, each offers distinct potentialities and also limitations (Jewitt et al., 2016: 3). This is exactly what I am pursuing in my ethnographic research: To use different modes alongside each other to reflect on and render productive the specific visual, sonic, material – and thus analytical – potentialities and limitation that writing, drawing, taking photographs, and producing audio recordings offer.

Therefore, besides the different modes that the research field itself offers, ethnographers themselves produce revealing modes that generate meaning while observing and analysing. This 'opens up possibilities for recognizing, analysing and theorizing the variety of ways in which people make meaning, and how those meanings are multimodality interrelated' (Mavers et al., 2018). With reference to Jewitt and Mavers, I claim that as a researcher it is important to reflect which modes are discovered in the field of research on the one hand, and which modes are used to analyse and in turn how to make them available as a result.

With regard to the approach of *Sensory Ethnography*, a central perspective in the methodological design of our project, it is especially relevant how multimodality as a tool can respond to a multisensory level of generating, negotiating, performing knowledge. With the perspective of *Sensory Ethnography*, we investigate sensory perception as a complex historical, social and cultural fabric. It examines not only the materiality of sonic perception and production, but also emphasizes sensory perception as constitutive of 'forms of sonic knowledge', as sound studies scholar Holger Schulze puts it (Schulze 2007). Cultural studies and sound studies scholar (and researcher in our project) Carla J. Maier writes that these multifaceted forms of sonic knowledge are generated in the 'process of listening to, producing, performing, and mediating sound – a process which is situationally, culturally, and spatially specific' (Maier [née Müller-Schulzke], 2012: 117). Relatedly, a part of *Sensory Ethnography* is the reflection (more precisely, diffraction by Barad 2007) of the ethnographer's methods, techniques and practices, that take place within socio-material and multisensory spaces – which Sarah Pink calls a 'social, sensory and material environment' (2015: 25).

I am drawing – being trained as a cultural anthropologist with a focus on the sociology of space – on a perspective that understands space as relativist, in which body and space depend on one another: actions and social processes shape and (re)produce space. Space derives for me from the relational arrangement of bodies. Since actions are constantly changing, space is also in a constant process of changing (Löw, 2001: 17), and so as part of space 'modes are not autonomous and fixed, but, created through social processes, are fluid and subject to change' (Mavers et al., 2018). Fiona Newell and Ladan Shams formulate it appropriately by relating sensory perception to spatial issues:

'When we perceive the world around us, our [...] experience is not of disjointed sensory sensations but is instead of a coherent multisensory world, where sounds, smells, tastes, lights, and touches amalgamate. What we perceive or where we perceive it to be located in space is a product of inputs from different sensory modalities that combine, substitute, or integrate.' (Newell et al., 2007: 1415)

Relating this perspective to Sarah Pink's *Doing Sensory Ethnography* it proves productive for my responsive research when she argues that sensory perception is inseparable from cultural categories, which 'we use to give meaning to sensory experiences in social and material interactions' (2015: 32). Our sensory perception and the interpretations of sense or performing knowledge in understanding the social, material or intangible elements of our spatial environments is not dominated by one sensory modality (see Pink, 2015: 32).

Perspectives of *New Materialism* are compatible with perspectives of *Sensory Ethnography,* because bodies, sounds and spaces are regarded as multi-faceted forms of materiality, performativity and knowing. Material Feminist Carol Taylor states as a scholar in education studies that materiality cannot be separated from the world (our spatial environment) and from our knowledge and the sense of it (Taylor et al., 2013: 667). In Taylor's words:

'matter is not inert, neither does it form an empty stage for, or background space to human activity. Instead, matter is conceptualized as agentic and all sorts of bodies, not just human bodies, are recognized as having agency.' (Taylor et al., 2013: 667)

I would argue, together with Taylor and Pink, that every mode has it's own agency and that the matter of a mode is part of generating meaning. Without simply adopting the modes of the field, but responding on the research field, transferring and bringing them to a new layer of interpretation, my aim is to show or open the multisensory and socio-material assemblages of daily situations and phenomena in the research field, focusing also on materiality and media as modes of communication, revelation and meaning.

Fieldwork and writing process
Examples of multimodality as an analytical tool

In the following, the research project Transcultural Practices in Postmigrant Theatre and in School (funded by the German Federal Ministry of Education and Research) will be described in more detail, in order to provide the backdrop against which the examples of multimodality as an analytical tool in the writing process work. The project leader is Prof. Dr. Birgit Althans, set in Lüneburg at Leuphana University in the Institute of Education studies. The analytical focus of the 'responsive research' (Althans et al., 2016) project is on the 'method mixing'[11] dealing with young refugees and children with migration background in schools and theatre productions that we grasp as transcultural arenas. We use method mixing as an operative term. The term means for us on the one hand the methodology to be developed by the researchers, on the other hand the methods of the research field. We relate both – the methods used in the field and those developed in the context of research and analysis – in response to the method mixing of the field. Method mixing includes performative practices like body techniques as well as practices of dealing with things, texts, speech and (digital) media, visualization strategies, sound practices etc., through which cultural transformation processes can be generated – and so the term also includes the methodology of multi-modal approaches. We ask how such methods are used, in particular, how they are performatively and medially shaped and how they are aesthetically worked out on the (rehearsal) stage or in the classroom.

The material generated in the fieldwork process is analysed through theoretical perspectives such as *Material Feminism, Cultural Studies, Sound and Sensory Ethnography* with the aim to work out specific methods of (trans) cultural education, knowledge production and negotiating meaning. We ask, how can we describe and visualize these fleeting situations, which take place in the 'in between' and which change constantly? How can these socio-material and acoustic assemblages be researched in which body, sound and materiality affect knowledge and learning (see Taylor et al., 2013: 669)?

This Paper aims to use multimodality (as one part beside others of 'method mixing') as an analytical tool to reflect processes of conducting and presenting ethnographic research and writing, by conducting a close analysis of my ethnographic practices especially during the writing process of fieldnotes. While making my field recordings and taking pictures as part of the participant observation of the rehearsal process, I mainly produce written notes and drawings. To me, drawing offers the possibility to visualize the cognitive images that occur while observing in a different way than writing allows me to do. Both the verbal and the visual modes of documentation and interpretation offer specific material and discursive qualities and can thus complement each other productively. In the subsequent process of revisiting and analysing the fieldwork material, I use drawing as an analytical tool, processing the photographs and other graphic material on the basis of sketches, memos or edited field-notes.

In the following part of this paper I will use multimodality as an analytical

---

11. Birgit Althans introduces 'method mixing' as an operative term – which encompasses both the methodology of the researchers and the methods of the research field – within the research project 'Transcultural Practices in Postmigrant Theatre and in School' (2016-2019).

tool to reflect my strategies in my fieldwork, described as three iterative steps made during the research process: (1) using pictures and drawings[12], besides written accounts, as an integral part of the field-notes, (2) bringing them into interplay with the ethnographic writing as a distinct tool for interpretation and thus (3) creating a research outcome that includes textual production as well as collages of pictures and drawings that aim at extending and refining the analytical scope of the ethnographic study.

Although there are more differentiated mutually conditional steps in research processes, for the purpose of presentability and legibility, I decided to display my research process in the described three steps. In opting for these three steps, I agree with Stefan Hirschauer, who defines the ethnographic writing process in (1) handwritten fieldnotes during participant observation and in the elaborate 'postscript' of the memory protocol, (2) the analytical notes (with its memos) and (3) the fully articulated 'thick description' (Hirschauer, 2001: 431; Geertz, 2003; Geertz, 1973).

Research field: the rehearsal process of a theatre production
In this paper, I aim at demonstrating how multimodality is used as an analytical tool, which is exemplified with regard to research I conducted on the theatre production *Still Out There* by theatre-collective *kainkollektiv* in cooperation with Young Theatre Bremen, one of the case studies of our research project. Set in Bremen, and based on a re-narration of the fairy tale 'The Bremen Town Musicians' by the Brothers Grimm, a tale about exclusion and self-empowerment, the production *Still Out There* creates a sonic-material narrative between fact and fiction, and in this way, explores the (post-)migrant and personal stories of the 9- to 19-year-old actors and a Croatia-based dancer and performer. Besides dancer, actors, microphones, video projections, etc., the three musicians from the Syrian Expat Symphonic Orchestra (SEPO) build another layer in this theatrical (and in itself multi-modal) assemblage.

In the following examples, I focus on how fluid socio-material assemblages, in which meaning and knowledge is articulated through different modes, can be researched and analysed in a multisensory way.

(1) Using pictures, drawings and graphics, besides written accounts, as an integral part of the field-notes
In the first step of my ethnography I am using pictures and drawings, besides written accounts, as an integral part of the field-notes on the example of the fields 'trying-out-situations' and the developing of a scene through trying out special elements of using space with body during the rehearsals of the theatre

12. In my methodological approach, I use figures without explaining them in the text as they are considered to have, in interplay with the text, their own signification in description and analysis. All drawings, photographs, collages, graphics by Janna Wieland (2017-2018)

production *Still Out There*. The written accounts as data type are descriptions which were generated in participant observations (Hirschauer, 2001: 431). While making my field recordings and taking pictures as part of the participant observation of the rehearsal process, I mainly produce written notes and drawings.

While observing the rehearsals certain situations repeat themselves, e.g. situations of 'trying out' with voices, sounds, gestures, texts, movements, choreographies, exercises, light, materials, props, etc. The examples of 'trying out' are taken from the development of one scene, which was presented in the final theatre performance. The scene as an aesthetic assemblage of choreographed bodies and music will be shown in the following illustrations.

In the following part I show a fragmented version of my field-notes, that represent the situations from my perspective. The descriptions and illustrations are intertwined with me and my body as a research instrument. This entanglement can be seen in the aesthetic staging of the field of research and my response to it.

The notes are rewritten field-notes which were summed up using notes taken during the participant observation and for this paper translated into English. Parts of my rewritten field-notes of the rehearsal of *Still Out There* of *kainkollektiv* during December 2016 to April 2017:

Rehearsal I:
It is one of the first rehearsals of the rehearsal process of the play *Still Out There* by *kainkollektiv*. The rehearsal stage is relatively bright, light wood, large windows, a mirror that extends along the entire length of the room (see photo below). Light floor, ballet bars on the walls. The children and adolescents who take part in the play and this rehearsal are very different in age from 9-21 years old.

The stage director says that she wants to try out different things with the group. She emphasizes no one has to prepare anything for it, she and the dancer will give some impulses, so they can see what is possible to work on.

The dancer, who is standing nearby, walks through the group of children and adolescents (actors), into the middle of the group and introduces herself. With an impulsive voice, she says that there is no stupid question, no stupid movement if you take yourself seriously; you have to believe in yourself and feel it.

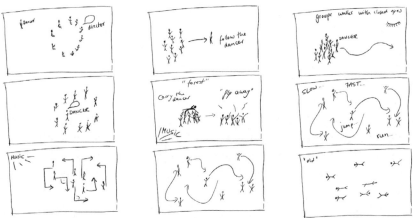

Figure 1: Drawing as part of the field-notes, moving bodies in the rehearsal space

Then the dancer gives the order. Atmospheric music in the background is turned on. At first everyone should walk normally and use the space in the hall. Then each participant runs straight ahead for themselves. Whenever the dancer gives the instruction, the participants change direction at an angle of 90°. Then the dancer goes back into the crowd and everyone follows her. At first like a bunch of grapes following her back and forth, then she goes into the middle of everyone, they automatically form a circle around her, fast moves, moves are getting louder. She starts to put her hands up, all of them follow her. The dancer gives a cue: 'forest'. The dancer climbs into the group and they carry her (see picture).

Figure 2: The participants carrying the dancer Ina Sladic

Then she crawls out of the 'wood' and 'trees' which the actors build and imagine with their bodies. Like an animal, like a lion. She says some participants should follow her. Then the forest dissolves again after the dancer says that the actors should perform like birds. In flowing 'flying' movements, everyone now moves through the room. Guided by the beat of atmospheric music in the background. Beside the music I can hear the steps, the creaking of the floor, the occasional rustling of clothes, the dancer's instructions. Then the actors should run normally again, each for him-/herself, then at different speeds. Then, running alone, then as a group, following the dancer, then closing their eyes and working as a group in a slow tempo. Slow, fast, normal, slow-motion, freeze, jumping, running, then letting everyone go very slowly. Then the dancer says imagine you are very old and weak. Slowly they all become slower and eventually fall down and try to get up and don't make it, because gravity seems to make them stick to the ground. Then, music off.

This was the dancer's first attempt, she says, to see what and how she can work with the young people and children's bodies in the course of the project.

Rehearsal II:
The rehearsal takes place on the rehearsal stage, a large room with black wooden floor, black walls (see photo). The room is brightly lit and almost resounding from the acoustics. I feel like I can hear every sound. The test sequence begins with the instruction to cross the room as a group. 1-3 people should cross the room one after another without touching the floor – climbing over the others. The movement through the room, which seems raw, rough and unfinished to me, is accompanied by noises: like touching the floor by footsteps, creaking, shuffling, noises of clothes rubbing together, e.g. jeans rubbing against jeans.

Short break.

A small table with a projector is already set up in the back of the room. The directors' assistant brings in a white box that is used as a screen. The director shows the young people and children an example why they have worked so much on 'going' and 'moving' in and as a group. On the screen, they all watch a theatre project called 'Peep Box Circuit'[13]. They watch the video projection together. The director says that they want to do the same with the actors and that's why they are trying all the moving with the body in previous rehearsals.

---

13. 'Peep Box Circuit' can be watched on vimeo: https://vimeo.com/206125538

Figure 3: QR-Code to watch 'peep box circuit'

I watch the teenagers and children watching the video projection. I feel, and see in the faces of the participants, that the previous questions 'why do we do this?' appear and a kind of 'aha' and 'understanding' takes place. When the video is finished, everyone jumps up right away. Someone shouts: 'We can do that too', someone else shouts: 'I want to be person who's carried?'

Figure 4: the participants carry another participant

In the background, the assistant director turns on the song 'Mount Kimbie – Taps'[14]. The music sounds loud and rhythmic from the large loudspeakers on the rehearsal stage. Now 'Peep Box Circuit' is being replayed in a transformed, personal way, by the actors. Or as they call it:

14. 'Mount Kimbie – Taps' can be listened to on youtube: https://www.youtube.com/watch?v=yff-7CYEOcI

'the phases'. The phases include running, hugging, controlling, running into one corner, then running into the other corner and lifting one person (see picture above), then running into two different corners and dividing the group, then 'landscape' (climbing on top of each other from one direction to the other in the room), then crossing during climbing and handing over or hugging the climbers, then running, then freeze, then everyone falls down, except one person, then up and down always in the other direction.

Figure 5: QR-Code to listen to 'Mount Kimbie – Taps'

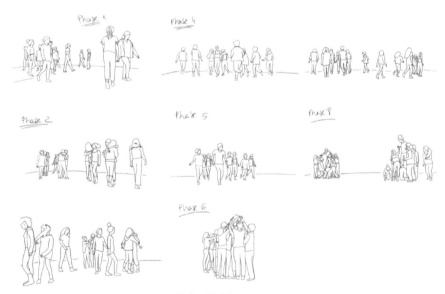

Figure 6: Drawing as part of the field-notes

In this part I showed the combination and the antra-action (Barad, 2007) of the different modes writing (field-notes), drawings and photos, and also if the reader watches or listens to the links in the footnotes, on an auditory and audio-visual level.

An essential point while doing participant observations is to make decisions – or agential 'cuts' as the concept of Karen Barad describes it (see Taylor, 2013: 689; Barad, 2017) – about what one perceives and especially focuses on when using video, photo, sound or written accounts. Taylor et al. define these situations of decision making as 'cuts' in reference to Barad in the following words:

'researchers […] become ethically responsible, via the material-discursive 'cuts' they make and the interventions they enact. These cuts produce the world we inhabit. The emphasis in new material feminism on 'becoming-in-relation' to/with matter and meaning has the potential to re-cast and reinvigorate an ethic of care by installing an ecological perspective – rooted in a respect for the vitality of all matter – at its heart.' (Taylor et al., 2013: 667)

For example, in situations that happen very quickly, a different mode of recoding or note taking is called for, or in situations that are particularly poignant, theatrical, intimate, or situations that repeat themselves. Also, for situations that are difficult to rewrite spontaneously, but which can be better captured on a visual or auditory level, it is helpful to use different media to be able to reveal or capture the different modes of generating meaning. As a researcher, I must be aware that I am in a multi-sensory experienced space and must always choose the more suitable mode of transcription for observing.

While observing the rehearsal process one (agential) cut, as response to the research field, I made had to with repetitive situations in which the participants were trying out different elements. I interpreted these situations as significant for the participants and the director as productive way of producing knowledge and ultimately the final performance. In the extended field-notes I discussed above, I decided to show the rehearsal process as a process of 'trying out'. This assemblage of 'trying out' situations – in which bodies are choreographed, the materiality, the moved bodies and the rehearsal space, and well-rehearsed music is played – will be analysed in the following part by bringing photos and drawings into interplay with the ethnographic writing as a tool for interpretation.

(2) Bringing photos, drawings and graphics into interplay with the ethnographic writing as a tool for interpretation
Both the verbal and the visual modes of documentation and interpretation offer specific material and discursive qualities and can thus complement each other productively. In the subsequent process of revisiting and analysing the fieldwork material and the interview material, I use drawing as an analytical tool, processing the photographs and other graphic material on the basis of sketches, memos or edited field-notes.

In the rehearsals, I observed several times that the director came to rehearsal with a new idea, suggestion or vision, explained it and then said: 'I would like to try this out with you now'. At this level of observation, my focus (among others) is on situations of trying out. In an interview with the director she said that 'the rehearsals have always been well prepared in the sense that you know what points you are trying today' (interview director, 2017).

Working on the analysis of repeating 'trying out' situations in the rehearsal process, I use field-notes, memos and interviews with the two directors of *kainkolletiv* and the participants, focusing on material and sonic aspects of education and formation.

Figure 7: Photo and drawing as integral part of the analytical part. It shows the moving bodies and the light reflections of the light on the floor

Analysing from the perspective of the materiality of light in the rehearsal space
Rehearsal one takes place in a bright, light-flooded room. The second rehearsal takes place in a 'large room with a black wooden floor, black walls' (field-notes Wieland, 2017). The light immediately creates a staged effect by setting the

participants in a scene. The contrast of bright light in dark space has an effect that is materialized in an intensified focus on the movements and sounds of the moving bodies: 'The room is brightly lit and almost resounding from the acoustics. I feel like I can hear every sound/noise' (field-notes Wieland, 2017). In an interview with the participants, one young person described it as follows, 'totally more beautiful with the light and I noticed, so now we really slowly finish the play' (interview participants, 2017), through the use of light a simple, basic scene becomes a direct staging. The director also describes that this is exactly the question: when does the work with basic things become a staging, at what point does the picture become coherent (interview director, 2017)?

Figure 8 & 9: On the left rehearsal one in the light room is shown, on the left the right room of rehearsal two with its contrasts is shown as integral part of the analysis. It shows the moving bodies and the light reflections of the light on the floor.

Analysing from the perspective of the materiality of moving and choreographed bodies

The participants move their bodies on command of the dancer's instructions, with the rhythm of well-practised music and without music: 'running alone, as a group, following the dancer, closing their eyes, walking as a group in slow tempo, fast, normal, slow-motion, freeze, jumping, running, climbing over the others' (field-notes Wieland, 2017). The moment of 'closing their eyes', I perceive as a moment of trust. The participants follow the dancer as a group, all with their eyes closed. On the one hand, the group must move very carefully and each individual must also respect and perceive themselves and the others. Since the group cannot see anything, they have to pay more attention to each other's sounds and movements, focus and concentrate, touch and hold each other.

One of the participants said in the interview, 'What I found a bit difficult is that we had a hard time trusting each other and we thought we could hold on to each other and not let go' (interview participants, 2017). Another one said, 'I remember somehow at the beginning when the dancer was leading us with eyes closed. At the beginning, I wasn't really suspicious' (interview participants, 2017). For both participants, the situation of trust and walking with their eyes closed seemed to be a challenge. Also carrying the dancer and another participant (see pictures above) was connected with a high degree of trust.

At the same time the physical exercises were repeated in the rehearsals: 'We had to walk all the time, climb on top of each other all the time and somehow it was very exhausting and I think even in the first or second rehearsal we had to form circles and climb out of the circle together [...]. This physical work with body and walking and climbing and so on dominated the rehearsal' (interview participants, 2017). On the level of moving bodies through the room, the 'trusting', 'being able to rely on each other', as well as the mindfulness to each other and the concentration on different senses, also with regard to physical contact, and the repetition of these sample sequences seem to be a special component of the physical rehearsal experience.

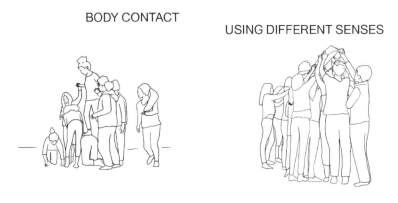

Figure 10: Collaged photos with written accounts. Two examples of the analysis of the moving bodies

Analysing from the perspective of the materiality of sound guiding the bodies
Sound appears in the rehearsal situation on different levels: on a verbal level (instructions and talks by the director and the dancer/choreographer), on the auditory level of music and sounds played over loudspeakers, as well as the soft sounds of movements (creaking of the floorboards, steps on the floor, rustling of clothes, low hum of lamps). In the rehearsal process sound and voice are used as an aesthetic-dramaturgical medium. One of the participants said that it was a different situation when the music and sounds were played over loudspeakers: 'I have a different attitude' (interview participants, 2017), it made her more focused and alert.

Moments of trying things out take place on different levels. These moments are part of an assemblage of materiality of light in the rehearsal space, the materiality of moving and choreographed bodies, and the materiality of sound guiding the bodies. These, in turn, are in constant change and bundling, recursively assembling and re-conceptualizing themselves in the process (Deleuze and Guattari, 2005). In summary, these situations of 'trying out' with voices, sound, gestures, texts, movements, choreographies, exercises, light, materials, props, etc. take place and these modes have their own capacity for action, agency and impact. This effect of things materializes on the transforming levels of trust and confidence, distances to each other, common goals and ideas, as well as the aesthetic-dramaturgical handling and agency of things, sound and bodies is negotiated.

Figure 11: Collaged photos with written accounts and drawings. An assemblage of trying out situations

In this part I show the combination of the different modes of writing (analytical notes), drawings and photographing, which support the analytical writing process.

(3) Creating a research outcome that includes textual production as well as collages of photos and drawings
The research outcome that includes textual production as well as collages of photos and drawings has the aim of extending and refining the analytical scope of the ethnographic study. According to my research and analysis (which of course is just a small part of the overall project), I understand 'trying out' as a method to improvise, reinterpret, confuse, repeat and stage oneself, perform: The unusual is confronted, conceived, deliberately negotiated and staged.

Through experimentation and 'trying out', the imagination is stimulated and things are reinterpreted and aesthetically shaped, and sound is used as an aesthetic-dramaturgical means. By trying things out, things will be negotiated (feedback is given if something fits or not), things are reinterpreted, questioned, put into new contexts, and also these trying outs impart the imaginative examination of things and movements (as in this example also the imagination of making a 'forest' out of the performing participants' bodies). Using the body as an aesthetic-dramaturgical means (movement, dance, touch, all part of an aesthetic experience in which the body is tried out and consciously moved and staged), transforming levels of trust and confidence, common goals and ideas (for example climbing over each other and learning to trust each other) are negotiated. In the rehearsals, the participants are dealing with an open 'trying out' process and thus with ideas and things that are larger and that cannot be understood directly – but that will develop over time – and take place in the negotiating and handling of things, sounds and bodies in an aesthetic-dramaturgical way.

Proposition: The theatre offers potential for transformation processes, especially in the rehearsal process, since different roles are reinterpreted, tried out, assumed, negotiated and questioned. The educational scientist Hans-Christoph Koller conceptualizes transformation processes as an essential part of education. The concept of transformational education describes the 'process of experience' by which a subject 'emerges changed'. The process of change refers not only to changed thinking, but also concerns the changed relationship of the subject to their world, to other people and things, as well as to their own selves (Koller, 2012: 9).

In the context of the overall research project I would continue to ask about topics such as embodiment, materiality, and the question of effect, agency, the impact of light and the support of rehearsal situations through well-rehearsed sounds. In addition, the question of repetitions including trying out processes ask what kind of transformational educational processes can be developed. These and similar questions will be discussed further in future reports on the overall research project and can only be touched on here.

THE UNUSUAL IS CONFRONTED, CONCEIVED, DELIBERATELY NEGOTIATED AND STAGED

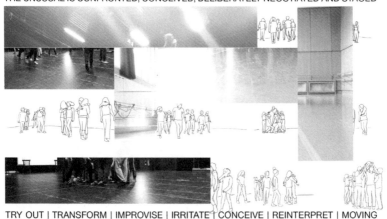

TRY OUT | TRANSFORM | IMPROVISE | IRRITATE | CONCEIVE | REINTERPRET | MOVING BODIES | DANCE | TOUCH | CLIMB | LIGHT | SOUND | MATERIALITY | IMAGINE | TRUST | REPEAT | CONFRONT | DELIBERATE | NEGOTIATE | STAGE

Figure 12: Collaged photos with written accounts and drawings. An assemblage of 'trying out' situations

Outlook
How can I reveal to others what I have observed 'going on'?

This study gives insights into sensory, medial, spatial and multi modes of thinking as part of multimodality as an analytical tool on conducting and illustrating ethnographic research and writing, by conducting a close analysis of ethnographic practices, especially during the writing process of the field-notes and analytical notes.

Based on and entangled with material *(Material Feminsim)*, spatial *(Sociology of Space)* and sensory *(Sensory Ethnography)* approaches, my claim is that a use of multimodality as a tool leads to a deeper or thicker form of analysis and interpretation.

Mulitmodality, so my conclusion, offer the possibility of revealing the different layers of performing knowledge – of social-spaces that can be analysed in socio-material assemblages from another theoretical and analytical perspective. We perceive with all senses, some of which can hardly be translated into language. Therefore, it is advantageous to use different modes and forms of revealing that include – depending on the research field and the modes I choose to represent it with – writing, drawing, photos, collages and other modes of cultural expression.

Multimodality can support the research process whether based on writing or some other mode. As the paper has shown the term multimodality offered the possibility of reflecting on my research processes and the modes I use more specifically while including perspectives of *New Materialism, Sensory Ethnography* and *Sociology of Space*. And at the same time, to reflect on my own actions as a researcher in my usage of research methods and techniques. For me as a researcher, I use different modes to reflect and analyse my own research and writing process, thus the ethnographic writing process implies interpretative modes that creates a multi-modal (and aesthetic) product. I see the potential of multimodality as an analytical tool in the different modes allowing different levels of reflection, diffraction, remembering, memorizing and questioning one's own point of view as part of a responsive research.

Ethnographic writing is also a 'trying out' of an approach to combine *Sensory Ethnography* as analytical tool to reflect on a multisensory experience in multi-material research field and – from the spatial analytical perspective – thus an exploration of the spatial assemblages in which cultural transformations take place. As an ethnographic researcher, I have to react to forms and modes of generating meaning which appear in the research field with comparable research modes.

Certain modes or resources of negotiating meaning have their advantages and disadvantages and can complement each other. For example, in researching sound aspects, it might make sense to work with a combination of fieldnotes, audio recordings, and their transcription. When investigating materiality issues, it may be necessary to draw or photograph them and thus to establish connections on a spatial-theoretical level. Or in order to capture not only descriptions of social processes of interaction, which are often very fleeting or repetitive, it is useful, for example, to make video recordings in addition to written accounts, which in turn complement the descriptions in note taking and might produce different meaning or evoke different interpretations through their combination. The cuts and decision making in response to the research field concerning which modes are used in which research situations – also by extending the field-notes, the analytical notes and the final outcome – will be analysed further in the overall research project.

In the examples presented in this paper, I use drawings in combination with photographs as an analytical tool in the research and writing process. And this these products and research outcomes will also form an integral part of the final publication of our research project. Thus, in addition to a written text, there will be different formats that function in part like ethnographic texts while diffracting and entangling each other, supplemented by photos, graphics, drawings, collages, as well as auditory material, e.g. in the form of an audio paper. So, the further aim is to develop an extended form of 'thick description' (Geertz, 2003; Geertz, 1973). Finally, the research results produced by this description – as a 'thick', 'semiotic' and 'microscopic' description (Geertz, 1973; Bezemer et al., 2018), which includes textual, visual and auditory accounts – should be regarded as aesthetic products or artifacts of responsive research (see Althans et al., 2016). These artifacts can also help us to give a more comprehensive account of the complex processes of cultural transformation that we encounter in our research project, and in a world shaped by migration and globalisation at large.

Bibliography
Althans, B.; Engel, J., (ed.) (2016) *Responsive Organisationsforschung. Methodologien und institutionelle Rahmungen von Übergängen. [Responsive organisational research. Methodologies and institutional frameworks of transitions]*, Wiesbaden: Springer.
Barad, K., (2007) *Meeting the Universe Halfway: Quantum Physics and the Entanglement of Matter and Meaning*, Durham, NC and London: Duke University Press.
Barad, K., (2017): *Agentieller Realismus. [Agential Realism]*, Berlin: Shurkamp.
Belting, H., (2001) *Bild-Anthropologie. Entwürfe für eine Bildwissenschaft. [Visual Anthropology. Designs for an image science.]*, München: Wilhelm Fink.
Bezemer, J.; Burn, A.; Pahl, K., (2018) *Glossary of multimodal terms: Ethnography* [online], URL: https://multimodalityglossary.wordpress.com/ethnography/ [Accessed Date: 1.6.2018, 17:00].
Causey, A., (2017) *Drawn to see: drawing as an ethnographic method*, Toronto: University of Toronto Press.
Deleuze G.; Guattari, F., (2005) *A Thousand Plateaus. Capitalism and Schizophrenia*, Minneapolis: University of Minnesota Press.
Dicks, B.; Flewitt, R.; Lancaster, L.; Pahl, K., (2011) Multimodality and ethnography: working at the intersection, in *Qualitative Research*, Sage, 11 (3): 277-237.
Geertz, C., (2003) Thick Description: Toward an Interpretive Theory of Culture, in Denzin, Norman K.; Lincoln, Y. S., (eds.) *Turning Points in Qualitative Research: Tying Knots in a Handkerchief*, Lanham: Alta Mira Press.
Geertz, C., (1973) *Description: Toward an Interpretive Theory of Culture: The Interpretation of Culture*, New York: Basic Books.
Geertz, C., (1999): *Dichte Beschreibung. Beiträge zum Verstehen kultureller Systeme. [Thick Description: Toward an Interpretive Theory of Culture]*, Frankfurt am Main: Suhrkamp.
Hirschauer, S., (2001) Ethnografisches Schreiben und die Schweigsamkeit des Sozialen. Zu einer Methodologie der Beschreibung, [Ethnographic Writing and the Silence of the Social. Towards a Methodology of Description], in *Zeitschrift für Soziologie [Journal of Sociology]*, Bielefeld, 30(6): 429-451.
Howes, D., (2014): Anthropology and multimodality. The conjugation of the senses, in Jewitt, C. (ed.) (2014) *The Routledge Handbook of Multimodal Analysis*, New York: Routledge, 323-334.
Jewitt, C.; Bezemer, J.; O'Halloran, K., (2016) *Introducing Multimodality.* New York: Routledge.
Klug, N.-M.; Stöckl, H., (ed.) (2016) *Handbuch Sprache im multimodalen Kontext. [Handbook of language in multimodal contexts]*, Berlin/Boston: DE GRUYTER.

Kress, G., (2011) Partnerships in research: multimodality and ethnography, in *Qualitative Research*, Sage, 11 (3): 239-260.

Kress, G., (2014): What is mode?, in Jewitt, C. (ed.) (2014) *The Routledge Handbook of Multimodal Analysis*, 60-75.

Latour, B., (2007) *Eine neue Soziologie für eine neue Gesellschaft [A new sociology for a new society]* Frankfurt/Main: Suhrkamp.

Lindner, R., (1981): Die Angst des Forschers vor dem Feld, [The researcher's fear of the field], in *Zeitschrift für Volkskunde [Journal of Ethnology]*, 77: 51-65.

Löw, M., (2001) *Raumsoziologie [Spatial Sociology]*, Frankfurt/Main: Suhrkamp.

Maier, C. J., [née Müller-Schulzke] (2012) *Transcultural Sound Practices: South Asian Sounds and Urban Dance Music in the UK*, PhD thesis, Frankfurt/Main.

Massey, D., (2005) *For Space*, London: Stage.

Mavers, D.; Gibson, W., (2018) *Glossary of multimodal terms: Mode*, [online], URL: https://multimodalityglossary.wordpress.com/mode-2/ (Accessed Date: 1.6.2018, 17:15)

Miller, D., (2010) *Stuff*. Cambridge: Polity Press.

Newell, F.; Shams, L., (2007) *New insights unto multisensory perception, in advances in multisensory research* [Guest editiorial in special issue on advances in multisensory research], 36(10): 1415-1418.

Pink, S., (2015) *Doing sensory ethnography*, London: Sage.

Taylor, C. A., (2013) Objects, bodies and space: gender and embodied practices of mattering in the classroom, in *Gender and Education*, Routledge, 25(6): 688-703.

Taylor, C. A.; Ivinson, G. (2013) Material Feminisms: New Directions For Education, in *Gender and Education*, Routledge, 25(6): 665-670.

Figures 1-12: All drawings, photographs, collages, graphics by Janna Wieland (2017-2018)

The research project on which this paper is based is called 'Transcultural Practices in Postmigrant Theatre and in School', a project funded by the 'Federal Ministry of Education and Research' (BMBF) at Leuphana University Lüneburg/Germany. Project leader is Prof. Dr. Birgit Althans. Interviews were conducted as part of the research project – in this study are parts of the interview with the two directors of *kainkollektiv* (2017) and the young actors/participants (2017) shown.

Ethnographic writing: Fieldnotes, Memos, Writing Main Texts and Whole Narratives
Bob Jeffrey

An earlier version of this article was first published in Beach, D., Bagley, C., Marques da Silva, (2018) The Wiley Handbook of Educational Ethnography, *Wiley/ Blackwell, Hoboken, NJ, USA*

The writing of ethnographic fieldnotes is an essential part of the ethnographic process. For the purpose of this chapter we can identify five types of writing: descriptive fieldnotes, reflective fieldnotes, reflexive fieldnotes, memos, writing main texts. In the main this chapter focuses on descriptive fieldnotes, but we do provide examples of all the other categories.

A major concern regarding observational notes written in the field relates to the nature of these fieldnotes; whose reality do they represent, how is this reality portrayed and who judges its validity? Qualitative research, unlike quantitative research, does not have a mathematical scientific epistemology upon which to validate its activity. Ely et al (1997, p.64) argue that '(N)arrative is a method of enquiry and a way of knowing' – a discourse and analysis – just as scientism and quantitative research have methods and ways. The ethnographer is the analytical instrument; their perspectives, analyses and re-presentation are the main methodological instrument that carries out the research. The validity of their representation cannot be seen as 'a true account', but it can be a 'subtle reality' (Hammersley, 1992), in which the representation is seen as relevant, plausible and creditable and validated by the ethnographer's peers through review and critique. This subtle reality will appear to the readers of these representations as a *vraisemblance*, a representation of a situation or context as a valid account according to their experiences in similar situations or those similar experiences described in the literature.

Atkinson (1991) suggests that to achieve descriptive authenticity ethnographic writers can legitimately use such rhetorical devices as hypotyposis.

> The rhetorical device of hypotyposis – the use of a highly graphic passage of descriptive writing, which portrays a scene of action in a vivid and arresting manner, used to conjure up the setting and its actors, and place the implied reader as a first hand witness............There is therefore a close relationship between the authenticity of these vivid accounts and the authority of the account – and hence of the author. Authenticity is warranted by virtue of the ethnographers own first hand attendance and participation. It is therefore mirrored in the presence of the reader in the action that it reproduced through the text. The ethnographer is virtuoso

– a witness of character and credibility. It is therefore important that 'eye witness' evidence be presented that recapitulates that experience. (p.71-73)

Ely et al (1997) suggest that all knowing is a transaction between what's out there and the self. They go on to argue that the difference between facts and truth is that 'Hamlet', 'Anna Karenina', and 'Middlemarch' are fictional but true to the psychological processes of their characters and the societies in which they live – they captured essence. By contrast works of non-fiction are sometimes factually correct but not true in the sense of getting at the essence. They suggest some questions that one might ask during drafting: what forms will do justice to the research; what data will help the reader; how to create a partnership with the reader; how to keep thinking openly; from whose point of view will be the narrative; how can I come across as a researcher and a person? They argue that stance rather than bias is better understanding of researcher position; context is experienced and the ethnographer is the creator of knowledge; valuing both subjective and objective knowledge is a form of knowing. Qualitative research is more analogies with film and snapshots.

Van Maanen (1988) proposes that the researcher should write a direct account of personal experience as they lived through it, before talking to participants.

> We might think of narrative as a bundle of elements useful in storying – structures, points of view, spatial and temporal devices, characters, plots, themes and of course, a narrator or narrators. The particular version of the story is located in some partial knowledge so we cannot say that narrative reflects *a reality* but we can say that with the help of the reader, narrative produces meaning and creates a *version of reality*. The reader participates vicariously – living the experience figured through narrative rather than standing on its periphery. (pp. 64-5)

The way these representations are constructed is a vital factor in constructing the *vraisemblance* and although we are seeing new forms of representation being used in this new technological age the literary approach, writing fieldnotes, is a subject matter of this chapter. Atkinson's book, published in the 1990s, *The Ethnographic Imagination* (1991) is a vital source for analysing the process of written fieldnotes. He highlights the poetics sociology, the poetics of authoritative accounts, the representation of reality, voices in the text, narrative and representations of social action, character and type – the textual construction of actors, and member and stranger issues – difference, distance and irony. Woods (1996) talks about 'seeing into the life of things.' Ely at al (1997) suggest the writing experience is 'like cooking, digging deep, feeling the work, shaping, tasting and smelling' (p.9). They go on to talk about narrative as a bundle of elements useful in storying - structures, points of view, spatial and temporal devices, characters, plots, themes and of course a narrator or narrators.

Denzin in Ely (1997) describes thick description as more than a literal recording of what is witnessed. It is a matter of ascertaining multiple levels and kinds of meaning in a culture. There are four contexts in every situation – history, power, emotion reality and knowledge. Wolcott (1995) suggests that literary style is not absent in our work, descriptive accounts often provide at least a "dash of panache". He suggests that our accounts often include poignant elements related through anecdotes vignettes or expressive language of those whose lives we examine. He suggests that we think of the ethnographic task as composing rather than doing your study. Atkinson (1991) suggest that language is a repository of shared experience, a vocabulary of motives and is fundamental to social actors' way of rendering action rational, accounts are to be understood as social action rather than taken at face value. He further suggests that if language is left unstudied it comes to control its creators as the sorcerer's apprentice. Walcott (1995) suggests that fieldwork presents an unusual opportunity to gain some insights into the content of life, literally through living fully contextualised research. Regardless as to how the experiences are later written up, the thinking that accompanies fieldwork must be one's own. Everything is filtered through what Geertz (1973) calls it 'I – witnessing'. The self becomes the referent and the context where all other actions are played out, all other meanings discerned. Our work is always unique in time place. Art, he argues, draws always and only upon three elements – experience, imagination and emotion. Imagination draws attention to how experiences are joined together and subsequently revealed to the viewer or listener. Emotion opens the way for feeling, tone is necessary to temper the wholehearted embrace of scientific objectivity.

Atkinson's (1991) major and perhaps most controversial proposal is that ethnographic writing should not only be rhetorical but persuasive. His argument is that the ethnographic text proceeds not by the accumulation of evidence as discrete elements in an inexorable progression either of hypothesis-testing or of inductive reasoning. The text, he suggests is not built up from the marshalling of evidence in an addictive manner but its argument is essentially rhetorical. It is persuasive. It is therefore the function of exemplar to contribute to its persuasive character. Atkinson draws upon Edmonson (1984) with regards to the exemplar,

...it can thus help to guarantee for the reader that the text reports a recognizable shared world of mundane experience. Its use is one way in which the author and implied reader can repeatedly renew the narrative contract. It is by no means universal but the repeated use of exemplars allows the text to project a world of observable reality against which the 'news' of the sociologists commentary can be constructed (ibid. p.95).

Atkinson summaries the voices in the text thus, 'The persuasive force of the ethnographic argument is sustained by the repeated interplay of concrete exemplification and discursive commentary (the histoire and the discourse– Edmonson). The text moves from level to level and from voice to voice. The reader is to be persuaded of the veracity and authenticity of the portrayal by the use of actual types, (ibid. p.103).

This perspective may be very challenging to those steeped in social science, such as the author of this chapter. During my 25 years of research with Prof Peter Woods and Prof Geoff Troman and advised by Martin Hammersley, I focused upon collecting rich data and presenting an analysis of it as our major findings. The analytical characteristics and features of our research sites we formulated from the data, were supported in articles and books, by exemplifications from the data. The data was, to some extent, seen as data, neutral, to be worked on and sifted, categorised, analysed, tested, refined and metamorphosised into new analytical characteristics, findings and features. However, I was also aware that we were using literary forms, persuasive rhetoric, metaphors and empathetic expressions as we documented in detail the lives of the people we researched. I became aware that any credibility, plausibility and validity attached to my work, was not only due to my analytical insights, but also to the literary forms I used in the representations of people's lives. I recognised, as Van Maanen (1988) suggests that I did not do fieldwork because we were artists and we did not become artists through our accomplishments at fieldwork, but I did not hesitate to nurture and draw on whatever artistic talents, gifts or abilities I possessed that helped me to achieve the full potential of fieldwork approach. My re-presentations of the reality of the situations I researched were both analytical and rhetorical, intended to persuade the reader of the voracity of *vraisemblance* of these contexts.

The rest of this chapter will analyse and reflect some of the ways in which I carried out my literary ethnographic research, using examples to represent the five types of writing identified in the first part of the introduction.

Fieldnotes

Writing ethnography covers a wide field from thoughts and ideas prior to site visits, through fieldnotes written on site focusing on social settings, theoretical sampling, reflective and reflexive notes, post fieldwork notes, memos, literary experimentation with data and categories to final writing of the ethnography inclusive of literary genre, tropes and re-presentation. Many of these overlap, as the ethnographer carries them out in similar time periods, as experiments in literary description and analysis. Whilst much is written in the field, some is also written travelling to and from the field and in the ethnographer's working space at home or at their institution, and sometimes in cafés or pubs, or conjured when walking the dog.

The main part of this chapter has, nevertheless, tried to delineate some of the main categories of writing and provide exemplars from research carried out by the author from 1992 to 2008. We firstly explore what I call descriptive fieldnotes from the field, reflective fieldnotes, reflexive fieldnotes, memos and end with examples of writing main texts.

Direct/Descriptive Fieldnotes

This category refers to fieldnotes written on site and is a description of the context and social relations. It differs from Clifford's (1990) 'description' which is 'the making of a more or less coherent representation of an observed cultural reality', (p.51). I would call this re-presentation, or analysis and writing up and I have a section devoted to this definition later in the article. It seems to me that common usage of the term 'description' today in the field of ethnography means observational writing not re-presentation of observations so I will continue to use the term descriptive fieldnotes. They contain exemplars that emphasise: situation, environment and setting; atmosphere, noise and movement and relations – work and people, people with people.

Situation, environment, setting

In surveying a scene, the ethnographer has many choices on which to focus and they should experiment with different aspects as well as integrating them from time to time. This exemplar shows the ethnographer providing an overall re-presentation of an environment.

> The computer suite consisted of three hexagonal workstations over a metre high with the children sitting on high chairs sharing a computer between two of them. It looked like the central control panel in Doctor Who's Tardis and the head teacher told me it had specifically been designed to be attractive to young learners. It was a light airy room with lots of computer designs and relevant vocabulary spread around the walls. The hexagonal design encouraged the children who sat round it to consult and collaborate with each other easily. The learners pressed their fingers to their lips as they gazed at the screens exhibiting puzzled brows, balancing on the edges of their stools as they slowly revolved them backwards and forwards. One hand covered the mouse with a constantly twitching forefinger stabbing at its shoulder and the other hand occasionally dabbed at the screen or

searched for an appropriate button. They debated and evaluated choices, quality and techniques (FN-17/03/03-S) (Jeffrey and Woods, 2010).

These detailed descriptions of a setting are the basic activity of the ethnographer and they should work on it tirelessly as it will pay dividends in re-presenting vraisamblance. The latter is the plausibility of a text, that is: its relation between given text and public opinion; the degree of correspondence to the expectations or conventions of a given genre and the extent to which the texts masks its own textual conventions, appearing to conform to a 'reality' (Todorov 1968, in Atkinson, 1991, p.39).

Creative engagement

I visit a year 2 class who are sat in a horseshoe of tables so they can carry out some still life drawing and painting being led by an arts specialist. The still life collection is a computer screen, an audio speaker and an iron and another electrical piece for their topic/theme this term is electricity and the whole school has begun to integrate their curriculum plans. The learners have sketched their perspective of the still life and are mixing paints when I arrive to paint it with the arts specialist moving around the middle of the horseshoe talking to the learners and occasionally an adult will stop the children to make a specific point.

There is a low background chatter audible as the artists put out their tongues a little, lick their lips slowly and bite their lower lips in concentration. Heads bend over their paintings as their eyes skim to and fro over the picture evaluating and deciding what to do next, talking quietly to themselves. "I don't find it very easy to make silver," one girl tells her teacher. A mouth is screwed up to the right and both arms are stretched upward as one painter contemplates her piece. A mouth is left open as he wonders what to do next and another leans over closely perusing their picture and quietly talking to both their neighbour and themselves as they decide what to do next. Another appears to be enjoying the swish of the brush as he takes it back and forward over the same area a number of times. Another delicately fills in some detail with a pointing action and yet another puts his head into his hands in apparent frustration and then tells a neighbour his problem. Dabbing with the point of the brush is tried while another sits back and taps the wooden end of the paintbrush on the painting a number of times as she wonders what to do next. A thoughtful look focuses on a nearby painting as she watches the artist making vigorous circular strokes and another drips paint onto the picture by shaking the brush up and down.

There is one handed painting with the other arm wrapped round the chin and the head resting on it. A teacher says, "Don't worry about the paint on your hands", and one boy rubs the paint onto his fingers and smears it on to his picture and then admires his fingers and shows them smilingly to a friend. (Jeffrey, 2014)

Atmosphere, noise, movement
Another focus could be the sounds and movement of a setting.

The London fire houses are laid out in the centre of Hall on a road map drawn on to a carpet. The children come to collect them to take them back to their classrooms for the burning in the afternoon. One child can't find his. He wanders around saying, "It smells like a chocolate, it is brown. I am staying to keep an eye out for it". He marches around the paths. "It couldn't have moved because it has no legs. Perhaps it has fallen into the sea. Perhaps someone else has taken it by mistake. We'll act like sniffer dogs. Maybe a magician has disappeared it".

Talking about his house Joe touches the double sets of chimneys and says "My mum made it. It took a very long time and my dad finished it one at night". Samantha has spent over an hour writing about her house, sitting alone in front of the building after drawing a picture of it. She is five years old.

Outside at the burning, children sit on Arthur's seat, singing London's burning. They move around smiling as a fierce wind cuts in to their ruddy cheeks. They jump up and down from time to time.

I talk to some grandparents and they approve of this new form of teaching. (see the tape)

Four children are taken away to the playground to help the adults put on sawdust. The music teacher sings some fire songs and Jenny teaches the Mexican wave and all the children laugh and giggle as the do it. It is bitterly cold.

The houses are alight "the one next to me is on fire", "wow, look at them fly into the sky. They're gliding." "Bye Bye. Some people have escaped by flying. They're witches". There are smiles, cheers and loud laughs as one collapses. "My one is burnt to bits. There is no more life". There are loud 'oohs' as one of the last houses eventually succumbs. There are no complaints about the cold bitter wind. There is a loud whoo as the wind suddenly blows the ash towards the children. The Church is the last to go. After the burning the children and parents disperse. Some back to the classroom others to buy hot dogs for sale in the car park. (Jeffrey and Woods, 2003)

Relations – work/people, people/people
A third focus could be the relations the site's members have to their activity and to their peers.

From 3.30 to 4.15 p.m., 10 teachers drift in and out of the staff room. On this dip day some just wanted it to end. "I'm just getting through it, getting on with life. It was an horrendous build up and I just want to get it over and look forward to doing something else."

At 3.43 Aileen brings up her news, "I saw the inspectors go into Tracy's room. Is everything all right?" Evelyn is sat at the table, Aileen stands with her back to the radiator thinking and Lional enters and yawns reflecting his tiredness. The phone rings and no-one answers it which is unusual. It rings again and Aileen says vehemently "Oh God go away." Lional tells his tale of working in someone else's class on some maths with some children and how badly it went.

At 3.45 it is noted that the inspector is talking to another teacher. A regular cover teacher – partner of one of the teachers – has had his class for the day. "I had inspectors all day. I wish the inspector could see the children with the deputy as well as me to show how difficult they are. There was a stand up fight in PE and some children refused to do PE. It wasn't a very good today." Esther has difficult children too. "Isn't the weather horrible. It's so windy it's affected the children. Inspectors don't care about the weather."

At 3.50 there are six teachers present and the depressing climate is enhanced by more stories, "A child hit an inspector with a ball in the playground and had to write a letter of apology. The PE skills paid off then!" says Jennifer (Ironic). "Ignoring their commitment feels particularly debilitating. I'm pissed off. I stayed up till 3 am this morning because I lost the science lesson on the computer and it was a blinding lesson and nobody came." Other close encounters of a different nature are recounted, "I'm glad that they didn't see my RE. I had the book on my lap as I did the lesson. A child opened the door and I jumped. I feel I don't really want to do any more tomorrow."

She leaves the room. Letica comes in. "The kids were horrible. My maths lesson was horrible." Laura arrives with the only positive reactions, "I've been a real teacher all week". "I haven't," says Esther depressingly. "The music inspector has seen no evidence of appraisal or composing and that because it's not in the plans she is going to report there is none." The others try to help by offering examples of evidence but she doesn't write it down. Instead she rails against the process. "I'm fed up with having to show evidence. They must see it. She wants it given to her on a plate. She won't delve into people's records." She then remembers a family commitment, "Oh no! I forgot to phone the doctor for my son. I left him at home ill. He shouldn't be ill when we're having Ofsted." Laura contrasts this by announcing her evening plans, "I'm going home to make a pair of trousers," but Esther maintains her theme with more assertiveness, "I don't want her to get away with saying there isn't any music here." Someone else does some analysis: "What has to be accepted in an inspection is that some lessons are better than others. I had one or two like that. Why should this week be any better?" And irony sums it up for many of them, "Is it only 4.15? Doesn't time fly when you're having fun!" (Jeffrey & Woods, 1998).

The direct descriptive fieldnote is the main observational writing carried out by an ethnographer. While hanging around ethnographers should be active using every opportunity to experiment with different writing forms and subject matter. This time in the field is one that allows the ethnographer to be creative with their re-presentations, to build a large database for the project and to hone their ethnographic practice. Keep busy by writing and developing as an ethnographer.

Reflexive Fieldnotes

This category is one where the ethnographer acknowledges that they are the research instrument and that all descriptive fieldnotes are filtered through the person/ethnographer. According to Wolcott, 'Observation cannot proceed without an idea in the observer's mind what one is to look at and look for in qualitative research any more than in quantitative' (p. 163). After arguing that the latter is wrought with issues of 'bias' Wolcott (1995) sees 'bias as something we should guard against, I have come to think of it not only as something we must live with but as something we cannot do without' (ibid.). The reflexive fieldnote is one way in which researchers can meet and deal with their 'bias'. It is in addition to Clifford's (1986) 'six ways that ethnographic writing is determined: contextually; rhetorically; institutionally; generically; politically and historically', (in Atkinson, 1990: p. 25). Reflexive writing means ethnographers writing about their personal relationship to the site, the people and their relations. These can also provide insights and the ethnographer may find reflexive moments happening at any time as in this exemplar.

> I left the school, on that Friday before the inspection, at 5.30 to go to Swan Lake at Covent Garden and I found out later that Cloe was the last to leave at 9.45. As I enjoyed the invigorating and delightful music of the first Act of Swan Lake with its party atmosphere I began to feel quite close to the Trafflon teachers and felt angry that they were not part of this very jolly and uplifting environment. Later, over the weekend and on the first day of the inspection I put together some thoughts about why I really liked these people......... I am moved by the pain of it all, by the stress, by the plummeting of self-esteem, by seeing how their cherished values in terms of pedagogy are being marginalized, by their fear of failure, and by the tensions created. I am particularly moved by the way these people have committed themselves to their pupils and gained over the years some measure of confidence about what they do and what they can contribute to society, find themselves to be no more than units to be examined, observed, scrutinized and assessed. This particular week was the lowest time for them as they entered into the fringes of the central spotlight of power – the Ofsted inspection. (Woods, 1996)

Reflective Fieldnotes

This category is also a large one in which the ethnographer mixes ideas, theories, empirically grounded research findings, subjective reactions with observations as in theoretical sampling, carrying out experimental analysis. The term reflective is a problematic concept and defined in many different ways, for example it seems similar to Clifford's (1990) 'inscription' where 'a moment of abstraction.... when a participant-observer jots down a mnemonic word or phrase to fix an observation' (p.51). Clifford sees 'inscription' as having 'turned to writing' from 'the flow of action and discourse', whereas our general activity in the field is 'writing' supplemented by interviews or conversations, which Clifford calls 'inscription'. We therefore differ in the use of these terms and feel that 'reflective fieldnotes' will be more relevant a term to today's ethnographers.

Description is used here to show the critical voice of the ethnographer; critical in the sense of examining their observations/ descriptions as they record them. In the main the ethnographer tries to describe their situations from the point of view of the participants but in reflective moments they test out some hypothesis or bring some possible analytical categories and features to the scene. Ethnographers don't always split their activity between collecting data and then returning to the office to carry out analysis upon it. They often do both at the same time trialling ideas and insights as they occur to them in situ. These kinds of fieldnotes could be called analytical fieldnotes in the methodological description of an ethnographers work but this conveys a rigid process whereas in the research context it is much more fluid. I will stick with the term, albeit, one that is used in many different ways, because it is defined in this written article by the descriptions given to other sorts of fieldnotes, direct descriptive, reflexive and reflective. Each category being a heuristic attempt to describe in more detail the nature of the ethnographer's writing, although we are aware that constructing any typology of fieldnotes shows how any attempt to separate the research process into 'data collection followed by analysis' is futile as this process is on-going all the time. Nevertheless, this categorisation may assist neophyte ethnographers understand how to carry out their work. The example below shows the ethnographer trialling some ideas about 'what's going on here'.

1) SATs revision and preparation – Friday 11 May

They use the Ginn science books – all facts, 'there are a lot of facts and you've just got to learn them', 'whatever subject you're doing it's the same story.' I asked if any of them wanted to stay in at break to revise with me but they declined saying 'they were not allowed to, they needed fresh air'.

They seemed cool, downtrodden, or repressed, resigned, accepting of a fact based life of quizzes, facts, tests. What you know is the priority – not how you feel. (I devise some value priorities for them to put in order of priority in conversation with them later – knowing a lot, being a level 5, being considerate to others, being a hard worker, behaving well, being good at something, being creative and imaginative.

Elishe says 'I have chosen a subject I struggle with – teeth – so I am going to write out the questions to answer. I got muddled up with incisors and c?? (*I don't know either*), I am not sure which is which. We had a human question sheet and I got nearly all of them right except those on teeth'.

They are handed back their science mock tests from yesterday and they finish those they didn't do and check them. Francis says make sure you fill in all the parts. ....They are onto 'the earth' and Francis, their teacher, says, "If you put a circle as the answer you won't get a mark. Is the sun hidden behind the moon at night, true or false? It should be false because the moon's light is reflected from the sun". A boy offers the answer that Mr Wilson told them it was true during a solar eclipse. *They don't appear concerned about this contradiction.* Another asks how many marks she would get if she answered 4 out of 5 of the questions for this section and Francis says there are only 2 marks overall. *(Even I cannot work that out. Does this make any more sense the operation itself?).* Lloyd thinks the picture of the cloud is wrong and Francis agrees but they plough on.

He asks Jack to tell them the answer to a gravity question. *(I am overwhelmed as I understand little of it and logical questions from the children are passed over quickly.)* Joshua pushes his paper away when he gets to the point where he stopped yesterday. I ask if he wants to do it with help. He says 'no' and looks tired. I ask him if he is and he says 'a bit'.

Are they fascinated by filling in the boxes as they put in a zero if they get it wrong. It doesn't seem to bother them what they get right or wrong. They just appear to accept failure. Does the performance implant an acceptance of failure rather than stimulating them to try harder? They play a game of success and failure and you can't have one without the other. (Jeffrey, 2014)

Memos

Memos are used to experiment with a particular perspective, theory, insight, analytical category. They are written during the process of data collection and may have been stimulated by ideas in the field. They may or may not become part of the final ethnography but they open a perspective for critique from colleagues and the ethnographer. Some groups, like ours, share these and use them to, again, trial analysis and understanding. There is even a space for them in the computer based qualitative programmes such as Atlas-ti. The first memo arose from studying the digital presence of a school in an educational market.

Open Performances – performativity and openness

   Parents and the community are invited into the school more often and visitors, including parents, see more of the school's work and the way teachers teach as the classrooms are more open. Teachers have to accept an array of visitors into their schools and classrooms and actually invite strangers in at a moment's notice.

   Teaching has become a public affair. Even the private reports to parents are now virtually open with every parent knowing the school statistics on its SATs performance, Ofsted assessments and children and parents talk openly with each other about the child's 'level' both in and outside the staffroom, the classroom and the school grounds.

   Meetings now often take place in public not in the head's office, which in one of our schools was only used to house her two dogs, with the door open of course. One such meeting we noted was in the school café and included a DfES person and another meeting constituted six local headteachers.

Qualitative and quantitative performance is now encapsulated into a discourse concerning the school's performance and openness is the key which validates the school's interest in performativity. (Jeffrey, 2014)

The second memo arose from examining the number of public events in a school programme and noting a heavy reliance on a tight timetable. It represented school life as similar to a productive company rushing to ensure high productivity through intensification of work.
Fast teaching for fast times.

There was powerful energy flowing through these schools that reflected the urgency of a dynamic culture of busy organisations incorporating many active and exciting daily events, 'They support International Book day. Many days are filled with one off activities that ring out across the school. In the classrooms during routine times they still exhibit a youthful energy generating dynamic activity. A speed filled sense of urgency to get on and move on infected the learning culture. Fast teaching resulted in which as many as ten changes of activities taking place in a day, the multiple events, curriculum and assessment imperatives lead to intensive time filled experiences.

The quiet slow pace of a silent writing lesson is quickly contrasted by a fast action maths lesson. The fast change is an inimical part of primary education in these fast times. The fast pace cuts across creativity and performativity.

Whole day projects add to the dynamism. National celebrations are taken up and add to the fast experiences. Week long projects add to the ever changing experience of a fast education.

There are a plethora of outings and school journeys, 'I spy 30 cases in the staff room corridor indicative of a school journey and find out that year 4 are going to a Norfolk activity centre for 3 days' (FN-C-3/3/07) and they sometimes spread into the holidays, 'It's Oxford singing week and all classes engage in singing activities during the week ready for a whole school sing along on Friday. Some teachers/TA's have signed up for a sing-along during half term, another activity similar to Coombes, always something going on and they have to fit in the curriculum' (FN-23/5/07).

The dynamism of the institutions is structuring phenomenological time – subjective time – into an experience of a polychromic time frame spurred on by the established dynamic culture. Teachers and schools, striving to be open, inclusive, caring, aspirational and entrepreneurial are creating a polychromic time frame that they believe is an appropriate culture for schools and learning. The difference between the polychromic time of the primary school teacher prior to the reform programme in the UK was that the class teacher was in charge of the polychromic, flexible time frame and now they are not so much in control.

Being successful adds to the pace of life. This fast pace is dynamic, exciting but it has an internal tension. Fast teaching leads to a fragmented education and a fragmented pedagogy.

This fast education and fast teaching was supplemented by the fast tracking of careers. The fast tracking involved fast procedures. The fast pace is the norm. However, there is sometimes a regretful tone as the next topic or initiative takes precedence.

The open, inclusive, caring cultures full of aspiring and entrepreneurial agency are also places that operate at a dynamic fast pace, a reality of modern life elsewhere as well as in schools. Primary schools polychromic time frames today are both a mixture of management directed initiatives and creative endeavours that provide satisfaction and energy for the teacher. (Jeffrey, 2007)

Writing Main Texts
The actual ethnography is a collection of fieldwork ideas, exemplified by memos, analysis of the data into categories and sub categories that re-presents the qualitative life of the context under study bounded within the focus of the research. Literary devices are used to trial possible re-presentations. These literary adventures have been broken down into six categories, light narratives, evocations, vignettes, metaphoric analogies, simple narratives and whole narratives. Needless to say they all overlap in some way or another but it may help the literary process to categorise them as such.

A] Light narratives (playfulness)
Qualitative researchers are beholden to seek new ways of describing and analysing their sites of research, particularly if they wish to publish in journals where they are expected to bring new insights to add to the knowledge base of the area under study. Ethnographers are also keen to re-present their research

122

sites from new perspectives, which may well add to the reader's understanding of the nature of that site and the relations therein. The following extract was an attempt to do this but was also using a literary playfulness to enhance the new perspective.

An Appreciative Ethos

Coombes' ethos is also 'appreciative'. The ecological environment, social interactions, spiritual narratives, the skills and crafts of the community, cycles of life and annual cultural celebrations are all appreciated for their uniqueness and their signification. Everyone, including parents, enjoy the 'grand' events that permeate most weeks of the year and the policy of a 'hands-on' approach ensures that children's curiosity is stimulated and satisfied. Pleasure is gained from many adventures: seeing a 'Coombeshenge' rise before their eyes in the grounds; helping to cut down the Christmas tree, planting daffodils, potatoes, sunflowers; 'beating the bounds' of the school site with long sticks and returning to one of the many annual events, such as the Epiphany march around the grounds in January. Appreciation involves understanding, awareness, discernment and insight as each new engagement not only reveals features and qualities but they join with all the other engaging experiences to comprehend the breadth of the world and the delights of learning.

Every week, people visit the school to talk about their lives, perform their skills and reproduce their crafts – Irish dancers, Scottish bagpipe performers, harpists, artists, stone masons, a military band, a bell ringing group, a vet ministering to the sheep, a member of the Cromwell society on a horse, a crew in an army helicopter, a juggler on a one-wheel bike, a specialist in children's playground songs and rhymes from America, a Muslim woman talking about her faith and culture. There are also environmental maintenance events such as sheep shearing, hedge building, and willow arch weaving. These talks, demonstrations or performances engage the children's interest and take them on something akin to a 'Grand Tour' of the world outside the school. (Jeffrey and Woods, 2003)

This playfulness may well take over the ethnographer as they stretch their literary enjoyment beyond the acceptable, as in the example below, but nevertheless it is all part of enjoying the literary process in pursuit of *vraisemblance*.

The head teacher of one of my research schools had asked me to hang around so I could introduce myself to the RgI (lead inspector). She had shown the Chief Inspector a letter I had sent her outlining the project and assuring her that I would not interfere with the inspection.

As the chief inspector left the parents meeting at 5.10 p.m. followed by two other inspectors, both women, they proceeded along the corridor, where I was lurking, followed by the headteacher who said, as they approached me, 'This is the researcher who wrote the letter I showed you'. The inspector smiled, held out her hand whilst continuing her march towards the governors' meeting in the other building. I shook hands, and without interrupting her step, she passed by without an acknowledgement, a spoken word or a receding glance. The entourage followed with the Headteacher muttering 'I've got tea and cakes ready for you', as they passed into the playground. I, meanwhile, didn't quite know whether to be grateful that I had been privileged to touch the hand of this busy august personage or whether I should feel appreciative of her busy schedule. I felt as though I was in a Tudor film, lining the streets as the Royal entourage passed by, feeling gratified at the opportunity to be recognized for a brief second. Or was I in a fantasy wonderland with Alice (Jeffrey, 1995).

B] Evocations
Evoking the atmosphere of a situation, or context is very much part of the ethnographer's tool kit, using literary forms to garner more *vraisemblance*. Woods (1996) notes that novelists such as Somerset Maugham, D.H. Lawrence are all examples of raising 'empathetic understanding' (Eisner in Woods 1996, p.82). He goes on to argue via Rose (1990) that such works 'help us to understand because their creators have understood, and had the skills and imagination to transform their understanding into forms that help us to notice what we have learned not to see' (Rose in Woods, 1996, p.82).

The aim of evocative writing is 'to conjure up the very feel of people's experiences, to recreate atmospheres and convey ethos (Woods 1996, p. 84). Using this form gives the ethnographer full reign to re-present the situation in prose that is near the poetic. Ethnography is a super ordination of the consequence of its imperfections. It is neither self-perfecting in the manner of scientific discourse, nor totalising in the manner of political discourse either by reflexive attention to its own rules nor by the performances' instrumentality of those rules. It transcends instead by evoking what cannot be known discursively (Tyler, 1986), and accepts that each description has been constructed to evoke the setting by a writer.

The dance circle
The children are learning how to work in a circle, going in and out and circling round in different directions. Their faces are serious as they have

to concentrate on the beat and the direction of turn when the circle goes round in the opposite direction. They are learning about unity and unison in the universe. As they practice their universe 'birth and sound' sequence they watch the leader with a studied intent as they perform the flash jump, the smooth roll, the scrunch role and the flame leap. Their eyes follow their arms looking into space with slow stretched turns. Nadine smiles as she explodes and follows this with a spiky roll and a swirl (FN-21/11/03). (Jeffrey and Woods, 2010).

These evocations are often constructed in the field when very little is actually going on and the ethnographer feels beholden to being doing something while hanging around. The following extract was written on the Saturday prior to a government inspection of a primary school by the UK organisation The Office for Standards in Education.

It's ten past ten on Saturday morning. I'm sitting in the infant hall with my back to the windows facing the display boards. It is very quiet and a contrast to the normal buzz and chatter of a school. I can hear a blackbird singing in the garden. The light, albeit filtered through tall pot plants climbing up the large window frames, shows up the highly polished floor. Every display board has uniform three centimetre borders made from black sugar paper – one was removed because it didn't conform. The contents of the displays are all mounted and uniform computer printed labels explain the contents or challenge the reader to respond mutely. There are very few written labels written by teachers. All is nearly ready for the inspection event........ As I contemplate the school's quiet confidence the calm is punctuated by; the moving of furniture, the playing of some music, the hammering of a staple gun, or the sudden whistling of a teacher leaping briskly down the stairs. Or more unusually the burst of laughter from two or three teachers gathered in a corridor or in someone's classroom.

The silence is again disturbed by the low hum of two petrol lawn mowers as they circle the lone willow tree cutting the grass of the main green play area. This is Saturday morning and one wonders if the workers are being paid overtime rates. The Premises Officer is playing his full part in the preparation. The teaching staff have already commented on the surprise of having new locks on the loo doors. All is nearly ready for the inspection event...... The main hall in the upper school is totally covered with a school journey display that spills out onto the corridor. Every piece of wall is covered with over 400 treble mounted pieces of work and photographs representing this year's journey to Kent. The windowsills are used to display artefacts and folders of children's work. All is nearly ready for the inspection event.

The hall is set up for assembly on Monday. There is a newish lectern bought by the head after she first heard about the Ofsted visit and in keeping with the school's developing emphasis on religious assemblies. (She hoped that the lectern would bring 'a sense of awe'. Some teachers would have preferred the money spent on books.) There is a matching chair and another one on the other side of the lectern. There are two tall pot plants behind the chairs flanking the lectern and the chairs. A music stand is to one side waiting for a child to play some music. Large printed numbers have appeared on the walls in recent days to indicate where each class should sit. I thought, at first, they were hymn numbers. All is nearly ready for the inspection event. (Jeffrey and Woods, 1998)

C] Vignettes
Vignettes are compact sketches that can be used to introduce characters, foreshadow events and analyses to come, highlight particular findings or summarise a particular theme or issue in analysis and interpretation. Vignettes are composites that encapsulate what the researcher finds through the fieldwork. In every case, vignettes demand attention and represent a growing sense of understanding about the meaning of the research work (Ely et al, 1997).

Aspirations and Entrepreneurialism
Members held personal aspirations for career, for the learners, for their school and community and the values underpinning these aspirations were at the same meritocratic, egalitarian and humanist. There was clearly a technicisation of work represented by levelling assessment procedures and target setting but general educational values were present with passion, which to some extent, counters some of the literature showing primary schools and teachers as depressed and stressed resulting in a loss of commitment (Troman and Woods 2001). Our schools were littered with cultural and educational homilies exhorting its members to think and act positively, to see learning as a comfortable but challenging journey made easier through self-assessment and through co-operation with others, identifying mistakes as learning points and generally celebrating the joy of learning and education and downplaying authoritative power relations. These homilies were for adults as well, some of them placed in staff toilets. An aspirational culture was prominent throughout with a celebration of continual improvement as each member arrived at a station on the never ending journey through professional and personal life. These school cultures

are positive learning based communities in which every unscheduled stop or diversion was an opportunity to review, reflect and renew progress and opportunity to increase self-aspiration and personal responsibility.

Added this we identified an educational entrepreneurialism, an energy to be innovative, to drive along new initiatives and to develop original strategies and activities. Acting as commissioners of services schools focused on a variety of funding streams to develop their institutions, to engage in local partnerships, to raise the quality of training for everyone to develop skills and enterprise. These schools are imbued with visual energy, with visual celebrations of their values, work and life, with visual examples of joy and contentment, of order and care, of excitement and dedication to learning and the humanity of life. (Jeffrey, 2014)

D] Metaphoric analogies
Literary expression is littered with metaphors, almost all writing is metaphoric, meaning that one topic may lead to another through their similarity whereas metonymy is used because of its contiguity. According to Atkinson (1991) the former tends to be used in poetry and the latter in prose. Two examples that differentiate them quoted by Lodge (1977) via Atkinson (1991) are the *Ballad of Reading Gaol* by Oscar Wilde as poetic and metaphoric and the description of a hanging in *The Guardian* newspaper, some time in the last century, being a metonymic one. Atkinson argues that the latter is mainly seen as synecdoche, the presentation of a small part of a scene to represent the whole. Ethnographers use both, more metonymy and synecdoche in their everyday descriptions, of say a revision lesson for SATS tests to represent the whole of the national SATS programmes, values and technology. However, from time to time they may wish to construct an overt metaphor, using an unrelated concept or experience to describe an unrelated situation.

Again, ethnographers experiment with them and some may come to be included in the final ethnography and some may not if they seem contrived and possibly overbearing. The first example was published and the second was not. The first was stimulated by a trialing of the panoptic effect of regular inspections of schools and the second by the notion of an inspection team poring over and testing every element of a school to satisfy worthyness. They may be too much for some readers but they are examples of the ways in which ethnographers can experiment with different metaphors to try to re-present *vraisemblance*, a semblance of authenticity and truth.

Wearing in a new suit – However, there is something fundamentally different. The school and the teachers have been re-dressed by Ofsted. The clothes may look the same but they have been re-dressed with Ofsted's hands of approval or disdain. There is a new inner lining to their clothes. One which reminds them constantly that Ofsted's priorities and pedagogy are paramount and that Ofsted has the power to undress you, gaze at you and, in the spotlight of their supporters, re-dress one with care or brutality as they see fit. They have effectively colonized (Hargreaves, 1994) the primary teacher's domain, their classroom and their identity. (Jeffrey, 1999)

The similarities between a Ministry of Transport Test (MoT) for a motor car and an Ofsted inspection are that the mechanic has a set of components to investigate and he is looking for those component parts that are failing. Ofsted inspectors have a framework that identifies parts of a school or classroom activity and they, like the mechanic, attempt to identify the failing parts. The mechanic marks certain components as failing and then leaves it up to the car's owner to go and get the components fixed, as does the Ofsted inspector. It also has to be noticed that a mechanic in pursuance of his investigation climbs into the body of the car to check various components, into its bowels. They shake components, tap various parts of the bodywork and swivel moving parts to test their functionality. In a similar fashion the inspector creeps into the body of a teacher's classroom, observes and evaluates working activities, questions and examines the children, and investigates activities for functionality but unlike the mechanic, with no indication of what kind of evaluation they are making, (Jeffrey, 1995).

E] Simple Narratives
In order to unpack the complexity of school organisations and the lives of its members it was initially helpful to describe some aspects of the culture in discrete terms while accepting that the reality is a welter of action. The metaphor of policy tracks has been used to highlight the nature of the research into the ways in which performance and creativity policies permeate these school cultures but also to examine their separate existences, cross-overs and conjunctions. Tracks and tracking is a well-used term in policy and education, particularly in the new performative discourse and the use of the metaphor is provide us with a starting point – the schools as a busy station terminus with many policy tracks leading from it which sometimes maintain singularity but where various crossing points and mergers take place.

The Performance Track
At the same time the performance track runs parallel to the creative teaching and learning track occasionally crossing each other or running

together for a few miles. School cultures are imbued with awards and rewards, of cracking learning barriers, producing performances for each other, for parents, for the community, for funders, for celebrations, for targets, for corporate image, against each other internally in the shape of sports and other competitions and against other schools. A powerful discourse of 'learning to strive' brands the journey through the pervasive homilies and target setting for learners and teachers. There are performative collaborations between learners and teachers and schools in clusters, performative selection is open and accepted across the intellectual divide, a multiple series of tracks on which learner's travel at different speeds with differing cargos. Each school, Key Stage, teacher, group and individual have targets to achieve concerning effective teaching and learning, levels of achievement and behaviour. People, including learners play the game and gain satisfaction from the process of perform-ance and performance outcomes with apparent joy and the raising of self-esteem at the climax of any performative journey. There is a constant power drive to push and pull the train along to the next station, to celebrate the change in distance covered and to improve the speed on the next leg of the journey. An improving life is being lived out by everyone in the institution and this has now become an institutions main objective – that of improvement, a constantly moving vehicle or momentum only pausing for fresh energy at each station.

Journeys are travels through space and time and timetables are drawn up to plan the journey and test the performance of the school or class. The emphasis on teleological time is an indicator of performance and the time taken varies, according to the set timetables and to the interruptions to service, that exist in the modern dynamic primary school. There is fast education, fast teaching, fast tracking but time for a laugh and some fun although initiative overload causes breakdowns and feelings of frustration. The tick-tocking of the improvement clock permeates every day and every space even when the signals are against and diversions have to be taken. These time conflicts add to the frustration and the appropriate elapsed time for learning is often compromised. Phenomenological – subjective - time is marginalised to the slow track and sometimes side-lined in favour of technical rational time (Hargreaves 1994) but all in all a polychromic time is the major experience, (Jeffrey, 2014).

The metaphor of time was used across all the data of one research project and in the following case applied to the people involved.

Staff and Passenger Identities

Schools and teachers aim to balance the two, to ensure both have their place but also to join them together when possible crossing over for a brief spells, but more often than not reverting to their own tracks again. Each of these identities, the creative teacher and the performing teacher is a challenge to the self, to maintain and develop the former and to meet the challenges faced by external demands and the progression of their learners. There are professional debilitating tensions and mixed emotions about their role of teaching, their passion for creative pedagogy and their commitment to improve the lot of their learners. There is some private performative anxiety in the face of performative failure and this affects their interest in professional care and educational development. However, they have also developed a professional ease with their situation, an acceptance of their lot but a desire to maintain some control over it, a professional pride at any resulting performative progress and they maintain an interest in any professional progress and at the same they value the solidarity of values and professional aims in today's collective enterprises. They are imbued with the discourses of the day as they replicate the language and aims of the policy discourses, both performative and creative but they seek to manage any conflicts between them as best they can and at the same time act creatively to overlay them as the new flexible opportunities present themselves. The amount of work and the desire to achieve difficult crossings are wearisome but challenging. They accept the fast moving situations and use their energy and commitment to manage them replicating the fast moving policy and economic global scene. Fast teachers for fast times, (Jeffrey and Troman, 2017).

Whole narratives

During the process of data collection and analysis the ethnographer uses many literary devices, as exemplified earlier, to enhance validity and authenticity but at some point they have to produce an article or a full ethnography. This activity is end of experimentation and the act of re-presenting the life of the context being researched. While the ethnographer will use many of the literary devices used during fieldwork and analysis a whole story has to be constructed for readers. It is not enough to re-present data from the field under contextual headings such as; 'The art lesson', or 'Maise's story', or 'Working with peers'. A narrative must be original and reflect the new knowledge produced in the analysis of the data. Contributing new knowledge, mostly in an incremental manner, to the field of published research or theories is, in our view, the way in which an ethnographer's re-presentations are legitimised in the academy, by peer review. An ethnographer may not wish to gain this legitimation and in which case they can re-present raw data without bringing new insights to the field of research but in our case adding to new knowledge has been a key objective.

One of the main ways of adding to knowledge is through the creation of a compelling or at least new perspective on a specific context, a new way in which the reader, who is probably familiar with the research context, can add to their store of ways to interpret that context.

This process involves to some extent the telling of a story using a holistic narrative that constructs a way of 'seeing into the life of things' (Woods, 1996).

Some examples are given below of the narratives we have constructed for our articles and books.

The reconstruction of primary teachers' identities. (Woods and Jeffrey, 2002)
1. The primary teachers' Plowden self-identity –
    a. Humanism,
    b. Vocationalism
2. Challenges to the Plowden self-identity –
    a. The assault on child-centred philosophy
    b. Diminution of 'elementary trust'
    c. Changes in the teacher role
    d. Teacher Dilemmas
3. Identity Work: meeting the challenges –
    a. Self-positioning
    b. Self-Assertion
    c. Identity Strategies
    d. Self-displacement
    e. Game playing
    f. Realignment

This chapter begins by outlining the teacher's core values of humanism and vocationalism and secondly describes the challenges to those educational values from the intensification of work, the regular inspections by Ofsted and the increasing priority given to testing. We identify two characteristics of that challenge and then give examples of changes in the teacher's role and the dilemmas facing teachers in managing a clash of values. The third section then describes the effects on the teachers as they manage this crisis and the strategies they employ.

We see this as a literary device to tell a story from our research which adds to the body of knowledge of teachers experiencing change in their working lives. Every ethnographer or qualitative researcher, who wishes to gain recognition from the academy, and their readers, needs to re-present a new way of perceiving this particular context. It is here that the hard work in research is carried out, whereas the writing of the data and experimentation is a practice of delight and fun.

This second example does something similar to the first by telling the story of deprofessionalisation, its emotions and coping strategies.

Feeling deprofessionalised: the social construction of emotions during an Ofsted inspection. (Woods and Jeffrey, 1997)

Emotional Reactions
    a. Anxiety
    b. Anger and resentment
    c. Guilt
    d. Grief at the loss of pedagogic values
2. Deprofessionalized Feelings
    a. Professional inadequacy
    b. Anomie
    c. Dehumanization
    d. Change of Commitment
    e. Loss of Self
3. Coping Strategies
4. Mutual Support

Again a story is told, albeit, an analysis of categories and sub-categories to show the qualitative nature of particular contexts and situations. The ethnographer/writer has to strive to tell a story, developing their literary practices during the process of field work and analysis. The ethnographic writer also draws upon theories such as Anomie, to show how the latter works in this particular situation and hopefully also adds something to the theory itself.

A third example shows how an ethnographer can add to a particular theoretical area, in this case that of institutional cultures. Drawing on research identifying some particular characteristics of institutions such as 'The Total Institution, (Goffman, 1961), 'The Greedy Institution' 'Coser' (1974) and the 'Re-inventive Institution (Scott, 2010) we identified a new type called 'The Embracing Institution'. This type of institution was one in which the market place played a vital role through competition for pupil places, league table positions following annual testing and publications of Ofsted reports. Schools we argued had to compete in an open market, displaying their credibility and in order to do this they embraced the outside world through promotion of their successes and pedagogies in digital forms for the world to see and at the same time ensured that all the workers in the institution were embraced in the vital act of team work to maintain their successful global visibility.

The Embracing Performative Institution (Jeffrey and Troman, 2012)
    Embracing openness
    Embracing members
        - Team work
        - Nurturing
        - Distributed leadership
    Embracing performativity and aspiration

We hoped that this analysis would add to the body of knowledge about institutional cultures. However, the narrative of the chapter still told a story of embracing the outside world as they had to in a competitive market place, how embracing each other as an encultured group pursuing the same goal of improving market position resulted in everyone embracing performativity and aspiration. The story, written by the ethnographer, showed the influence and power of culture in organisations.

Conclusion

Being an ethnographer requires imagination, literary skills and development, a passion for literary expression and experimentation and an abiding interest in storytelling. It is a qualitative life full of qualitative experiences, judgements, expression, wonder, delight, being captured by the joy of writing and an abiding desire to re-present their sites and situations as authentically as possible; to give the reader a detailed, informative and long lasting understanding of people's lives.

An issue that arises from this approach to ethnographer is that of writing in a home language or native tongue. It is clear that using literary forms have to be those that are inherent in the particular tongue of those writing the ethnographies. It is crucial that the ethnographer describes situations, re-presents contexts and plays with a variety of literary forms, firstly, in their home language. This is not a problem when publishing in the ethnographers' language but international ethnographers are often required to publish in English language journals and books. As most international ethnographers are bi-lingual in their native tongue and English, there may a temptation to carry out the research in English, in order to by-pass the translation phase. This approach should be resisted as the indigenous ethnographer's written forms must be in their first language. The good news is that some international journals and publishers – Taylor and Francis for *E&E Journal* – have agreed that articles may be firstly published in an ethnographers' home language and then translated for the English publications. The article is then seen as a 'first' publication of the article and therefore acceptable to journals who demand articles are new for the international market. Our experience is that those that have agreed to this protocol also agree that if an article is first published in an English language journal, a translated version in the home language of the ethnographer will receive automatic permission for publication in a home language journal. All authors will need to ensure this is the position of all publishers to whom they submit articles but it is worthwhile pressing them on this matter.

The consequence of this type of agreement ensures that ethnographers are able to use the literary devices, forms and style of their native tongue firstly to re-present a re-presentation of research contexts authenticated by their native peers.

Enjoy.

Bibliography

Atkinson, P. (1991) *The Ethnographic Imagination: textual construction of reality* (London Routledge)

Coser, L. A. (1974) *Greedy institutions: Patterns of undivided commitment* (New York, Free Press).

Clifford, J. (1990) Notes on (Field) notes In R, Sanjek (Ed.), *Fieldnotes: The makings of anthropology* p 47-70.

Clifford, J. and Marcus, G.E. (1986) (Eds.) *Writing Culture: The Poetics and Politics of Ethnography*, Berkley: University of California.

Denzin, N. (1997) *Interpretive Ethnography: Ethnographic Practices for the 21st Century*, London: Sage.

Eisner, E.W. (1995) What artistically crafted research can help us understand about schools, *Educational Theory* 45, p. 1-6.

Ely, M., Vinz, R., Downing, M., Anzul, M. (1997) *On writing qualitative research: Living by words*, London: Falmer Press.

Geertz, C. (1973) *The interpretation of cultures*, New York: Basic Books.

Goffman, E. (1961) *Asylums*, Harmondsworth: Penguin.

Hammersley, M. (1992) Some reflections on ethnography and validity. *Qualitative studies in education* 5(3): pp.193-203.

Hargreaves, A, (1994) *Changing Teachers, Changing Times: Teacher's work and culture in the Post-modern age*, London: Cassell.

Jeffrey, B, (1995) *Memo – Ofsted Project*, New Cottage, Painswick, GL6 6UA.

Jeffrey, B. (1999) 'Sidestepping the substantial self: the fragmentation of primary teacher's professionality through audit accountability' in M. Hammersley. (Ed.) *Researching School Experience: Ethnographic studies of teaching and learning*, London, Falmer.

Jeffrey, Bob, (1995) *Fieldnote – Ofsted Project*, New Cottage, Painswick, GL6 6UA.

Jeffrey, Bob (2007) *Memo on Fast Times – Capital Project*, New Cottage, Painswick, GL6 6UA.

Jeffrey, (2014) *The Primary School in Testing Times,* Painswick, E&E Publishing, p. 15

Jeffrey, B. Troman, G. (2012) The Embracing Performative Institution, *Journal of Organisational Ethnography* 1(2) pp.195-212.

Jeffrey, B. Troman, G. (2017) 'The governance turn, institutional embrace and the postmodern professional' in Borgnakke, K., Dovemark, M. and Marques da Silva, S. (Eds) *The postmodern professional:Contemporary learning practices, dilemmas and perspectives* 4-32. London: Tufnell Press 4-32.

Jeffrey, B. Woods, P. (1998) *Testing Teachers: The effect of school inspections on primary teachers*, London: Falmer.

Jeffrey, B. Woods, P. (2003) *The Creative School*, London: Falmer Press.

Jeffrey, B., & Woods, P. (2010) *Creative Learning in the Primary School*, Abingdon: Routledge.

Lodge, D. (1977) *The modes of modern writing*, London: Edward Arnold.

Rose, D, (1990) *Living the ethnographic life*, London: Sage.

Scott, S. (2010) Revisiting the total institution: Performative regulation in the Reinventive Institution, *Sociology*, 44(2), 213-231.

Troman, G, and Woods, P, (2001) *Primary Teacher Stress*, London: Routledge/Falmer.

Tyler S. (1986) 'Post-modern ethnography: from document of the occult to occult document' in J. Clifford and G. Marcus, *Writing Culture*, Berkley, CA: University of California Press.

Van Maanen, J. (1988) *Tales of the Field: On Writing Ethnography.* Chicago: University of Chicago Press.

Wolcott, H.F. (1995) *The Art Of Fieldwork*, Walnut Creek, CA, AltaMira Press.

Woods, P. (1996) *Researching the art of teaching*, London: Routledge.

Woods, P. and Jeffrey, B. (1997) The social construction of emotions, *Cambridge Journal of Education*, 26(3), pp 325-343.

Woods, P. and Jeffrey, B. (2002) The constitution of teacher identities, *British Journal of Sociology of Education*, 23(1), pp. 89-106.

SECTION THREE

Researcher-member
relationships and writing

Writing as new understandings of social phenomena: The practice of including children's perspectives

Diana Milstein, Angeles Clemente, and Alba Lucy Guerrero

Introduction

The collaboration that occurs during fieldwork between ethnographers and their participants, and how they dialogue, exchange, discover one another, and share activities, has been a topic of debate over the past few decades on the academic agenda. This debate has caused the collaboration of the 'natives' with the researchers to become public, tangible and recognizable in ethnographies done some time ago as well as those that are more contemporary. At the same time, discussions have opened up on epistemological and methodological aspects relative to the writing that emerges when the investigative work is recognized as collective. There are debates about the way in which an ethnographer decides which voices will be included and in what ways they will be included, the relation between the voice of the researcher and his or her interlocutors, and the somewhat participative modalities of the interlocutors in the authorship. In these debates, the collaboration of children has emerged with some delay, even though the topics that have constituted Anthropology as a discipline, such as parenting rituals, upbringing, socialization, among others, 'native' boys and girls have been included in ethnographies since the early decades of the twentieth century. In this article, we analyze the continuous process of fieldnote writing that registered encounters with children which, in turn, resulted in opportunities of discovering for the researchers.

The explicit incorporation of children as interlocutors and collaborators in ethnographic field work – including the relevance this has on the processes of writing fieldnotes, papers and monographs – dates to the end of the 1960s. Over the last thirty years, the sphere of Ethnography and Education has been enriched by the different ways children have been incorporated as collaborators, the reflections on these collaborations and how the perspectives of children on social phenomena that we study are woven into ethnographic texts.

Hirschfeld (2002) pointed out that the lack of interest that anthropologists have shown towards children is related, partly, to the little appreciation they have of their cultural imprint in the configuration of what he called the culture of adults. In fact, when we interact with children, in certain moments, when faced with a comment or 'unusual' interpretation of a child, we researchers find it difficult to write, because we do not know how to do it, how to incorporate this way of acting, perceiving and understanding in fieldnotes. The process of writing itself has allowed us to objectivize the understanding worked with children and discovered the richness of the displacements. We have enriched this objectivization process by developing a collaborative work between the three authors of this paper. Our work has been central to help us uncover the subjective relationship of each one of us with her object. The first experience of this kind was developed by two of us and consisted in the analysis of some fieldnotes of a short dialogue between Guerrero and a Colombian girl in a displacement situation. This kind of practice that generated successive rewritings to come to an interpretation of an uncommon observation of a girl, allowed us to re-elaborate the question of internal displacement (Guerrero & Milstein, 2017).

The collaborative work we are proposing consists of analyzing individual fieldnotes of projects that we have developed in different places. We choose fieldnotes that involved certain kind of mystery or enigma in relation to a specific interaction with or between children. We read and discuss our fieldnotes in order to discover more creative forms of incorporate to our writings the wealth of children as co-producers of our adulthood (Johansson, 2012). This is one of the most challenging aspects of our collaborative work, to include the children in the process of writing.

Through two examples, we will show in this paper some of the ways in which children participate as collaborators/interlocutors in ethnographic research, and how they have made us deconstruct our schema and ways of thinking when we are in the process of writing down our interpretations of the social phenomena that we register and attempt to analyse for understanding.

Although children express their visions in a way that is often ephemeral, we want to highlight that children *do by saying*. We find Austin's expression (1962) very useful to emphasize the performative character of what children say, which is generally taken as temporary, secondary or irrelevant. The challenge consists on developing modes of writing that include these ways of *doing by saying*. In addition to including what children say, the performative writing transforms children words and interpretations into permanent and relevant contents. What apparently has little importance because it is said by children, results in a performative writing that affirms the content as relevant, important and permanent. "Words and language have a material presence in the world; words have effects on people; words matter", (Denzin 2001:24), stating that the interactions that we carry out with the subjects of the communities we study are the outcome of performative events that transform the information in shared experience (Denzin 2001:24). Our aim is to use the advantages of performative writing to find ways to represent those shared experiences with children.

The ethnographic text is not the only outcome of analysing what was said and done during the fieldwork, but the manner in which it was said and done implies changes in the adult-ethnographer's frames of reference and preconceptions. Canagarajah (2002), a sociolinguist from Sri Lanka, calls *connecting the word to the world*, which, for us, means much more than connecting the text to the context (p.1). It is, in fact, putting into words how the world of the children participating in a specific investigation changes the adult world of the ethnographer and influences the written word, that is, the product of that investigation.

In the next two examples, we will discuss fieldnotes writing processes that make an attempt to account for the first annotations of the situation that distorted how it was enunciated and of the writing process that followed. In the following two examples we will show how in the first writing of fieldnotes there is a certain distortion of what children said about their experiences and about their understandings. These distortions are clearly mediated by our position as adults and by our personal experiences. In the first example, the process of successive writings allowed the researchers to notice and correct their interpretation of the social practices in the classroom. They became aware that this interpretation minimized the relevance of children's and adults' experiences outside the classroom. It illustrates how valuable is the practice of going back to the fieldnotes and to share them with research participants in order to make sense of the data and to re-write the initial interpretations. Moreover, it show that the analysis emerged from performative interactions, and not from the authority of our singular perceptions (Fabian, 2007). The second example describes the way the researcher, throughout successive writings in which children also participated, reconstructed her idea of politics as confined to social life for the children understanding of "politics as a kind of employment". Thus, it was possible for her to apprehend to what extent spaces like school classrooms could be researched with a focus on politics as a dimension that entails relationships, disputes and tensions that are not those from the spaces customarily associated with politics.

In the next section, we present the elaboration/deconstruction that each researcher carried out in order to incorporate children's interpretations as data that allowed for the reconsideration of some aspect of the research problem and show that we can represent with writing positions that we would not easily be able to act out in "real" situations. As adults, we already have our own way to think, however, we can invite children to co-write the world.

Re-writing monsters
For two years, we (Clemente, Dantas & Higgins, 2011) tracked a group of students through their fourth and fifth-grade classes in an urban primary school in the city of Oaxaca. The Language Centre at the state university of Oaxaca has for the last several years been placing its student-teachers who are completing a bachelor's degree in TEFL (Teaching English as a Foreign Language) in urban classrooms to provide introductory classes in English. The class we have been observing is somewhat different in that the students come from very humble backgrounds and several of the male students are from the *Ciudad de los Niños*,

a children's shelter and orphanage in Oaxaca. Our intention was to explore the peculiarity of the school social practices in this classroom, but the particular situation we found there made us focus on issues of diversity and the body. The 18 children (4 girls and 14 boys) of this study came from the urban popular classes. Several of the boys were from the children's shelter, others were from single-head households and many lived in households where the fathers were working in the United States. Parents worked in a variety of jobs, common among the popular classes (construction workers, small scale vendors or domestic laborers). Health crises, economic scarcity, and domestic violence were a part of their everyday lives.

Yedani, one of the student-teachers, told us about her plan to do a class session on body parts. She was worried because two of her students did not meet what was assumed to be the norm in terms of a 'normal body'. A student named Arely had a misshaped hand and another, named Francisco, was missing an ear. After planning her lesson, she invited us (Clemente, Dantas and Higgins) to observe it. She taught the names of the different parts of the body with separate pictures of each of them, to avoid presenting a complete 'normal' body. Yedani knew that her students enjoyed making posters more than writing. Therefore, she asked her students to draw monsters using the vocabulary learned. The class was motivated, most of them working hard and talking to their peers about their productions. Several used collectible cards about popular TV and comics heroes to start their drawings. Others created their own monsters from scratch, adding features and details that contributed to their 'monster-ness'. The results were very attractive, varied and original.

We wrote our fieldnotes about the class observation and about the posters children had created with their monsters. Our notes showed phrases like these: "very lively class", "talk and interaction", "everybody working", "using TV heroes as models" "lots of scars". Later, we shared our fieldnotes with Yedani to discuss about our interpretations. Needless to say, our interpretations were done according to our own schemes of reference and within the framework of the task assigned by their teacher. According to Yedani's instructions, they were free to add or take away parts of the body when creating their monsters. That way they were learning the nouns and practicing the numbers. We noticed that most of the monsters had a human resemblance. We interpreted the decorative elements (graffiti, punk looks, tattoos, piercing) as part of the models that they are used to seeing in TV programs and movies. Usually, the 'bad guys' are depicted as part of subcultures (gangs and tribes) that are generally described as people with tattoos and piercings and who often paint graffiti as a way to communicate among themselves or to mark territory. For us, the high frequency of scars was a direct connection with a Frankenstein type of monster. We also thought that it was such a successful task because Yedani had focused on something different from a conventional task. Instead of asking for drawings of something or someone her students liked or admired, she had decided to work on the monster figure, a well-known antagonist of children's stories and movies. Not to deal with the 'good guy' allowed them to trespass the rules of the nice and good.

When we, the researchers, along with Yedani, the teacher, had written a more or less complete draft of our interpretations, we decided to go back to the school and shared our interpretations about their creations with the students. It was interesting that the students had so much say about their monsters. All of them, were very vocal about their monsters and were able to explain even the littlest detail in their drawings. We found out that their creations were monsters or monstrous not only because of the way they looked (what was actually drawn) but also because of their personalities (e.g., bad, weird) or their behaviours (e.g., trouble-maker, fighter, nocturnal, man-eater), all of which was not written but rather told us.

Another silent feature of this joint activity was the fact that most of them were able to talk to us about the added written texts to their creations. Before, we did not take into account these texts because they were illegible (to us) because they had either been erased, or were unfinished, misspelled or crossed out. We learned that some of these texts consisted of coded graffiti (which, as they told us, was only for the members of the gang to know), the odd names of the monsters, or even the score of the Sunday football match.

Thus, we realized that this activity was more than just a ludic English-learning task. It was the opportunity for the students to express themselves in significant ways that we had been ignoring before. The most developed poster was Jesus Eduardo's Pandy. Pandy did not have anything apparently monstrous about it. He was clearly a man. He had one eye not because he was a monster but because he was a fighter. His hair was arranged in a punk style and dyed in two different colours. He had a long scar from his neck to his waist. He was also characterized as a wrestler, bare to the waist, with tight leggings and high-top tennis shoes. He was wearing a belt with the word CHOLAS written in it. His white face resembled a mask. Jesus Eduardo completed his creation with some drawings in the background: a bear face, a container and a sign. He explained to us that the bear was a Panda bear that connected the monster with its name; the container was labelled PANDA and held the chains that Pandy used to fight. There was also a triangle sign that read CHOLAS. Its function was marking territory and preventing trespassing. He told us that the CHOLAS are people hanging around in the streets where he lives.

Nobody mentioned Victor Frankenstein's monster, and some had not even heard of him. This made sense to us when we shared our view with them and realized that the scars were meant to represent something different. The scars were not the cause of surgical interventions of a mad scientist. They were the result of frequent streets fights, in the actual streets of the working-class suburbs of Oaxaca city. These scars were salient in the students' lives, and were traits to be proud of, as some of them attested. The researchers included the drawings with their writings and the explanations of the children to their fieldnotes. This collage of expressive modes made of this process of writing a performative event. By means of their visual language, along with the saying and the writing, the children were reproducing their everyday realities, the lives that they live in the poor suburbs of Oaxaca city. Lives that they are proud of, where they learn survival skills, secret languages and corporal signing, social membership and turf issues. Finally, the researchers understood that those drawings and those words were transporting them to the street, producing a shared experience that perform their understandings of the street life, and hence, the school and classroom life.

The children also were happy to tell the researchers about their aspirations for their future lives. They wanted to be part of the Cholas and other local gangs. They also aspired to be graffiti artists, to draw "monsters properly in huge walls" and "when nobody is watching". Moreover, they also showed us that bodies are not only about parts and functions. Bodies, according to them, tell stories and describe identities.

Since both, ethnographers and students, were co-participants in the encounter, the children were able to represent, with their drawings, writings and conversations, identities that were not possible to perform in the "real" life. With their writings, the researchers were not only able to uncover a dimension of the classroom social practices that was unknown for them, but also they were able to place the children in a location of knowers and writers.

Re-writing politics

During 2004 and 2005 Milstein carried out ethnographic work in Villa La Florida, Quilmes, located 25 km to the south of the city of Buenos Aires, Argentina as part of a research focused on the politics of daily school life that showed the diversity of social roles that come together and play a part in this routine, as well as profiling a variety of political aspects, tensions, and disputes' (Milstein 2010a: 1). An important part of this research was done with children, students of the elementary schools who work with me as co-researchers. These children had a prominent role as interlocutors in my work process and the documents produced with and by them were essential to knowing and registering versions and interpretations of life -in the local street and school areas- from their own perception of the social world dominated by the feelings, language, and acts of adults.

The researcher worked with 10 to 13 year-old children studying the last three years of elementary school. The aim of the study was to know the ways neighbours, children and adults, thought of the place they lived in and the school they studied in. One of the main issues was to know 'how it was before and how it was now to live in La Florida'. Some of the research activities involved teamwork and others were individual. Later, we would socialize our audio and photo registers in our meetings. They rarely took written notes and I always shared my fieldnotes. I also transcribed the recordings of their fieldwork and of our meetings and we read these together. During these reading sessions, the researcher wrote down notes about the discussion, and sometimes children dictated phrases or expressions that the researcher included in her notes. As illustrated in the following excerpts the notes took the form of a collaborative written text.

One day, listening the recording of a girl interviewing her aunt Ana, the children had the following interaction:

She's lucky, working in politics- said Patricia

Why? – I asked.

She is always in an office – said a smiling Camila.

With documents, talking on the phone, receiving people- added Leonor.

What people? – I asked

She gives bottles of milk to people in line…and other things. She chats with them. Sometimes she has to take them out because there are so many, and she can't deal with them. They told me that Cristina went there once – added Leonor.

The researcher was already aware that in Villa La Florida the impact of the 1990s socio-economic policies implemented in Argentina were coming clear. Many men and women worked in big factories that were forced to close, which left 40 percent of the neighbours out of employment. I also was aware that, in spite of the rejection to politics and politicians' worlds by most of the people in the 2001 'pueblada', the power of the 'punteros políticos' (party members of the local branch that work to keep the State territorial power and political clientelism) was strengthened in communities like this. What really shocked me was the content of the conversation and that for the children, politics was a very important employment. I proposed to talk about the work of their relatives and neighbours. We also decided to visit some people around the school to get to know more about "the employments of the grownups ideas". During one of our team encounters, we listened to the interviews and interchanged some ideas that we wrote altogether. One of the girls was in charge of the writing while the others focused on organizing the grownups ideas. The fieldnotes include the following excerpts:

Patricia says that her family is very hard working "I do not have time for myself and my siblings and, now that I am part of the team of the anthropologist and my friends, they are like a second family to me."

Daniela's father works with air conditioning: "My mother is a housewife and sometimes I help her. When I grow up, I want to be somebody important. That's why I have to study. It's also important to be a truck driver like my father who didn't study".

"All parents' employments are important because my mother now stays in the place she works and I would like her to be more time with me and my siblings because she works a lot, like my father".

Some days later, the children and I met in the park to tell stories. While doing this, a car with a megaphone passed by, inviting people to vote for a certain candidate. One of the children began to imitate the invitation. Everybody laughed. A girl said:

It must be Ana, your aunt.

I looked at the niece who said:

My aunt says that Cristina gave her the things to give away, for people to vote for her. My aunt is in the 'Program' because she needs a house and she has nine children, and it´s very difficult for her. My aunt is in this 'Program' and it was Cristina who gave her the stuff and told her to vote for Cristina, my aunt told me. After this, they put her in the office. That´s a better employment.' The conversation went on with comments about their parents' employments. One of the girls said:

I don't care about politics because I´m a foreigner and we can't vote, and they will never give employment to my mother because she is a Paraguayan, and she works cleaning. She doesn't sleep at home because she sleeps at work.

The fieldnotes on this conversation with the children were considered so important that they decided to include the topic of politics in 2 of the 6 sections, which they entitled "The employment of parents and the politics" in the rustic publication that we did together.

Working on my notes, I attempted to understand this concept of politics as a kind of employment. Politics had to be approached, rather, from the deeds of those who lack the conditions and attributes to develop it, preventing the reproduction of perspectives that stigmatize, marginalize and/or victimize them, which, in turn, distance the children from the political world.

Reflecting on what is written

Merleau-Ponty (2003), when discussing the Cartesian perspective, states, 'we do not live first and foremost in our own conscience nor in that of things but rather in the experience of the other.' The emphasis given to the experience of the other is then completed by the statement that 'our reflections are always ways of getting back to ourselves, a fact that is primarily due to our frequenting the other' (p.53). Under this perspective of the experience and frequentation of the other as ways of living, perceiving and understanding ourselves, what we have presented here are two illustrations of processes in which we as researchers write down, along with our descriptions, the barriers that we build and tear down in order to return to ourselves in as much as we are mediated by the experiences of others. Following Paul Willis, the opportunities that fieldwork provide 'to re-create the creativities of human practice in context (…) the point of engaging in field work, what impels [us] to face its difficulties, dilemmas and jeopardies, is to give [ourselves] the chance of being surprised to have experiences that generate new knowledge not wholly prefigured in [our] starting out positions (…) [We] cannot be surprised unless [we] thought that [we] knew, or assumed, something already which is then overturned, or perhaps strengthened, or positively diverted, or fulfilled in unexpectedly elegant ways' (Willis 2000: 113).

In the case of Yedani's class, the returning to ourselves was more in the sense of getting closer to the children and letting ourselves being taught by the young participants, in order to illuminate the interpretation of their productions, their cultural artefacts that had much to do with their everyday lives. The novelty, for us, was that, to be taught by the children, we had to add their writings -in drawings, words and sentences- to our writing because those were actually their ways of representing, and of performing their ideas. Thus, we were able to build a proper way to understand how the classroom practices were crossed by "the life in the streets".

In a similar way, Milstein encountered herself back in the writing process. In this case, children participated as co-researchers who engage with the researcher in the process of writing. The ethnographer revised her first interpretation, prior to the encounter with the children, who illustrated that they thought that politics happened in everyday family life. This gave space to a new perspective of how to think about politics, which was supported in successive writings. This experience shows that children's 'political talk' is largely idiomatic and does not, on first hearing, conform to received notions of the political even when they were talking about institutional politics (Nolas, Varvantaks & Aruldoss 2017:

78). As in the first example, this new understanding emerged from the children's quotidian routine, particularly from the domestic situations they are part of.

In the first case, the children turned into collaborators that forced the writers to include her drawn, written or spoken expressions to the ethnographic accounts and, hence, to modify the adult interpretation of the ethnographic event that allowed the researchers to reconsider the research problem.

When working with children, we need to produce events that generate their perspectives. Although this is a task that ethnographers do when conducting research with other groups, with children it implies questioning the ideas that we as adults have about the children's discourses as naive occurrences, without relevance and not well informed. The performative writing that we have discussed in this chapter leads us to define what children say as performative statements. In the examples presented, this was possible because of the context of collaboration where children participation went beyond participant observation.

In the second case, a comment from a co-researcher girl astonished the ethnographer, which leaded her to question her own concepts which, in turn, gave space to the meanings children gave to politics in quotidian spaces. In this way, the recognition of the children's interpretation altered the first interpretation of the researcher. Writing with them was essential to capture the connection between sense of politics and employment which allowed legitimizing practices valued by the community to which the children belong.

In both cases, the writing of fieldnotes is a privileged place for reflexivity, in which the researchers question their interpretations and allow themselves to be affected by the children's' understandings. These fieldwork situations, as many others that the readers may have experienced, illustrate the fact that in ethnography the problems and challenges that the different uses of language, in general, and writing, in particular, do not have anything to do with language as an abstract system but as 'language use for a purpose in concrete contexts of location and human action' (Willis 2000: 115).

In order to have access to such language use, the ethnographers of these two examples used their experience. Writing opened up the possibility of connecting experiences of our them with those of the children, always careful to take into account space/time locations and biographical perspectives. We attempted to show that by writing with children about our worlds, we make these worlds together.

When we work with children, it is not particularly strange that we, the adult researchers, become displaced in a situation in which the children behave as if it were frequent, regular or familiar. The behaviour of the children (the creation of monsters during an English lesson and the discussion about politics from the employments of family members and domestic situations, for example) does not necessarily reveal that what has happened is commonplace in the daily life of the people and neighbours of the place in question. There is, rather, an exposure in this behaviour of the capacity and strength that what the children do and say has in contributing to the shaping of adult experience. When we are aware of the collaboration of the children in fieldwork and pay attention to the way in which they cooperate when involved in the production of knowledge, we discover that they are co-producers of our adulthood. That is, what they say and/ or write reveals and allows us to unveil – in our own fieldnotes – facets and manifestations of our adulthood, useful for any topic that interests the researcher given the importance of reflexivity in ethnographic analysis.

Johansson (2012), in an article in which she discusses adulthood in the context of research done with children states that 'habitually, when children and adults are together, the relations of power and caretaking are more frequently built in the direction adult-child than the other way around because the categories of adult and child, as concepts locked in a black box carry certain suppositions implied in them with respect to the relations between children and adults. It is expected that adults teach, guide and provide for children, that they assume responsibility for them and that they be their role models. These are pre-established subjectivities, assigned, solicited so that adults become what is expected of them, materialized and stabilized for constant repetitions, and translated into laws, customs, family structures, literature, professions, etc.' (p.106, our translation). Taking into account the cases mentioned, we understand that one aspect of this problem can be addressed with fieldnotes. According to Johansson and others, it is difficult to find strategies for modifying the behaviours of adults in situ. But the productive work with fieldnotes and the successive written works give us the opportunity to change position and to read, see, hear, feel and think in order to understand. When writing, there is a negotiation between the understandings of adult researchers and those of the children who, in situations such as the ones described here, end up deconstructing the understandings of the researchers. In this sense, fieldnotes are not only constructed at the moment the lived experience turns into text, but also, they turn into a mediation for the researcher's estrangement and repositioning.

The process of writing collaborative ethnography when working with children is situated in the sense that the final text is performative, for it *does* reconstruct reality, taking the views of children as valid and meaningful. As we have seen from the two examples above, the process of writing is not an isolated activity; It is dialogical. However, this dialogue is not only with the future audience (as is most critical writing), but also with the very present group of children who are interacting with us, the adult ethnographers. They become, implicitly or explicitly, co-authors of the mediated construct (Canagarajah 2002: 5) called the ethnographic text. This ethnographic text, outcome of very intense dialogic activity among different people with diverse opinions and views, is 'a representation of reality, an embodiment of values, and a presentation of self' (Canagarajah 2002: 5). That is, it is and ideological construct, that, above all is historical.

Canagarajah defines critical writing, which entails 'an attitude and a perspective that enable us to see some of the hidden components of text construction and the subtler ramifications of writing' (p.1). Canagarajah develops an academic writing model for teaching academic writing. Although we are referring to this model, we are using it in a different way; for us, the academic writing students are us, the ethnographers, who are learning from the children working with us. Turning his model upside down, we contend that the collaborative process of ethnographic writing with children results in a text that 'is shaped by the disjunctions, fissures, struggles, and conflicts during its construction and reception' (Canagarajah 2002: 6). The same way Canagarajah depicts the relationship between academic writing students and their professors, we depict the relationship between us, the adult ethnographers, and our young collaborators. Paraphrasing the author, but switching places, we state that when writing ethnographic texts in which children are involved as collaborators, we the adult ethnographers, 'begin to see how writing is implicated in social conflict, material inequality, cultural difference, and power relationships (…) [During the process] we become sensitive to these factors' (Canagarajah 2002: 7) in a slightly (or broadly) different way from our perceptions before the interaction with the children. We adult ethnographers 'wrestle with textual constraints, tap the available material resources, and negotiate the conflict discourses in our favour to communicate effectively' the world in front of us. For Canagarajah, it is when teaching that instructors 'have to make students aware of these diverse constraints and possibilities as they strive for representation of knowledge that is emancipatory and empowering' (p.7). For us, it is the children who make us aware of the constraints and possibilities as we strive for the negotiation of diverse, and sometimes, opposite, representations of knowledge that the children-ethnographer encounters favours. Needless to say, that 'emancipatory and empowering' process allows ethnographers to distance themselves from their own schemes and preconceptions and, more importantly, 'to decolonize the control over knowledge production' (Clemente & Higgins 2010: 188).

Bibliography

Austin, J.L., (1962) *How to do things with words*. The William James Lectures delivered at Harvard University in 1955. Oxford: Clarendon Press. http://pubman.mpdl.mpg.de/pubman/item/escidoc:2271128:3/component/escidoc:2271430/austin_1962_how-to-do-things-with-words.pdf.

Canagarajah, S., (2002) *Critical Academic Writing and Multilingual Students*, Michigan: The University of Michigan Press.

Clemente, A., Dantas-Whitney, M. & Higgins, M.J., (2011) 'Queremos enseñarles que hay otras maneras': los encuentros etnográficos y la enseñanza de inglés en una escuela de Oaxaca (pp. 79-102). In D. Milstein, A. Clemente, M, Dantas, A.L. y M. Higgins, (Eds.) *Encuentros etnográficos con niños y adolescentes. Entre tiempos y espacios compartidos.* Buenos Aires: Miño y Dávila y CAS-IDES.

Clemente A. & Higgins, M., (2010) Performing methodological activities in post-colonial ethnographic encounters, in (eds.) Shamin, F. & Qureshi, R., *Perils, Pitfalls and Reflexivity in Qualitative Research in Education*, Oxford: Oxford, University Press.

Denzin, N., (2001) The reflexive interview and a performative social science. *Qualitative Research* 1(1), 23-46.

Fabian, J., (2007) *Memory against culture: arguments and reminders.* Durham: Duke University Press.

Guerrero, A.L., Clemente, A, Dantas, M & Milstein, D., (2017) *Bordes, límites y fronteras. Etnografía en colaboración con niños, niñas, adolescentes y jóvenes.* Bogotá: Editorial Pontificia Universidad Javeriana.

Guerrero, A. L. & Milstein, D., (2017) *Dialogar y producir alteridad. Un episodio de trabajo de campo con una niña de colombia in Bordes, límites y fronteras. Etnografía en colaboración con niños, niñas, adolescentes y jóvenes.* Bogotá: Editorial Pontificia Universidad Javeriana, 157-176.

Hirschfeld, L. A., (2002) Why Don't Anthropologists Like Children? *American Anthropologist*, 104, 611–627.

Johansson, B., (2012) *Doing adulthood in childhood research.* Childhood 19(1), 101-114.

Merleau Ponty, M., (2003) *El mundo de la percepción.* Siete conferencias. México: Fondo de Cultura Económica.

Milstein, D., (2009) *La nación en la escuela. Viejas y nuevas tensiones políticas.* Buenos Aires: Miño y Dávila.

Milstein, D., (2010) Children as co-researchers in anthropological narratives in education. In *Ethnography and Education*, 5(1), 1-15

Nolas, S, Varvantakis, C. & Aruldoss, V., (2017) Talking politics in everyday family lives, *Contemporary Social Science*, 12(1-2), 68-83, DOI: 10.1080/21582041.2017.1330965

Willis, P., (2000) *The Ethnographic Imagination.* Cambridge: Polity Press.

Competing power differentials in ethnographic writing; considerations when working with children and young people
Lisa Russell

Ethnographers should be aware of how fieldwork research and ethnographic writing construct and (re)produce relationships, day-to-day experiences, cultures, participants and the researchers' identities. All too often research methods texts remain relatively hushed about how fieldnotes are taken and how they are then used and often morphed for dissemination and publication purposes (Coffey, 1999). This chapter continues the debate around the challenges of how the ethnographer represents themselves, the field and young participants during the process of ethnography via the writing of fieldnotes and during the ethnographic output regarding dissemination.

In writing, ethnographers represent fieldwork experiences while simultaneously characterising their own self presentation and identity construction. This chapter explores how power differentials can be managed in the field while writing fieldnotes and problematises how the participants and the ethnographer can be fairly represented in dissemination. Participants are viewed as active agents who are knowledgeable about wider hegemonic inequalities and are capable of (re)producing inequalities themselves. Children and young people generate multiple voices which are negotiated within and sometimes beyond the field and it is the ethnographers' responsibility to be aware of these power imbalances, actively try and manage them and listen carefully to how marginalised groups such as children and young people articulate their positions (Lomax, 2011). Questions such as the effects of allowing participants to view, share and contribute to fieldnotes and the implications this has in terms of validity are problematised. As well as considering how the day-to-day activities, participants and ethnographers' identities are represented and (co) constructed in final PhD thesis, conference proceedings and journal and book publications.

This chapter does not draw on a singular research project and while I do draw upon my own ethnographic experiences of fieldwork and writing to include my ESRC (Economic Social Research Council) funded PhD 'Pupil Resistance to Their Schooling Experience' (Russell, 2005, 2011), an ESRC funded ethnography that explored the social inclusion of primary aged children through the arts with Pat Thomson and Christine Hall (Russell, 2007; Thomson, Hall and Russell, 2007) and a Leverhulme Trust funded ethnography with Robin Simmons and Ron Thompson that explored the experiences of NEET young people (Simmons, Thompson and

Russell, 2014), I do so in the context of the wider ethnographic literature. It is argued that the ethnographer should be aware and make steps to manage power differentials via their writing (in the field and beyond) so that a fair and balanced representation of the field, the participants and the ethnographer is recorded in situ and in dissemination. This is of particular importance when working in the area of social justice with young people, as the ethnographer is more likely to face negotiating competing power relations and interests between the participants (themselves), the field, the ethnographer's self (Coffey, 1999) and related university and funding affiliations.

Writing ethnography – a political act

Writing ethnography is complex, time consuming and hard work, but it also usually adheres to highly codified and institutionally defined categories that are institutionally (re)produced. Such conventions are so entwined that few, if any breach them, for to do so may have implications for an ethnographer's professional development (Coffey, 1999). It has long been acknowledged that how ethnographic texts are constructed in the field and then morphed in to publication outputs has a political power attached to it. The seminal book *Writing Culture: The Poetics and Politics of Ethnography*, edited by Clifford and Marcus (1986) acknowledged that 'enduring power inequalities had clearly constrained ethnographic practice' (Clifford and Marcus, 1986; p8), leading Coffey to surmise that writing is essentially a 'political act of meaning construction' (Coffey, 1999; p290). What we write matters, how we conduct ourselves in the field and represent those we come into contact with is of huge importance, especially when the ethnographer works in the area of social justice. When working with children and young people, power differentials in the field are amplified and if the ethnographer is trying to truly 'do' social justice (rather than simply write about it), how one represents themselves and the participants' cultural practices within and beyond the field should be taken seriously. How data in the field is collected, effects relations the ethnographer is able to foster and ultimately informs how the ethnographer presents the ethnography (and themselves) to the outside. Van Maanen in his book *Tales of the field* indicates that, 'ethnography is a written representation of culture' (Van Maanen, 1988), but ethnography is a process and a product and so may be better viewed as 'both a research paradigm and a way of writing' (Mahadevan, 2012). During the process of writing the ethnographer makes sense of what she has experienced, she analyses the data and gives thought to trying to accurately represent the field and its participants. Writing can transform, mutate and develop within and beyond the field. During this transformation there are power tensions at play that need to be acknowledged and managed within (and beyond) the context of them being written.

The crisis of representation

During the 1990s sociologists began to reflexively examine their writings and critically analysed how their writings shaped how certain cultures were being represented, understood and shaped. Influenced by the new literary movement and postmodernism, ethnographers became interested in a reflexive movement which involved directing their gaze at the process of how they construct their writings and analysed their texts. This 'linguistic turn' encouraged ethnographers to question the often previously assumed link between experience and text (Alder and Alder, 2018); authority and authenticity were challenged whereby a 'crisis of representation' (Clifford and Marcus 1986; Geertz, 1988; Van Maanen, 1995) ensued as ethnographers were encouraged to look at themselves and their institutions professional and political practices as means of shaping and (re)constructing 'reality'.

Ethnographers became increasingly sensitive to the idea that there may be multiple realities and interpretations at play, some of which may be in conflict with one another with privileged voices being heard and represented in privileged ways. Indeed, there are power relations at play within and beyond the field that become even more pertinent when working with groups that are usually given less dominance and command within the wider societal context, that is not to say that these groups are not aware of these imbalances, rather the ethnographer needs to listen carefully to how participants articulate and manifest these imbalances (Lomax, 2011). Children and young people know that they are often ignored, hushed and dismissed and sometimes they initiate imbalances amongst themselves. Children and young people engage with ethnography in unequal and different ways and operate exclusionary practices, they may verbalise wider socio-economic and political inequalities or indeed remove themselves from the research, they are active, knowledgeable and often capable of negotiating their own identity and position in the field.

Power differentials when doing research with children and young people

How people are viewed in society influences how they are understood and sometimes how they are researched, this has implications for the whole research process to include design, choice of methods, analysis, the consideration of ethics and how findings are disseminated. While much has already been written about methodological issues in relation to working with young people, far less has focused on how the ethnographer may manage power imbalances when representing the field both in situ and beyond in dissemination practices. The way the ethnographer perceives the status of participants within the field and within the wider societal context influences how writing is conducted and findings are disseminated. It is vital for the ethnographer to recognise that children and young people operate within a number of interacting and related power imbalances.

These power imbalances refer to how others perceive the participants in relation to unequal relationships evident in a wider societal context, relations between the ethnographer and the participants and importantly between the participants themselves. Writing can be used as a mechanism to actively reduce or indeed amplify these power differentials and speak to wider societal norms and values. The ethnographer needs to be aware that writing can also act to (re)produce hegemonic practices and values and be mindful that favour is often awarded to the ethnographer and their affiliated institutions.

It is the ethnographer and the affiliated institutions which are more likely to gain professional prestige and related financial gain, but more than this, it is how others view these groups which has implications for how the ethnographer positions themselves in their writing and how they position the participants within and beyond the field. The ethnographer must therefore view power as inherent to the research process and be particularly sensitive to how children and young people are positioned in the social world by others and by their very own actions. By accepting that there are power differentials in society and the research process, the ethnographer needs to carefully consider how they represent themselves and their participants' in their writing practices. If the aim of the ethnography is to give voice to children and young people, in addition to offering a bottom-up approach to understandings regarding their cultural practices and experiences, the ethnographer should actively mediate these power differentials in their practice and in their writing.

The ethnographer working in the area of social justice must do more than simply acknowledge these power differentials, they must actively try and manage them. The next section considers first how this may be made possible through the process of ethnography, as data is gathered via the means of fieldnotes and then how it is important to fairly represent the participants and the field during the dissemination of findings in conference proceedings, PhD thesis, journal articles and books. It is only by acknowledging and then trying to manage these power differentials within and beyond the field in the ethnographer's writing practices that the ethnographer can truly be working within the arena of social justice.

Such writing practices may bring into stark evidence wider professional, political and personal tensions between the ethnographer's stance, the affiliated university and/or funding body's position and the participants standpoint. Indeed, it may not always be possible to forefront the participants' outlook, but the ethnographer must try if doing research related to issues of social justice, since working in this area requires action, not mere acknowledgement (Bell, Lee Anne, Desai, Dipto, 2014). The ethnographer can try to manage power relations in their writing by constructing fair and realistic accounts both within the field and beyond it.

Writing fieldnotes

The writing of fieldnotes is central to the ethnographer, they are the record from which disseminated publications ensue (Walford, 2009). Different ethnographers have been recorded as using different fieldwork writing techniques and strategies, but there is general acceptance that most ethnographers feel the need to expand upon the notes taken in situ into a text which is fuller and more structured, as the very meaning which they hold may dissipate unless the ethnographer quickly expands and edits them after leaving the field.

During my own fieldnote writing process I, like my predecessors, enter the field armed with a notepad and usually a pencil – this notepad is solely used for writing fieldnotes, I start by writing the date, day of the week, time of entry, I sometimes contextualise the site's locality whereby I outline housing type, local population routine and rhythms and general local activity. I describe the field. If in a school I draw maps of classrooms, mapping where staff and pupils position themselves, and crucially where I locate myself. Time is documented, the frequency of which is dependent upon the occurrences being studied, but entry and exit times are always recorded so I can tally up how many hours have been spent in the field after fieldwork has been completed.

During my ethnography exploring pupil resistance to their learning experience (Russell, 2011) I sat with pupils in lessons, on the floor in the yard with them during break time and sometimes truanting with them in locations not permitted during teaching time. I documented participants' activities, experiences, perceptions and day-to-day routines, if possible I recorded verbatim, as well as non-verbatim speech. I document verbatim speech by simply using speech marks around what was said in the fieldwork log or via dictaphone if appropriate. Actions, behaviours and opinions are detailed and those I am writing about usually have access to my notes. Indeed, they are able to contribute to them, scribble on them and edit them in situ.

Some have criticised such writing practices as problematic, arguing that participants may self-censor and consequently effect validity and meaning of the raw data, I on the other hand argue this writing practice reduces power differentials between the ethnographer and the children and young people by aiding the ethnographer to build rapport. The ethnographer needs to build a relationship of trust with her participants, especially if seeking voices that are often hushed (Russell, 2005), but must also be aware that the children and young people themselves may hush one another (Lomax, 2011). In my experience participants soon get bored of the ethnographers' writing of the mundane day-to-day activities and initial fears regarding 'what is she writing?' soon disappear. During many of my ethnographic fieldwork experiences the children or young people ask, 'why are you writing that?' And I usually respond,

'I am interested in your day-to-day living, what may be boring to you interests me'. The data gathered with participants is influenced by their knowledge of their (and others) position in the research, the ethnographer can make steps to try and take the side of the children and young people by thinking carefully about where they locate themselves physically in the field, how they dress, talk, behave and indeed write fieldnotes.

Evidence of this is in Walker's Louts and Legends (1988) and Willis' *Learning to Labour study* (1977) and a further discussion regarding the positionality of the ethnographer can be found in 'It's a question of trust: balancing the relationship between students and teachers in ethnographic fieldwork' published in *The Qualitative Research Journal* (Russell, 2005). Of course most of my work involves working with children and young people and I usually purposely prioritise the young person's perspective. I use an array of participant-led research methods and am clear from the outset that gathering data with participants is key to obtaining valid, holistic data from the young person's perspective, but I am also aware that the children and young people themselves operate within realms of power differentials within their own friendship and family groups and within and through wider societal inequalities.

Whist writing in the field I am aware that the participants are part of my audience and that at certain moments they too contribute to the writing. During my ethnography exploring pupil resistance (Russell, 2011), I came across specific language challenges in my writing, especially in the Australian School as many of the pupils spoke Tongan, Lebanese or Arabic when insulting or discussing rumours, indeed language was used as a resistant strategy – a device to exclude teachers and sometimes other pupils from other cultures. Some Anglo-Australians spoke Pig Latin (a language where English words are altered by adding a fabricated suffix or by moving the onset of initial consonant or consonant clusters to the end of a word and adding a vocalic syllable to create such a suffix) to conceal what they were saying from others. This was just one of the power imbalances at play evident in this field amongst the young people themselves and against teachers that required careful management of reflexivity practices. There were clear exclusionary practices evident amongst the pupils themselves, the pupil peer groups operated in hierarchical positions with the FOBs (Fresh off the boat) or 'Islanders' (to include Pacific Islanders, people with Maori, Samoan or Cook Island ancestry) being the main group that seemed to stick together. Indeed, the pupils themselves were aware of this, as Juls – a New Zealander – describing her own peer group reveals in the following interview,

Oh like, FOBs they like to do things differently like they'll share and stuff, and they'll sing and dance and stuff at lunch (…) all the FOBs really do is sit there and bitch, and like, they talk and they're singing and dancing and they'll have fights constantly. (Cited in Russell, 2011; p 41).

The pupils also had knowledge regarding the power differentials between the adult esteemed ethnographer and the younger pupils, but they too exerted a degree of agency to try and reduce these imbalances in situ which had a knock on contributory effect to the writing of fieldnotes. Towards the end of a Physical Education class, Carl a New Zealander who spoke Tongan asked me 'can you say faiaka?' (pronounced fi-ak-o) as he wanted me to act as a lookout while he had a cigarette (rule-breaking behaviour). I did not know what this word meant or how to spell or pronounce it, but as the fieldnote excerpt below reveals, with Carl's help I learned.

Fieldnotes (21/03/03)
Carl asks 'where's Egerton (teacher) gone? I say 'I don't know I can't see him'; the two lads light up. Carl asks, 'Lisa will you be a lookout, can you say faiaka? I ask 'fi-ak-o what does that mean? Carl replies, 'teacher', continuing, 'shout fi-ak-o when you see a teacher'. Hoping that I won't need to and not wanting to get caught I say, 'ok', the other lad says, 'you're the first teacher who will be a lookout for us'. (Cited from Russell, 2011, p186).

It is later when I write up the day's events that I develop a fuller record of how I feel the participants' may have altered or responded to such data and why that might be the case, thus a reflexive journal is also written separate to, but alongside that of the original fieldnote excerpt to document mine and the participants' positionality, in addition to the actual fieldnotes to keep detailed systematic records of what is happening when and why. Context is important and is systematically recorded at every opportunity. During the above episode I reflected quite extensively about how I felt a degree of discomfort in that scenario due to the perceived danger of jeopardising fieldwork and the imbalances I felt between myself, the pupils and teaching staff. I was concerned that I may have been viewed as 'colluding' with the pupils, facilitating their rule-breaking behaviour, while simultaneously feeling good that Carl was finally starting to trust me. Reservations have been made concerning the feasibility of taking the participants perspective (Bryman, 1993) and indeed the uncritical assumption that by simply engaging in participatory methods that all children and young people's voices are heard equally (Lomax, 2011). Of course the ethnographer seeing through the eyes of participants, given the gendered and cultural differences is an issue that must be acknowledged, as must the participants' negotiation of their own identity conveyed and converted by their own agency. These power differentials must be acknowledged, understood and managed by developing thorough reflexivity accounts (Russell, 2005) and should perhaps be made more transparent in ethnographic outputs to add to the debate regarding the representation of participants, the field and the ethnographer. The ethnographer and the young people shape the writing process, but not always to equal degrees.

Once the ethnographer leaves the field, the participants contributing to writing usually starts to diminish. I, like other ethnographers, typically that night or the day after leaving the field immediately type up the fieldnotes. During this process the fieldnotes are already transcending into a neater form, I type them up, I map the drawings, edit spelling and grammatical errors, add parts that I was unable to include in situ due to the sensitivity of the situation or logistical and time constraints. I have symbols I use in the original fieldnote text to prompt my memory during the write-up or typing up of the pencilled fieldnotes. In this next text I may insert a reference to other sets of raw data obtained during the field visit, a photograph of a child's painting for example or a life cycle map used for interview elicitation purposes.

If working in teams, including the ethnography exploring NEET young people and their experiences (Simmons, Thompson and Russell, 2014) or the ethnography conducted in a primary school to understand inclusion through the arts (Thomason, Hall and Russell, 2007) I am also making the fieldwork log readable for others in the team, so that they too can gain a sense of the field and later use my notes for further analysis. The ESRC funded PhD ethnography that aimed to develop understandings regarding pupil resistance (Russell, 2011) did not demand this, I worked alone, and so less care was taken to correct spelling and grammar inaccuracies as my professional identity here was not being scrutinised by other academics (usually senior to my own professional position) in this particular version of fieldnotes. Ethnographer's must appreciate the difference between writing for the participants and writing for other academics. Audience matters and shapes the writing process and of course the interim and finished products.

This process of writing and re-writing matters as I am making sense of the data and analysis starts, indeed this sense making and knowledge production process may be viewed as 'inbetween writing' – the writing process that occurs between original records such as the raw data fieldnotes and how the ethnography is later represented, something which Coles and Thomson (2016) state is given scant attention in ethnographic and methodological texts.

Ethnographic meaning emerges between the ethnographer, the field and the audience. Ethnographer's study other people's day-to-day activities and cultures and carefully craft records dependent upon the aims of the study, the participants and the ethnographer's political, social and cultural background. Based on organisational ethnography, Mahadevan (2012) claims that ethnographic writing is a translation process that cuts across nodes of power to include the audience, the ethnographer and the field in the 'ethnographic triangle'. While it is useful for the ethnographer to acknowledge and in some instances conceptualise power as interactive and inherent in the 'ethnographic triangle' as it allows for the ethnographer to think about how certain rules of practice and institutional and hegemonic practices infiltrate, shape and interact with the participants and the ethnographer's agency it does this via taking for granted that writing involves two transformations. She claims, 'first, other is made sense of through self; and second, life is turned into narrative. The ethnographer is the one who is responsible for these transformations.' (Mahadevan, 2012; p119). Although problematised via the 'crisis of representation' literature as the ethnographer cannot speak in any other way than through her subjective self, these issues can be managed via giving participants more power in the field in the first instance, in the writing of fieldnotes in situ and by passing on some of the interpretative responsibility onto the audience during the subsequent versions of fieldnotes as they transform, not twice as suggested by Mahadevan but several times in a meaning-making process as suggested by Coles and Thomson (2016). The ethnographer is the main tool, but is not the only tool that can contribute to meaning making, for the participants can be involved in the writing of fieldnotes (even if in a minimal way) and in the analysis process (Barley and Russell, 2018).

Analysis and writing

Analysis is not a distinct stage that operates in separation from the research process (Becker, 1966; Burgess, 1984; Pole and Morrison, 2003), nor the ethnographic writing, it is on-going and arguably may occur before the ethnographer even enters the field. Thoughts about analysis and how what is observed in the field relate to key texts and theory occur also in situ. In my own fieldnotes such initial analysis, as well as thoughts about how my own positionality may be effecting young people's behaviour are written in the original fieldnote document and in later typed up versions. I separate such reflexivity notes under 'OC' – Observer's Comments, a practice developed during my PhD by utilising Phil Carpsecken's five-stage approach to 'doing' critical ethnography (Carspecken, 1996). These Observer Comments are the start of my documented analysis in situ and often act as starting point when I return to the data as a whole set later for further analysis, like Coles and Thomson (2016) I make sense of the data and look for themes and patterns, triangulating those themes and patterns where I can with other sets of data such as photographs, children's drawings, minutes of meetings documentation and life cycle maps – some of which have been produced with the participants. Thus data is created in and through interactions that occur between the ethnographer and the people in the field, if this is the case the ethnographer must accept the context bound nature of the multivocal meaning disclosed in research (Brewer, 2000). Little has been written about co-analysis in ethnography, but analysis, like writing is a process and the two go hand in hand, they are intertwined for the ethnographer.

There are continual debates about how ethnography should be conducted and presented (Walford, 2008), indeed there is an increase in the ethnographer's toolbox of late, with the advent of technologies, media and infiltration of expressive forms of ethnography to include mediums such as dance, text and drama (Barley and Russell, 2018), but Beach (2008) argues that it does not matter what research tools are used in ethnography, it is how they are used that matters. How data is collected, how it is analysed and then how it is disseminated matters. Co-analysis works in the field if it suits the aims of the study, but the ethnographer must be aware of the impact of audience, especially when power imbalances are evident. Audience can effect analysis and writing. During my work looking at social inclusion through the arts I spent time observing a resident artist working with primary age school children develop paintings of themselves and their families. I asked the children questions about their paintings during and after they had worked on them. Like photographs, children's paintings have multiple meanings that can change depending upon audience and time. Sometimes the artist and teacher misinterpreted the children's paintings, and the children's meaning or initial vision then changed as a consequence of that (mis)interpretation. Thus it is only by asking the children in situ what their paintings were that a misrepresentation of their work did not ensue. An example to illustrate this point can be found in Terry and his tents published in the Ethnography and Education Journal in 2007.

Fieldnotes 25/05/05
Terry is just putting the finishing touches to his painting before it is to be framed ready for exhibition. He walks over to the artist and shows her his work eagerly awaiting her approval and guidance. The artist asks if he has butterflies in his background. Terry nods his head to indicate that they are butterflies and the artist says, 'Shall I let you into a little secret? Butterflies have two sets of wings not one'. The teaching assistant then interrupts and reveals that Terry had previously told her that they were tents not butterflies. The artist asks Terry to clarify what the images are and Terry explains that they are actually supposed to be tents, as his

picture is of him camping. The artist then advises that he needs to make his tents a bit bigger so that they don't get mistaken for butterflies. (OC I wonder if Terry would have made them into butterflies if the teaching assistant hadn't have interrupted?)

The above extract indicates the complexities involved when trying to understand and analyse images produced by children. Like photographs, the children's images and their meanings were influenced by who was looking at the picture and for what reason. There were multiple cases whereby the resident artist and teaching assistant misinterpreted the children's images, the artist and assistant would question whether the child had sketched an arm or a leg, a shoulder or a neck. Moreover, the children's intentions and pictures developed and altered. Children would paint a pot and then later turn it into a tree or paint over it; they changed their work during the process of painting it. This decision to change was influenced by the peer group, artist's and teacher's comments, as well as their own decision to improve their work. And as Terry demonstrates, some may even have kept their images as they were but altered their meanings depending upon audience and circumstance (Russell, 2007).

Thus the children's paintings had multiple meanings that varied according to time, context and audience, the analysis here was occurring partly in situ and shaped the writing of fieldnotes and later dissemination of this work in academic, education and artistic forums. The children and the research team also had to think carefully about how they were representing the children in textual and visual form. The analysis in situ was context bound, just as the writing of fieldnotes, it is later during the re-writing and re-anaylsis that a deeper view was obtained, thought through and recorded. If the multiple interpretations are all seen as contributing to insight, the ethnographer needs to adopt an analytical framework (which usually informs written and visual outputs) that allows for participant and researcher subjectivities to be explored and understood.

Dissemination

Of course fieldnote data and meaning-making notes need to transform before dissemination to protect the participants and related institutions and also to transform into something that makes sense to its audience. It is not only the process of its creation (via the [re]writing of fieldnotes and the [re]analysis) that requires thought to power relations at play between the ethnographer, her professional and political standing, the affiliated university and funding body and the participants and the field, but also the end-product of writing. What, when and where ethnographic writings are disseminated are shaped by the ethnographer's professional and political identity and are usually done so in agreement with the ethnographer's affiliated university (Miller and Russell, 2005). Research outputs are given lots of attention under the current UK national research evaluation exercise, and indeed serve as a policy hegemonic frame that creates a simplistic construction of causality between research outputs and the way it might be picked up and used (or not) by others (Saunders, 2012). Ethnographers working in the tradition of social justice care about making a difference, and so this too may determine when, where and how dissemination occurs. For the novice PhD student differentiating themselves from the participants may be important if adhering to the traditional writing regimes. The ethnographer should try and maintain equality in her use of words and writing style even in dissemination should the hegemonic and academic writing regulations allow and meaning not be compromised. If for example, stutters, erms and dialect remain in the verbatim text of participants, perhaps they should too in the ethnographers.

Below are two fieldnote extracts taken from my work done exploring young people's experiences of churning between employment education and training. The first is close to its original hand-written format typed up immediately after leaving the field and the second is written for publication in the book *Education, Work and Social Change* (Simmons, Thompson and Russell, 2014). Analysis of the two depicts how the written word morphs, but also how the ethnographer can locate themselves and write in a way that privileges the side of the young person. Writing and indeed publishing may hold political meaning, the author (and the publisher) select certain aspects of an argument to emphasise. In the close to original fieldnote extract arguably a more positive representation of Cayden's life is depicted compared to the published version that later manifested in the book. There were lots of positive aspects evident in Cayden's life, such as the arrival of his new girlfriend, he conveys a happier state perhaps when describing her family as 'lovely'.

The published version arguably condenses this, with just a stunted reference to this aspect of Cayden's life at the end. The published version is shaped by wider hegemonic discourses regarding barriers to engagement, and despite the fact that the book criticises such discourses as deficit the book inevitably makes reference to them. As authors we were very aware of our practitioner and policy audiences and actively tried to move away from romanticised notions of not working. Not working has positive and negative aspects associated with it, it is nuanced and involves a complex interaction of agentic and structural cultural, economic, political, educational and work structures. We didn't want to represent Cayden as simply unemployed, inactive and draining state resources and thus ultimately contributing to the very wider political hegemonic discourses involving the unemployed young as lazy, at fault and a societal financial drain, that we were critiquing.

Fieldnote extract 1 – Lisa's typed log

06/10/11

9.00-10.00am

As I drive up to his flat I notice his curtains are drawn, the door is open as some workmen are doing some moving of furniture. He doesn't respond to the buzzer so I walk up to his room. He answers in his pyjamas bleary eyed clearly having just woken up. I apologise for waking him, he says 'it doesn't matter I'm not even bothered I need to get up'. He says he is supposed to be getting up between 8 and 9am, but as of late has been getting up later and going to bed later. He quickly gets changed and opens the curtains.

He tells me he has recently broken up with Sally (the girl who he was engaged with). She left him. He says they were always arguing. He is now seeing a new girl Jaimie-Lee who he met at college (even though he doesn't go to college). He says, 'me and Jaime-Lee-Laura haven't fallen out yet...nice girl...more quiet than me'. She works as a volunteer for Oxfam, she used to work two days a week but has recently reduced this to one day a week.

Cayden still sees his brother. He says they are planning another holiday away to Filey and Scotland again.

Cayden says he is happy at the moment, he says he is currently not looking for work as he is happy here, he is managing financially, his benefits have changed, he says he is getting more but cannot tell me what benefits he is getting. He talks about going out and seeing people, he has met some of Jaimie-Lee's friends and spends time at her parents' house, where she lives, he describes her family as 'lovely' – she also spends quite a bit of time round at his flat. He says she likes it here. He says they see each other most days in the afternoon. He says he hasn't time to get a job at the moment and feels he isn't ready due to his past – something he refers to a lot. He says, 'but I don't know when I'll be ready to work yet, no point I'm happy seeing friends and all that'.

He talks about him and his girlfriend moving in together, getting engaged and married and starting a family.

The above fieldnote extract is much more extensive, detailed and less well organised and scripted. It runs through events as they happened in situ and arguably gives a richer flavour of Cayden's life on that day. The published version is more condensed, and is written within the context of marginalisation and complexity. He was a young man with special needs who moved in and out of short term training programmes and volunteer work placements during the three-year ethnography. While the above gives a snapshot in time, the below by contrast better contextualises Cayden's moment with relevant literature and is edited so that the audience (in this case book readers) can make sense of his life path choices.

Fieldnote extract 2 – Published in *Education, Work and Social Change* book (p212-213).

As I drive up to his flat I notice his curtains are draw, the door is open as some workmen are moving furniture. He doesn't respond to the buzzer so I walk up to his room. He answers the door in his pyjamas, bleary eyed, clearly having just woken up. I apologise for waking him, he says, 'it doesn't matter I'm not even bothered, I need to get up.' He says he is supposed to be getting up between 8 and 9am but that lately he has been getting up later and going to bed later. He quickly gets changed and opens the curtains…He says he feels he isn't ready to get a job yet, due to his past – which is something he refers to a lot. He says, …I don't know when I'll be ready to work yet, no point I'm happy seeing friends and all that'.

All types of research (qualitative, quantitative, participatory or participant-led) are committed to the dissemination of knowledge with rigor, conscientiousness, and high ethical standards through a process of peer critique (Poortman and Schildkamp, 2012). Such scholarly debate has long been the mechanism to drive scientific discovery, facilitate public accountability and promote ethical practice. In an era whereby increasingly we are being asked to disseminate our findings to multiple audiences and even make our raw data readily available so that others can pick it up and re-analyse and subsequently re-write about our work, challenges for the ethnographer's dissemination practices ensue (Mosher, 2013).

The balance between communicating the scientific depth and rigour demanded by the research and academic arenas while simultaneously ensuring the research findings remain accessible, useful and representative of those it seeks to represent. Mosher (2013) explains that there is a trade-off here to be made, if audiences are broadened outside of that of the academic community the writer may decide to sacrifice depth of theoretical grounding which may conflict with institutional and academic requirements. There is a tension to be managed between serving the interests of those who partake in the ethnography and those who will more likely read to further the development of ethnography as an academic discipline. The ethnographer who works in the arena of social justice must negotiate these competing priorities and write in a way that prioritises and accurately reflects the field while also working in the confines of hegemonic academic and political structures so that the participants voice is not hushed to such an extent that it serves only to benefit those who have researched with them or serves to simply contribute to the status quo if that is the very thing the ethnographer is actively critiquing.

Conclusions

Writing matters to ethnographers, both in process and as it morphs in its inbetween writing stage right through to its end product. Ethnographers have longed problematised the link between experience and text, thus challenging writers to examine their politics and rhetoric. Issues of representation sensitised ethnographers to multiple and sometimes conflicting interpretations of reality and many have already acknowledged that some people and the interpretations they offer might be privileged over others (Alder and Alder, 2008). For those working in the area of social justice with groups perceived as less powerful in a wider hegemonic context, there is a need to be particularly aware, but also actively manage power differentials in ethnographic writing.

Ethnographers can do this during the onset in their writing of fieldnotes by allowing participants to see and in some circumstances contribute to the records and also by considering their positionality in the field, they can also do this during analysis by facilitating co-analysis of raw data should it be appropriate to the aims of the study. Power differentials are evident amongst children and young people themselves, as well as between the ethnographer, the field and affiliated institution. The ethnographer may manage or even actively reduce power imbalances in dissemination by accurately presenting themselves and the participants on equal terms quashing the façade of researcher prestige and actively resist always taking the path of least resistance. If ethnographers are to co-construct knowledge through their ethnographic writing, then meaning making and writing must be made to matter.

Bibliography

Alder, P.A., and Alder, P. (2008) 'Of rhetoric and representation: the four faces of ethnography' *The Sociological Quarterly*, 49(1), pp.1-30.

Barley, R. and Russell, L., (2018) 'Participatory visual methods: exploring young people's identities, hopes and feelings' *Ethnography and Education.*

Beach, D. (2008) 'Ethnography and representation: About representations for criticism and change through ethnography'. In *How to do Educational Ethnography*. The Tufnell Press. London.

Becker, H. (1966) *Writing for Social Scientist*. Chicago. University of Chicago Press.

Bell, L.A., and Desai, D. (2014) *Social justice and the arts*. England. Routledge.

Brewer, J. (2000) *Ethnography*. Buckingham. Open University Press.

Bryman, A. (1993) *Quantity and Quality in Social Research*. London. Routledge.

Burgess, R.G. (1984) *In the Field*. London. Routledge.

Carspecken, P. (1996) *Critical Ethnography in Educational Research, A Theoretical and Practical Guide*. London. Routledge.

Coffey, A. (1999) *The Ethnographic Self*. London. Sage.

Clifford, J. and Marcus, G.E. (1986) *Writing Culture*. Berkeley. University of California Press.

Coles, R., and Thomson, P. (2016) 'Beyond records and representations: inbetween writing in educational ethnography' *Ethnography and Education*, 11(3), pp.253-266.

Geertz, C. (1988) *Works and lives. The anthropologist as author* (1994 ed.) Stanford, California: Stanford University Press.

Lomax, H. (2011) 'Contested voices? Methodological tensions in creative visual research with children' *International Journal of Social Research Methodology*, 15(2), pp. 105–117.

Maanen, J. V. (1988) *Tales of the field: On writing ethnography*. Chicago. Chicago Press.

Maanen, J. V. (1995) *Representation in Ethnography*. Cambridge. Sage.

Mahadevan, J. (2012) 'Translating nodes of power through reflexive ethnographic writing' *Journal of Organizational Ethnography*, 1(1), pp.119-131.

Miller, H. and Russell, L. (2005) 'The personal, professional and political in comparative ethnographic educational research'. In: *Methodological issues and practices in ethnography*. Elsevier JAI.

Mosher, H. (2013) 'A question of quality: the art/science of doing collaborative public ethnography' *Qualitative Research*, 13(4), 428–441.

Pole, C.J. and Morrison, M. (2003) *Ethnography for Education*. Maidenhead. Open University Press.

Poortman CL and Schildkamp K (2012) 'Alternative quality standards in qualitative research?' *Quality & Quantity*, 46(6), pp1727–1751.

Russell, L. (2005) 'It's a question of trust: balancing the relationship between students and teachers in ethnographic fieldwork' *Qualitative Research*, 5(2), pp181-199.

Russell, L (2007) 'Visual methods in researching the arts and inclusion: possibilities and dilemmas' *Ethnography and Education*, 2 (1), pp. 39-55.

Russell, L. (2011) *Understanding Pupil Resistance – Integrating Gender, Ethnicity and Class: an Educational Ethnography.* England. E&E Publishing.

Saunders, M. (2012) 'Apolitical economy of university funding: the English case' *Journal of Higher Education Policy and Management*, 34(4), pp389-399.

Simmons, R., Thompson, R. and Russell, L. (2014) *Education, Work and Social Change: Young People and Marginalisation in Post-Industrial Britain.* England. Palgrave.

Thomson, P., Hall, C. and Russell, L. (2007) 'If these walls could speak: reading displays of primary children's work' *Ethnography and Education*, 2(3), pp.381-400.

Walford, G. (2008) *How to do Educational Ethnography.* London. The Tufnell Press.

Walford, G. (2009) 'The practice of writing ethnographic fieldnotes' *Ethnography and Education*, 4(2), pp.117-130.

Walker, J. C. (1988) *Louts and Legends: Male Youth Culture in an Inner City School.* Sydney. Allen and Unwin.

Willis, P. (1977) *Learning to Labour.* Farnborough. Saxon House.

The Entanglements of Collaborative Fieldworking: Using a 'Diffractive' Methodology[15] for Observing, Reading and Writing

Joan Parker Webster

Introduction

In today's world, the ethnographer has many different tools available to her for conducting research. Fieldwork once limited to in-person visits to geographic locations of study is now extended beyond the physical site through the use of technology. Classrooms and lunchrooms located within the larger school building and the outdoor classroom spaces of playgrounds, sports fields, and school garden plots coexist with online classrooms. These offline and online sites may be part of a curriculum blending face-to-face classes embedded with online websites designed to serve as repositories for course readings. Online websites may provide spaces for asynchronous class activities, such as online discussion boards (e.g. Blackboard), or provide a collaborative writing space for students to post class assignments (e.g. Google Docs).

Such blended classrooms may also incorporate other physical locations outside of the school building, which are "visited" in real time through synchronous online video conferencing spaces (e.g. Zoom, and group meeting platforms like GoToMeeting). As such, the educational ethnographer can now find herself moving within and across offline and online field(s) along with her participants in the course of the school day (Parker Webster and Silva, 2013). Therefore, rather than limiting observations and writing fieldnotes to an activity in a physical site like a school building, the field can be conceptualized as a 'field of relations' (Olwig and Hastrup, 1997) characterized by mobility. Acting-doing within these physical-virtual, synchronous-asynchronous, on-off-line spaces and places, become part of the connective networks of meaningful data that are produced by multiple contributors (Silva and Parker Webster, 2018). Given this fluid mobility, diversity of participants, and potentials for multidisciplinary of voices within these field(s) of research, it seems critical to re-conceptualize the notion of doing fieldwork and *writing* (in a multimodal sense) fieldnotes, which are mainstays of ethnographic research.

This chapter presents an approach to fieldworking – observing-writing-reading fieldnotes – that utilizes what Barad (2007; 2012) calls a diffractive methodology. Drawing from an ongoing ethnography with a "transdisciplinary" group of university scientists and K-8 teachers involved

---

15. Karen Barad (2007; 2012) uses this term to describe reading for differences that matter in their fine details.

in a Participatory Scientist-Teacher Action Research (PSTAR) project to develop a STEM-to-STEAM[16] science curriculum, I describe how dynamic relationships or what Barad refers to as *entanglements* are made visible through collaborative activities of observing-writing-reading fieldnotes. Through the practice of a "diffractive methodology", of reading (and writing) fieldnotes from multidisciplinary perspectives, the PSTAR team members sharpened their attentions to nuanced differences within the entangled disciplinary fields. This, in turn, contributed to deeper understandings of the transdisciplinary entanglements of scientific content, educational pedagogy and the social life of the classroom. The chapter concludes with a discussion of how such a diffractive methodology for fieldworking could offer an approach that extends and enhances ethnographic fieldworking activities through constructive engagements across disciplinary, situated-contextual and participant-researcher boundaries.

OneTree Alaska Project

The OneTree Alaska curriculum project developed as a partnership between university scientists, K-8 teachers and community members (visual and literary artists, citizen scientists) who saw a need to make science more relevant and multidisciplinary in scope in order to engage students in the classroom. The curriculum is placed-based, bringing the local boreal forest into the classroom and the classroom into the forest. *A Year in the Life of a Birch Tree* is based on phenology, the study of the timing of events in an organism's annual life cycle, which provides a means to track a species' ongoing responses to climate change. The lesson plans follow the natural progression of phenophases – from autumn leaf fall through winter dormancy, to the spring sap season and summer's bud-burst and leaf-out. A stated goal is to use the curriculum as a springboard for examining the multidisciplinary, crosscutting concepts embedded in the Next Generation Science (NGS) Standards.

Integral to the OneTree Project is a collaborative research component that involves scientists and teachers (the PSTAR team) working together to engage students in field-based scientific research and at the same time, conduct Teacher Action Research (TAR) in K-8 classrooms on the OneTree science curriculum. TAR, is a cyclic inquiry approach that involves planning, acting, observing and reflecting (Herr and Anderson, 2005). The purpose of TAR in the OneTree context is to examine the influence of the OneTree curriculum on (a) student learning of science in general and through a STEM to STEAM approach in particular; and (b) teacher practice in the teaching of science in

---

16. STEM is an acronym for Science, Technology, Engineering and Mathematics. STEAM is an acronym that adds the arts (A) to STEM. STEAM has been described as a movement to add art and innovation to the STEM subjects with a goal of transforming research policy, K-20 education and the economy.

the elementary classroom. Through discovery in the ongoing cycle of research then, as lessons are implemented and insights gained, changes, adaptations and revisions are added to the curriculum. In this way, the curriculum is a "living document" that is ongoing in its development.

Teachers participating in the PSTAR collaborative receive training in the scientific concepts of the curriculum and in the Grinnell System of Nature Journaling, which is a primary method of observing and recording scientific field data. They also receive training in conducting observations and writing ethnographic fieldnotes, which a technique also used in teacher action research methodology (Mills 2017; Cochran-Smith & Lytle 2009; Frank, 1999). The goal is for teachers to develop a multidisciplinary approach to inquiry and fieldwork so they are able to write ethnographic notes about teaching-learning practices and the social life in their classrooms and also record scientific fieldnotes using the Grinnell journaling system along with their students.

The concept of multdisciplinarity is a topic of many discussions about scientific literacy and programmatic attempts to bring the sciences and humanities together. Barad (2012) points to examples of institutions building educational programs that seek to either use the Humanities to think about the Sciences or use the Sciences to rethink the Humanities. What is problematic with these attempts, according to Barad, is that they seek to do this by synthesis. In Barad's view, framing these discussions in terms of synthesis implies "they were always already separate" rather than "always already entangled" (p. 51). In the case of the PSTAR group, what may have initially been conceptualized as a multidisciplinary collaboration between scientists and teachers (assuming separate entities), changed over time. As the team members participated in collaborative fieldworking, which utilized what Barad (2007) calls a "diffractive methodological approach", those always already entangled disciplines and practices were made visible.

A "Diffractive" Methodological Approach

In *Meeting the Universe Halfway: Quantum Physics and the Entanglement of Matter and Meaning*, Barad (2007) explains the need to "understand in an integral way the roles of human and nonhuman, material and discursive, and natural and cultural factors in scientific and other practices" (p.25). Drawing from scientific and social theories, she presents a "diffractive" methodology, whereby insights from different areas of study are read *through* one another, "building new insights, and attentively and carefully reading for differences that matter in their fine details" (Barad 2012: 50). This notion of "reading through" rather than reading against is integral to her diffractive methodology. The former is based in the notion of entanglements of matter and meaning; the latter presumes a set of dualisms that, in Barad's view, places nature on one side and culture on the other, resulting in a separation of matters of fact and matters of concern and care. This is manifested in the separation of academic disciplines "whereby the division of labor is such that the natural sciences are assigned matters of fact and the humanities matters of concern" (p.50). As such, this cordoning off of academic domains makes it difficult to see patterns of diffractions, or patterns of differences that make a difference, which make entanglements visible. For Barad, the Humanities and Sciences have not 'grown up separately from one another", rather they are always already entangled. This notion of entanglement is at the center of Barad's diffractive methodology and provides her rationale:

> My aim in developing such a diffractive methodology is to provide an approach that remains rigorously attentive to important details of specialized arguments within a given field, in an effort to foster constructive engagements across (and a reworking of) disciplinary boundaries (Barad 2007: 25).

As an ethnographer conducting research with the OneTree PSTAR collaborative, my focus is on how they work together as a teaching and learning community who are also engaged in research – both scientific field study and TAR. My fieldwork takes me into the PSTAR teachers' classrooms (indoor and outdoor). It also takes me to the university sites associated with OneTree. The primary site is the Tilly STEAM Studio – a multi-use teaching-learning space where curriculum development and implementation workshops are held for teachers in the OneTree Project; and where PSTAR group members meet for data analysis and writing workshops for presentations-publications; and where fieldtrips for students take place. There is also an outdoor experimental station, called the "T-field", where teachers and students participate as citizen-scientists with university scientists in field-based research.

Because we are all involved in conducting research (Field-based Scientific, Teacher Action Research and ethnographic), we are all entangled in doing fieldwork in these different field(s). Through our fieldworking together, it soon became evident that there were opportunities for "constructive engagements across disciplinary boundaries" (Barad 2007: 25). Though we were all approaching the project from different disciplinary perspectives – natural sciences, social sciences, education – and professional positionalities – university science-research professor, elementary teacher, ethnographer – our participation in the "research" on the project reworked these boundaries as we learned to read the insights from our different research perspectives through one another's fieldnotes. And, through this diffractive methodology, we began to learn how to be attentive to what gets excluded as well as what comes to matter, and recognize those differences that make a difference (Barad, 2012). In the following sections, I will illustrate how utilizing a diffractive methodology can produce new insights as we make visible those always already entangled disciplines.

Fieldworking: The Enganglement of Disciplines

Fieldwork, conducting observation and writing up fieldnotes, is practiced in many different disciplines for the purpose of conducting research. Writing formats and organization are varied, however, many share common elements. For this discussion, I focus on fieldworking approaches used by ethnographers and field-based scientists – how they engage in fieldworking and the different techniques they use to gather information, which reveal "insights" about the various aspects of fieldworking in both disciplines. The table below summarizes these key aspects.

Field-based Scientific Study	Ethnographic Study
Entering the Field In field-based scientific study, the scientist 'enters the field' of study with private, local, state or federal government permissions processes. Ethical standards are met through peer review-academy and/or private, local state or federal government funding agency.	Entering the Field Ethnography is field-based study. Gaining access or 'entering the field' is a primary step. Ethical standards are met generally through IRB processes. Ethical guidelines of funding agencies (private foundations, state, federal governments, school districts) are also followed.
Defining the field Can be defined by the focus of the researcher's expertise (e.g. forestry ecologists-botanists gain access to forested lands, etc.) or can also be defined by issue/problem, such as 'climate change' in which multiple scientific perspectives conduct inquiry in the same 'ecosystem'	Defining the field Defined by the research focus-question(s). This focus is usually aligned with the researcher's expertise and orientation to research and is often framed by social or policy issues related to the researcher's area of expertise and academic research focus.
Fieldworking over time Becoming 'native' to a place (*sensu*) depends on spending extended time in and interacting with the environment (biotic and abiotic) over time to come to know it intimately (Dawe et al. 2015). Traditional ecological knowledge and western science practices both depend on the familiarity that comes with intensive observation and documentation of relationships of the inhabitants in the ecological space-place over time.	Fieldworking over time In order to engage with people and develop relationships, the ethnographer must spend time "in the field". The essential element, time, is critical to defining what ethnographers "do". Ethnographic fieldwork involves some degree of direct participation and observation, and thus, constitutes a radically distinctive way of understanding social activity in situ (Atkinson 2015, 3-4).

Fieldnotes	Fieldnotes
In field-based scientific inquiry, the researcher records observational fieldnotes that include time, date, weather conditions, geographical locations, habitat, specimen measurements, etc. and other 'descriptive' observational data that may include multimodal representations such as drawings, sketches, plot maps, tables, graphic representations, sensory descriptions (e.g. bird song sounds, smells, tastes, etc.) (Herman, 1986). In the *Grinnell System of Nature Journaling*, there are four elements: (a) fieldnotebook (taken into the field); (b) a journal in which field observations from fieldnotebook are transcribed and reflected/elaborated on; (c) catalogue system for specimens; (d) cross-referencing index (Herman, 1986).	Thick description should not be thought of in terms of diffuse descriptive 'detail' "The thickness of ethnographic work rests on systematic attention to the 'thickness' of the multiple modes of order and action' (Atkinson 2015: 29). The material and sociocultural aspects of modes – visual images, language (writing-speaking), music, gesture, 3D objects, kinesthetic-bodily movement, etc., (Silva and Parker Webster, 2018) and multisensory data (Pink, 2015) contribute to 'thickness' of ethnographic fieldnotes. Ethnographers can record fieldnotes in real time and can also keep a separate researcher field journal in which journalistic notes are created from memory. There can also be a separate notebook-journal in which additional notes are written after review of original fieldnotes (Carspecken, 1996; Atkinson, 2015).
Significance of place and space Ecosystems-habitats have boundaries. Significance of place and space depends on the physical characteristics-the materiality of place overlain by biological imperatives of different species, which are always adapting to changes in that place. Thus species flow back and forth across space and time.	Significance of place and space Place and space – 'The materiality of place furnishes recourses that are used by social actors, and they are endowed with significance. They inscribe boundaries that are simultaneously material and symbolic. (Atkinson 2015: 29).
Fieldnotes in Cyclic Inquiry Process Tool to focus or bring new ideas/ questions into the field –this is accomplished through notes created upon review of observational fieldnotes previously recorded in field.	Fieldnotes in Cyclic Inquiry Process Tool to focus or bring new ideas/ questions into the field – accomplished through additional notes created upon review of observational fieldnotes previously recorded in field.

Table 1. Comparison of field-notes/fieldwork in Field-based Scientific and ethnographic study.

The above table suggests there are aspects the two disciplines share. Both require spending time involved in intense and focused observation of and participation in the field(s). Both require real-time observations, and involve asynchronous re-reading of fieldnotes and additional notetaking or resonses about those notes. And, in both disciplinary traditions, fieldwork and fieldnotes are cyclic, such that each observation and writing of fieldnotes inform the next observation and writing, which serve to focus and bring new ideas to the future observations in the field(s).

I then decided to do a side-by-side diffractive reading of the table representing key aspects of the two disciplinary approaches to fieldworking to help me build new insights into details of the "specialized arguments" of each discipline. A further close and attentive reading revealed nuanced differences that "matter in their fine details" (Barad, 2012). In the following discussion, I focus on an example from 'fieldworking over time' to illustrate how a diffractive reading could open up new insights and provoke new questions about the entanglements of these aspects of fieldworking within these two disciplines. This reading is limited in scope as it draws only from the summaries in the above table (see Table 1. Comparison of field-notes/fieldwork in Field-based Scientific study and Ethnographic study), and is presented only as an illustration of how a diffractive reading *through* these disciplinary approaches could be realized in practice.

Using the category 'fieldworking over time', I conducted a closer reading of the nuanced differences of the concept of *relationships* in the field(s). In field-based scientific study, becoming "native" to a place involves interacting with the biotic (living things, such as plants, animals, bacteria, fungi, etc.) and abiotic (non-living, such as sunlight, temperature, water, minerals in soil, etc.) elements in the ecosystem. The relationship seems to occur by interacting with the environment, and this interaction seems to be realized in the documentation of relationships *between* the inhabitants over time. The act of documenting done by the scientist as an observer of relationships between inhabitants of an ecosystem, seems to suggest separateness – between scientist as documenter and inhabitants of the ecosystem, setting up a dualism of subject/object. Therefore, the relationship seems to be viewed as between two separate entities.

The ethnographer develops relationships with participants over time. The doing is engaging in "some degree of direct participation and observation" in situ, which is how relationships are built. What seems to be distinctly a difference that makes a difference is the tacit understanding that humans communicate through language in a way that other biotic species do not. That does not mean that other biotic species do not communicate; quite the contrary. Therefore, rather than a linguistic-centered stance, the notion of a new materialism, which underscores Barad's (2007) conceptualization of entanglements, what comes to the foreground is that while language is a means of communication for humans, "we cannot center language in our understanding of social life writ large" (Dennis in press 2018: 3).

At question, particularly in relation to the concept of entanglements in both above cases (ethnographer and field-based scientist), seems to be the nature of the relationships – are they developed *between* separate entities of scientist and inhabitants of ecosystem or ethnographer and participants *through* interaction? Or, are these relationships always already entangled through what Barad (2007) terms *intra-action? Intra-action* "signifies the mutual constitution of entangled agencies". This is in contrast to the more commonly used concept of *interaction*, "which assumes that there are separate individual agencies that precede their interaction". Rather, intra-action "recognizes that distinct agencies do not precede, but rather emerge through their intra-actions". And, "agencies are only distinct in relation to their mutual entanglement; they don't exist as individual elements" (p.33).

The scientist, may consider herself one of the "biotic" inhabitants of the ecosystem at the time of observation-documentation. The ethnographer may consider herself a participant-observer, engaging in some degree of participation in the daily lives of participants. But, the question is, how are these relations conceptualized? In other words, are they an interaction *between* separate entities or are they mutually entangled through intra-action? This seems critical to a discussion of the potentials of a transdisciplinary approach to research that utilizes a diffractive methodology of *reading through* rather than *reading against* as put forward by Barad (2007); and particularly relevant and applicable to the notion of reading and writing fieldnotes across multidisciplinary perspectives.

Writing in the Fields: The Entanglement of Disciplinary Methods

Participant observations and writing of fieldnotes is a mainstay of ethnographic research. As Atkinson (2015) states, fieldwork requires "some degree of direct participation and observation", and as such, 'it constitutes a radically distinctive way of understanding social activity in situ' (p. 3-4). Being in the field and writing fieldnotes allows ethnographers to participate and observe in the context of people's daily lives. Field-based scientific fieldwork requires intensive observation of the ecosystem or habitat of study and recording fieldnotes that document these observations.

In situ observations and thick description in ethnographic fieldnotes
Ethnographic fieldnotes have a "very particular and distinctive character" and are not like other data (e.g. videorecordings, photographs, artifacts, etc.) because they are 'created by the ethnographer, translating what she or he has see, heard and done into a textual form' (Atkinson 2015: 51). The use

of "thick" description is also key to ethnographic fieldnotes, such that the notion of "thick" refers to multimodalities and requires attention to semiotic resources, such as sound, image, gesture, movement, and sensory data, such as smell, taste, tactility at play. This can apply to narrative re-presentation of the activity in the field; but also can take multimodal forms, such as drawings or maps of the physical organization of the classroom – how desks are arranged, quiet reading areas, etc. – and the material objects (e.g. the white-board or class computers) and their locations are also included to enhance narrative fieldnotes. Thus, fieldnotes, sketches, maps, etc. are all multimodal translations of what the ethnographer has seen, heard and done during fieldwork. The following is an excerpt taken from my fieldnotes recorded during a OneTree lesson presented by the scientists to a second-third grade multiage class illustrating a typical re-presentation of a classroom observation.

Scientists are teaching the lesson today in 2-3 grade multiage class. Second graders are new to the class – most third graders were second graders in this same class last year. Class starts in the 'indoor' classroom. Jan and her Research Assistant (RA) are at the "front" of the class near the large whiteboard. The classroom teacher (CT) and her student teacher (ST) are moving around the classroom passing out blank Grinnell journals to the pods – new journals for new school year. Students are busy getting pencils out of desks. There is a lot of noise as students open and close their desk-tops. There are five pods of desks – four desks-two facing two; one pod has a fifth desk at the end of the four. One desk is situated away from other students by the teacher's desk. All pods have good view of whiteboard at the "front" of the class. The teacher's desk is along the left side of classroom at a bank of windows that face out to the wooded outdoor landscape. As students get settled in for the lesson, Jan, lead scientist, starts with a question to signal the lesson is about to begin:

Jan: *Does anyone remember something from last year...when we worked together...studying the birch life cycle?*

Hands go up around the room. Jan points to students to answer.

We grew little trees from seeds...
We chose a tree to look at all year...
We counted catkins on a branch...
We got birch sap from our tree...

There are still hands shooting up and some students are jumping out of their seats in an effort to be called on.

Jan: *Okay, good start, thanks. Now, let' take a couple more minutes and talk with your pod group about what you remember about last year's study.*

Students begin to whisper-talk to their pod partners about what they remember – a buzzing sound fills the room; students seem engaged in discussion. CT, ST, Jan and RA are circulating around the room, stopping by pods to listen. I move my chair closer to the pod nearest me and ask if I can join their group for the discussion.

S1(m): *You're Dr. Joan, right?*
J: *Right! Thanks for letting me join your group. Are you all excited about the new year?* (all nod yes)
Do you mind if I take notes of what you talk about?
(all shake heads nonverbal "no")
S1: *We don't mind* (as if speaking for the group).
There is a brief pause as if they are waiting for someone to start, then S1 begins the discussion.
S1: *I remember when we tapped our tree last year...*
S2(f): *It was cold* (said in soft voice, barely audible)...
S1: (continuing as if not hearing S2)...*and we had to be careful to put the tap in just right to we didn't hurt the tree.*
S3(m): *And it took a long time for the sap to start running.*
S1: *Yeah, it first dripped slow, but then it really came out fast...*
S3: *And we had to keep changing the buckets...there was lots of sap.*
S2: *But, then the sap started to turn cloudy* (said louder than before)...
(S2 pauses, looks to S4 as if offering her a chance to contribute.)
S4(f): (looks down and does not respond; has been following conversation making eye contact with other students as they speak, sometimes nods, but does not contribute verbally)
(10 seconds pass. S2 looks at others and me.)
S1: (looks at me directly as if to see if I will intervene with a comment as the adult-teacher figure in the group)
S3: (immediately continues picking up conversation thread) *I remember all a sudden we had to stop tapping because...uh, because...*
S1: (jumps in to finish S3's thought)...*it turned cloudy...and tasted bad* (emphasis on bad; makes a face and sticks tongue out) *yuk.*

Everyone laughs. [Fieldnotes excerpt: August 29, 2016]

What I have noticed in my approach to writing fieldnotes, as illustrated in the above example, is at the outset of my observation I usually begin with a "big picture" description of what is happening in the classroom. I describe the physical space – how the room is arranged, locations of desks, whiteboards, etc., note any general prep activity, such as handing out materials. I also give a general description of the social context, who is participating, whole group, small group, teacher-driven, student-driven, etc. As I write, I use multimodal, semiotic resources to give a "thick description".

At some point, the focus shifts from the big picture to the micro – zooming in, as in the above example, on a group of students engaged in a small group activity. This zooming in and out are usually natural progressions of classroom instruction dictated by large and small group activities. I also write (as much as possible) participant talk with accompanying gestures and body movements indicated in parenthesis, even if there is audio-recording made. I find that capturing language with gestures, facial expressions, proximities of bodies to one another is key to a holistic re-presentation of the event and can then be used to enhance the transcription of an audio-file. I also note the gender of the participants (e.g. f or m), which is critical in the analysis process. All of these practices work together to create a "text" of what I have experienced as a participant observer within the daily lives of the teachers and students in the classroom.

In situ multimodal re-representations in field-based scientific fieldnotes

Observation and fieldnotes are also mainstays of field-based scientific research. A primary fieldworking tool utilized by students, teachers and scientists in the OneTree curriculum project is an adaptation of the *Grinnell System of Nature Journaling*. The Grinnell fieldnotebook brings together written scientific observations (e.g. bud or leaf count, limb measurements, etc.), with drawings or sketches of specimens with accompanying narrative descriptions. Entries are recorded on two-facing pages. On the left is a standardized format where biotic inhabitants and abiotic elements are recorded as lists or short phrases: time (in and out), date, locality, route (directions/map to local), weather, habitat, vegetation, general notes about insect activity, animal droppings, tracks, species seen, human disturbances and changes since last visit.

On the right is a blank page for scientists to create drawings or maps with labels and captions, write additional notes, observations and questions that are the focus of the day's observation. The following is an example of the facing pages of the adapted Grinnell fieldnotebook used in the OneTree project (see Figure 1. Grinnell Journal Entry (transcribed), July 7, 2014).

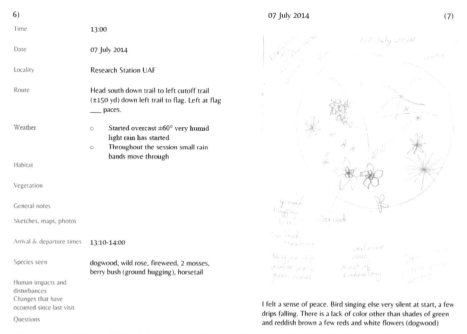

6)   07 July 2014   (7)

Time	13:00
Date	07 July 2014
Locality	Research Station UAF
Route	Head south down trail to left cutoff trail (±150 yd) down left trail to flag. Left at flag ___ paces.
Weather	o Started overcast ±60° very humid light rain has started o Throughout the session small rain bands move through
Habitat	
Vegetation	
General notes	
Sketches, maps, photos	
Arrival & departure times	13:10-14:00
Species seen	dogwood, wild rose, fireweed, 2 mosses, berry bush (ground hugging), horsetail
Human impacts and disturbances	
Changes that have occurred since last visit	
Questions	

I felt a sense of peace. Bird singing else very silent at start, a few drips falling. There is a lack of color other than shades of green and reddish brown a few reds and white flowers (dogwood)

Figure 1. Grinnell Field Journal Entry (transcribed), 7 July 2014

Looking that the left page, it is interesting to note that the headings of the format work together to provide a "big picture" account of the biotic inhabitants and abiotic elements present in the locale. Then, on the right page the detailed drawing of the species within a section of the forest floor, illustrates the focus (or zooming in) of the day's observation. What is also interesting, particularly in the sense of Barad's (2007) concept transdisciplinarity and the notion of "reworking of disciplinary boundaries" is the final addition of a more narrative, qualitative style of fieldnote writing that records a personal and multimodal-sensory experience: "I felt a sense of peace. Birds singing…very silent at start, a few drips falling".

Reading through fieldnotes: Meaning making across disciplinary boundaries
In addition to recording fieldnotes in a *field journal* like the one above, a key component of the Grinnell journaling system involves re-reading the observational fieldnotes, some time after the in situ observation (later the same day or evening); then transcribing data from the field journal into a separate journal for recording additional responses to the original observational data. In the OneTree project, because of its STEM to STEAM approach, these responses can also take the form of a literary genre (e.g. poem, story, essay); an image or drawing; a found object pasted in the journal; or, additional questions about the observation. The following example is from the same participant's separate

journal. Data from the left facing page of the field journal (8 July) were transcribed and recorded the left facing page. Then, on the right are responses to the earlier observation (see Figure 2. Fieldnotes Review (transcribed), July 8-9, 2014).

(14)	08 July 2014	08 July 2014 (15)
Vegetation	Height: Dogwood 18 cm Fireweed 63 cm Lowbush 17 cm	•How did things shape up today? •Did you notice something take shape as a developed definite form? •List how shape, outline, contours were used in art & science activities today.
Arrival & departure times	13:13-13:55	•In a real sense the day's activities helped me to make sense of
Species seen	Twinflower (*Linnaea borealis*) on trail to site Labrador Tea (*Rhododendron groenlandicum*) at site Fireweed (*Chamaerion angustifolium*) Dwarf Dogwood (*Cornus canadensis*) Lowbush cranberry "lingonberry" (*Vaccinium* *vitis-idaea* L.) Horsetail (*Equisetum arvense*) Red stem moss (*Pleurozium schreberi*) Lichen (*Cladonia* sp.)	yesterday's overload of information. The start of drawing helped me to see composition and using the shape of the plants and how to arrange them against the shape of negative space. The identification lab showed how the shape leaves and the arrangement of these leaf shapes are a large part of plant identification. •The leaves of the various plants we studied and identified today have definite shapes and characteristics that are the same for different specimens of the same species. We also saw that the shapes of leaves of plants in the same family also have similar shapes. So shape is important.
Human impacts and disturbances		•Shape was used in art to represent form. Outline and contour provided boundaries for form in art.
Changes that have occurred since last visit Questions		

Figure 2. Fieldnotes Review (transcribed), 8 July, 2014

In this example, you will notice the questions or prompts at the top of the right hand page, which are sometimes given to help focus students' re-readings and writing responses in their separate journal. These particular prompts, which focus on the element of shape in visual art, were generated during a training session as part of professional development training for participating teachers in the project. The prompts were designed to help teachers think deeply about constructive connections across disciplinary boundaries (in this case art and science) when observing and drawing images in their Grinnell journals and in turn, apply this knowledge to their teaching practices with their students. The participant first notes the connection of the visual element of shape help to identify species in the field.

> The identification lab showed how the shape leaves and the arrangements of these leaf shapes are a large part of plant identification.

He then goes further to describe the visual art element of shape as a way to scientifically understand and identify same species.

> The leaves of the various plants we studied and identified today have definite shapes and characteristics that are the *same* for different specimens of the same species.

This connection seems a concrete example of making visible the always already entangled disciplinary fields within the OneTree project. It seems also to mark a "moment" in the re-working of disciplinary boundaries.

In my ethnographic work, I keep a fieldnotebook for in situ observations and fieldnotes and a second journalistic record of events, which are re-presented from memory. These are usually informal conversations that are often impromptu, occurring in hallways, teachers' lounges, lunchrooms, coffee shops, etc., where in situ notetaking can be awkward or even become a deterrent to participation in these conversations.

I also maintain a third notebook, which is actually a Word file. This is where I record initial meaning reconstructions (Carspecken, 1996) on selected segments of the primary record or in situ fieldnotes. According to Carspecken,

> Meaning is understood in holistic and tacit ways during everyday life, and this holds for getting impressions of meaning from fieldnotes as well...Thus, you ought to begin meaning reconstruction by reading through the primary record and mentally noting possible underlying meanings (p.95).

This process of articulating meaning fields for me begins with a close re-reading of the primary record as soon as possible after the observation and fieldnote writing takes place. I then identify significant segments and copy into a Word file, keeping the primary record in tact. I then go through the segment and "articulate" the tacit impressions of meaning about what is occurring and bring these to the discursive. For example, the following is a partial articulation of a "meaning field" (MF) from my fieldnotes excerpt, August 29, 2016. (see page 14):

S2: *But, then the sap started to turn cloudy (said louder than before)...*

(S2 pauses, looks to S4 as if offering her a chance to contribute.)

S4(f): (looks down and does not respond; has been following conversation making eye contact with other students as they speak, sometimes nods, but does not contribute verbally)

(10 seconds pass. S2 looks at others and me.)

[MF: S2 has entered the conversation for the second time, speaking louder this time. Until now, the conversation the two boys as primary interlocutors have controlled the discussion. She looks over to S4, the other girl in the group, who has not said anything up until this point. S2 seems to have noticed that S4 hasn't had an opportunity to talk because the boys seem to be carrying the conversation. S2 has taken the floor and is holding it with a short pause. She non-verbally offers S4 the opportunity to contribute by looking directly at S2, as if to say, girls are allowed to talk in this group too and you can take your turn now. But, when S4 does not respond verbally, S2 doesn't pressure her by calling her out. Instead, S2 relinquishes the floor back to the boys.]

The reason I bring the notion of "meaning fields" into this discussion is that when I read through the two disciplinary methodologies of writing fieldnotes (ethnographic and scientific field-based), particularly the process of re-reading initial fieldnotes, transcribing selected sections, making new meaning and recording these insights a separate journal, I noticed the connection across the two disciplines. Through both processes another layer of meaning is added, which can reveal differences that make a difference and "how differences get made" and "what gets excluded" (Barad, 2007). These are ongoing processes – not a final step – that serve to bring new ideas/questions into the field of research.

The Entangled Ethnographer
So what does this mean for the educational ethnographer engaged in fieldworking and writing fieldnotes? Through my own ethnographic work with the PSTAR group, I have developed a better understanding of the concept of transdisciplinarity, particularly in terms of entanglements of disciplines, fields, and research participants and how this concept can contribute to the practice of writing fieldnotes. Reading multidisciplinary fieldnotes submitted by the PSTAR team of teachers and scientists *through* my own ethnographic fieldnotes, made visible in a very concrete way the entanglements of the different disciplinary perspectives and ways of writing fieldnotes.

This diffractive methodology provided me as the ethnographer new insights about those "important details of specialized arguments within a given field". For example, from reading Jan's fieldnotes, I learned there are very specific attributes to look for when choosing a specimen for the study of its phenophases throughout the school year. As an ethnographer, involved in studying the OneTree project and the PSTAR team, building on this new insight helped me focus my attention to these important details so that I could better understand how students, teachers and scientists are acting-doing as social beings entangled together with biotic and abiotic matter and meaning.

Interactions and Intra-actions

Reading through the progression of my own ethnographic fieldnotes over the course of the project, I also noticed how working within a multidisciplinary project like OneTree and with the PSTAR collaborative influenced how I conduct fieldwork. In particular, how the fluid movement back and forth within indoor and outdoor classrooms and online spaces, which are marked by different materialities, revealed differences that make a difference in the way I observe and write. The differences in my mobility influenced the tools I used and how I used them – computer and Grinnell-type notebook and pencils.

These in turn influenced style and organization – from descriptive narrative to a more Grinnellian shorthand of phrases or words, which increasingly included scientific concepts, with drawings of the specimens encountered in both indoor and outdoor classrooms. I also noticed the increase in descriptions, sometimes accompanied by a sketch, mapping students' *intra-actions* with the material objects in their situated context, instead of the more commonly used mapping of *interactions between* students-students or student-teacher.

In her discussion of Barad's theory of new materialism, Dennis (in press 2018) builds on the concept of *intra-action* as signifying relations that are not composed of external, additive, atomistic entities, but instead are internal actions co-constitutive with one another. In other words, relations are thought of as *within* rather than *between* subjects, and Dennis uses the term *intra-relational* to describe the internal actions that are co-constitutive with one another, which indicates "boundaries presumed to distinguish subject from object, text from context and so on are actually porous, re-constitutive, and active, not binarial (3). Dennis goes on to explain how entangled bodies and material objects intra-act with one another.

> We can think about this with respect to locating our bodies in a desk and understanding that the opportunity of our bodily movement and feeling is now partially bounded by and constituted of its being with the desk (3).

In my fieldnotes, *intra-actions* seem to be made visible most often in the outdoor classroom, perhaps because of the differences in the material objects in that environment, and the different forms of communication occurring within these situated contexts. In the outdoor classroom students' (and my own) bodily movements, rather than being bounded by desks and the socially acceptable ways of negotiating the space, are bounded by and constituted of their entanglement with the biotic and abiotic materiality of the natural forest environment. The following excerpt from my fieldnotes taken in the outdoor classroom (the boreal forest next to the school) illustrates this concept.

Two students have stopped at a birch that is set apart from its neighbors. Due to its size – at least 1.5 to 2 times larger – probably claimed more ground and canopy space from nearby siblings. It is sunny, and the angle of the sun creates a dappling effect on the forest floor. A very light breeze is rustling the trees. Student A sits on decaying log – close proximity to path right next to the trunk. He focuses on peeling bark (touches it) may be recalling birch exfoliate to aid growth. Runs hand across groundcover. Student B has wandered off the path and sits about 20+ feet away, on the groundcover – half lying down looking up at the canopy, shading his eyes from the sun. I am sitting mid-way between them on a soft patch of plurozium – moss. Both students take some time to observe, just look at their surroundings before picking up their journals to record their data observations on left side of Grinnell journals. There is no verbal or even non-verbal student-student communication. They are intensely involved with observing and writing about the specimen they have chosen. It is quiet except for the music of singing of birds and swaying branches, [Fieldnotes excerpt, May 5, 2017].

In these ways then, fieldworking that incorporates transdisciplinary writing of fieldnotes and a diffractive methodology of writing-reading through these fieldnotes contributed to more comprehensive multidisciplinary accounts that made visible the entanglements of the social and the scientific. I would also argue that practices such as these could potentially inform the "doing" of educational ethnographic fieldwork in general and the writing of fieldnotes in particular.

Returning to Table 1, *Comparison of field-notes/fieldwork in field-based scientific and ethnographic study*, the notion of transdisciplinary research practices seems particularly important to consider for educational ethnographers whose studies are conducted in fields where various content areas are the focus of the research. In such fields, it is therefore important to consider those content area specialists, or other professionals who are working in the field, who may be trained in disciplinary research techniques compatible with ethnographic techniques, as co-participant-researchers that can contribute to the research through their specialized disciplinary arguments. This can potentially contribute to thicker, richer and more comprehensive fieldnotes as well as sharpen and expand the observational capabilities of the ethnographer.

Making visible the entanglements of the material with the social life of the classroom (indoor and outdoor, virtual, synchronous and asynchronous) seems critical to the ethnographic researcher. While thick and rich description is integral to ethnographic fieldwork and writing fieldnotes, Atkinson (2015) states the material is often absent and, according to Dennis (2018) even when well described, the material context has been unproblematized and not discussed part of the social action that takes place in a classroom.

How the classroom is arranged can offer insights into the social life that is enacted there. Equally important are the "other" places and spaces in which participants – students, teachers, lunchroom attendants, recess monitors, etc) "intra-act" with the materiality of the environment – lunchroom, playground, outdoor classroom, pathways, or the multimodal affordances within an online classroom (Silva & Parker Webster, 2018). All are entangled within and contribute to the social life of the participants in educational contexts and must be considered a necessary part of any ethnographic study.

Conclusion

Because we, as educational ethnographers, work in multidisciplinary fields, I suggest making visible those always already entangled relationships that exist within the natural and social worlds should be of primary interest and concern as we engage in fieldworking. If, as Barad (2007) suggests, we are to think about the social and the natural together, then we need a method for theorizing this relationship "without defining one against the other or holding either nature or culture as the fixed referent for understanding the other" (p.30). In her view, what is needed is a "diffraction apparatus" in order to study these entanglements. What has been described in this chapter are my first efforts with thinking about and putting into practice such a "diffractive methodology"; and as such these represent early thoughts. My emergent understandings are also underscored by many questions concerning the many nuances of the concepts and philosophical underpinnings within Barad's theory of new materialism.

However, I do think that there is much promise in a "diffraction apparatus" that means reading insights through one another in ways that illuminate how differences get made, what gets excluded and how these matter for ethnographic fieldwork. Such a "diffractive methodology" can serve to sharpen the ethnographer's attentions to those differences that make a difference and make visible the always already entangled disciplines and practices within ethnographic fields of study.

Bibliography

Atkinson, P. (2015) *For ethnography.* London: Sage.

Barad, K. (2007). *Meeting the universe halfway: Quantam physics and the entanglement of matter and meaning.* Durham, NC: Duke University Press.

Barad, K. (2012) "Interview with Karen Barad". In Rick Dolphijn and Iris vander Tuin, (eds.), *New materialism: Interviews and cartographies* (48-70). Ann Arbor, MI: University of Michigan Library.

Carspecken, P.F. (1996) *Critical ethnography in educational research: A theoretical and practical guide.* NY: Routledge.

Cochran-Smith, M., and Lytle, S. (2009) *Inquiry as stance: Practitioner research for the next generation.* New York, NY: Teachers College Press.

Dawe, J., Meyers, Z., Parker Webster, J., and Pastro, C. (2015) *"What did they learn? Using multimodal analysis of student work to document STEAM learning".* Paper presented at the Teacher-Scientist Partnership Conference, San Francisco, CA, February 11-12, 2015.

Dennis, B. (in press 2018). Context and materiality: Inclusive appropriations of new materialism for qualitative analysis. In R. Winkle Wagner, J. Lee Johnson, & A. Gaskew (Eds.), *Critical Theory and Qualitative Data Analysis in Education.* New York, NY:Routledge.

Frank, C. (1999) *Ethnographic eyes: A teacher's guide to classroom observation.* Portsmouth, NH: Heinemann.

Herman, S, G. (1986) *The Naturalist's Field Journal: A Manual of Instruction Based on a System Established by Joseph Grinnell.* Harrell Books.

Herr, K., and Anderson, G.I. (2005) *The action research dissertation.* Thousand Oaks: Sage.

Mills, G. (2017) *Action research: A guide for the teacher researcher (Sixth Edition).* Edinburgh, UK: Pearson Education Ltd.

Olwig, K. F. and Hastrup, K. (eds.) (1997). *Siting Culture: The shifting anthropological object.* London, Routledge.

Parker Webster, J. and Silva, S. M. da. (2013). Doing educational ethnography in an online world: methodological challenges, choices and innovations, *Ethnography and Education*, 8(2), pp. 123-130. DOI: 10.1080/17457823.2013.792508

Pink, Sarah. (2015). *Doing sensory ethnography*, 2nd edition. London, UK: Sage.

Silva, S.M. da, and Parker Webster, J. (2018). Positionality and standpoint: Situated ethnographers acting in on- and offline contexts. In Dennis Beach, Carl Bagley and Sofia Marques da Silva (eds.), *Wiley Handbook of Ethnography and Education* (501-512). London, UK: Wiley.

Fieldnote issues, collegial support and collaborative analysis

Andrea Raggl

Introduction

Fieldnotes seem to be an often neglected part in ethnography (Wolfinger, 2002). As Van Maanen (2011) points our fieldnotes are 'one of many levels of textualization' (p.153) in ethnographic work. Ethnographers usually write notes when they are in the field and these 'jotting notes' (Emerson et al., 1995: 17) or 'aides-memoire' are often re-written into more elaborated fieldnotes out of the field. In research books published in Germany a distinction is made between notes taken in the field called 'fieldnotes' and notes re-written out of the field 'Beobachtungsprotokolle' (observing protocols) (Streck et al., 2013; Breidenstein et al., 2015). Writing notes in the field and re-writing them out of the field are active processes of interpretation and sense-making: noting and writing down some things as 'significant', noting but ignoring others as 'not significant' (Emerson et al., 1995). This process of 'textualization' (Clifford & Marcus, 1986) can be seen as translating experiences into a text. Fieldnotes are 'local documents' (Rapport, 1991) and 'inevitably reflect the ethnographer's background knowledge, or tacit beliefs' (Wolfinger, 2002: 93).

However, in spite of their crucial role in ethnography there seems to be a 'suspicious silence' around fieldnotes. Nevertheless, in the last years more attention has been paid to the messy practice of writing fieldnotes. Walford (2009) interviewed four experienced ethnographers in the field of education in 'The practice of writing ethnographic fieldnotes'. One of the interviewees was Sara Delamont who explains that her notes taken in the field 'are very impersonal – very factual' and her notes out of the field are more 'reflexive': She writes 'up the one-word, scrappy, abbreviated scribble into a longhand, grammatical narrative account' (p. 129). Jackson (1990) interviewed anthropologists and concludes: 'Virtually all respondents expressed strong and ambivalent feelings about their notes. The subject of fieldnotes is clearly complex, touchy, and disturbing for most of us' (p. 9). For Jackson's interviewees this ambivalent feeling about their notes is because 'fieldnotes reveal what kind of person one is: messy, responsible, procrastinating, exploitative, tidy, compulsive, generous' (p. 21).

Fieldnote issues

Fieldnotes play a crucial role in ethnographic research. Ethnographers often put a lot of time and effort in writing notes in and out of the field. This section delves into the messy practice of actually writing fieldnotes in situ. How and when do we write notes? When is it better to stop taking notes? How far are we disturbing the situation when we sit there and take notes? How much pressure can it put on teachers?

Disturbing the context

In research projects carried out after my time in England, after completing my PhD, I became much more aware of my role as an ethnographer in the field. In a learning community with experienced ethnographers I developed a strong identity as an ethnographer. I was able to distance myself from my former 'teacher self' and changed gradually into a participant observer (Raggl, 2015). This helped me to start further research projects right from the beginning as a note-taking participant. However, the field itself positions former teachers into a certain role, as a doctoral student I have worked with, explained in a memo on fieldwork:

> Since teachers knew that I myself was an English teacher, I was often asked to listen in dialogues of students during speaking activities as to make myself 'useful' in the classroom. I was also asked to read out books to the students in English (Charlotte).

Fieldworkers experience situations where it seems to be better to lay down the pen and stop taking notes, such as the following fieldnote of a project on establishing a 'class' with children who had just changed from kindergarten to Year 1:

> 3rd day in the first week of school. The teacher has changed the seating of the pupils. She has put names on each desk so the pupils know where they sit now. Shortly after the lesson started she looks at one table and asks: 'What has happened here?' Leyla answers: 'I was sitting here yesterday and now I have put this (the piece of paper with her name on) here.' The teacher explained: 'I did that. And do you know why? It was too loud yesterday.' She takes Leyla to a table in the front where Eniz is sitting. She speaks quietly with him. He is shaking his head and is holding himself at his chair. All the children are now looking at the two of them. The teacher says again something to him but he very clearly shakes his head now. She tries to get him from the chair by pulling him but he shows with his whole body that he is not willing to move. It is totally silent in the classroom – all of us watch the spectacle what was going on between the two. The teacher gives up and leaves the place. Shortly afterwards she comes to me and explains that she wanted Eniz to sit back between the two girls where Leyla was sitting.

At the end of the morning I had a little chat with the teacher. She explained: 'This class is difficult. In my last class it was much easier. I don't want to be the bad one but they have to know that I'm the one who makes the rules.' She obviously felt bad about how the situation in the class developed. I asked her: 'How do you feel about me being here?' She answered: 'Actually quite good' but then she explained: 'I would probably have reacted differently had I not been observed. I would have pushed that through if you had not have been there.' She then added thoughtfully, 'I don't know why I actually agreed to take part in the project'.

Ethnographers can become part of rather difficult situations when they are in classrooms. The teacher here agreed to take part in the project but questioned it after our 3rd day together in the classroom. She had not expected that things would be so difficult in this new class. Having an observer in the class taking notes all the time had put additional pressure on her.

In this particular situation I stopped taking notes. I felt it was inappropriate to take notes when all of us were watching what was going on. From my conservations with her I knew that she was trying hard, she wanted to be good teacher and felt bad appearing as a 'bad teacher'. This episode shows a lot about teachers' vulnerability (Kelchtermans, 2009).

I have not found anything yet in the texts on practices of writing fieldnotes concerning this issue as to when ethnographers should lay down their pen and stop writing notes in the field. There are also fields where note taking is not possible at all although schools are described as rather easy places to take notes because writing is a common practice in classrooms (Breidenstein et al., 2015). Taking notes is part of the teachers' job. However, it often has a controlling or judging function in schools if carried out by a third person and I found it rather difficult as a novice ethnographer to take out a notebook and write notes in classrooms where it appeared I was disturbing the situation. As a former primary teacher I was observed and judged when I was teaching and later as a novice teacher by the head teacher or an inspector. I am very aware of the practices of writing notes in classrooms and the meaning it can have for teachers. Therefore I would argue that schools are not easy places to take notes. Paul Connolly mentions similar feelings in an interview with Geoffrey Walford (2009): 'So the classroom was a bit different as was the staffroom. It wasn't easy to pull out a notebook at the start ... because the teacher ... would take that personally' (p. 124). The doctoral student I worked with wrote a memo on doing fieldwork concerning the tense moments in the classroom where she felt uneasy taking notes:

In lessons in which one specific teacher was teaching, I had to come up with a very specific technique of taking notes. In crucial moments in which the situation in class got tense between teacher and students for example I would pretend to describe the interior of the classroom instead of paying direct attention to the conflict in front of me so as to not increase pressure on the teacher. I was, however, trying to listen close to what happened and take notes (Charlotte).

The student underlined: 'My priority is not to make anyone uncomfortable with my presence in their class.' Disturbing the field; making the teacher uncomfortable by being there as a participant observer is an important issue in doing fieldwork. With another teacher the student felt very much controlled in her note taking as a participant observer.

I tried to make it a habit of not closing my notebook when teachers approached me because I did not want them to think that I wrote about them in a bad way. However, my notes of students and situations are very private and I feel that I have a right not to show them.

Charlotte had the experience of teachers trying to justify their actions in the classroom.

Teachers have come up to me and tried to explain why they did one thing or another in class to justify their decisions. In one classroom a teacher felt increasingly under pressure whenever I took out my notebook. She would shoot down the aisle and make comments on her teaching to me.

These struggles show a lot about the field itself, that it is not a daily practice in most schools to have researchers there and being observed is not something many teachers feel comfortable with. Being observed maybe felt as a power struggle with researchers sitting there quietly – although sometimes not comfortably – without showing a lot of themselves. They are not passive but more reserved, whereas teachers are very much 'in action' and show a lot of themselves. In classes where things were running more or less smoothly, where the teacher was rather relaxed and self-confident it was easier to take notes. In classes where the teachers struggled and where things were running out of order, it was much more difficult to be there at all and the wish to escape from difficult sites, for the researcher was strong. In the case of my own research and of the doctoral student visits in the challenging research sites were reduced because it was difficult for both researchers sitting there for hours. The researchers may sometimes feel sorry for the children who could not escape unlike the participant observer who can find many reasons for not being there. The knowledge that the researcher sitting there and taking notes may be putting pressure on teachers and also affecting on the relationship between them. Difficult situations which emerge during fieldwork have to be lived through together. It seems to be important that we still engage in an exchange with teachers about what happens and how the teacher feels about it.

The importance of self-discipline to ensure maximum of productivity

Consequently, in my first ethnographic project CLASP I hesitated taking notes in the classrooms. Instead I engaged in lots of conversations with students and teachers and acted more as a teaching assistant by helping out in the classroom. There was, on reflection, too much familiarity to the field as being a former primary teacher. I found it hard to make the shift to the new role of an ethnographer, whose main tasks were participating, observing and writing notes in the classroom. Looking back at these beginnings of doing ethnography I realised that it needed a lot of self-discipline to stick to these main tasks in the field. On the one hand we are trying hard to get entrance into a new social setting and establishing new relationships there; building up trust with participants to become a partial member of the new world. On the other hand we must learn how to represent, in a written form what we have seen in the field (Emerson et al., 1995).

Doing fieldwork involves 'writing' notes in the field and afterwards, observing specific scenes or being involved in formal and casual conversations. Fieldworkers often have to choose between join(ing) conversations in unfamiliar places and distancing themselves from the scene to write about what they have observed. In different phases of doing fieldwork the interrelated tasks of participating, observing and writing can be lived differently. At the beginning of the fieldwork it can be appropriate to be more a participant than an observer when building up relationships. Later on one can concentrate more on the observing. However, it seems to be important as Jackson (1990) points out that my 'behaviour, especially my fieldnote-taking, serves to remind me, and them, that I am in the field, but not of the field' (p. 10).

In many research books it is highly recommended to re-write the notes from the field as soon as possible (Emerson et al., 1995). Breidenstein et al. (2015), for example, suggest it is better not to tell the tales of the field to someone but to directly write them so that the narrating is put into the writing and not lost by telling. In my own research practice, I tried to write the notes most of the time right after leaving the field. In the few cases where I did not do this, I found it very hard to do it even one day later through use of recall. Notes from the field that were not written right afterwards were easily 'forgotten' and not written at all. I forced myself to write them up following an unwritten rule that, if I have not done something with the notes from the last field visit, I did not allow myself to go back to the field. This helped me to take the writing of the fieldnotes seriously and to do it as quickly as possible. I started to plan my field visits to ensure that there was time for rewriting the notes from the field immediately afterwards.

Delamont lists different forms of textualization which she uses in her fieldwork: (1) notes taken in the field, (2) notes written up in the out of the field book, (3) field diary which is used for reflections and for remembering ideas and (4) another book for titles, pseudonyms etc (cited in Walford, 2009). I always start very enthusiastically with similar strategies at the beginning of a new research project but it needs a lot of self-discipline to keep on writing all the different texts throughout a project. The re-writing of notes taken in the field as quickly as possible after leaving the field needs quite a lot of self-discipline, but it does make fieldwork much easier when I am still fully absorbed by the field itself. As Van Maanen (2011) points out: 'In the field, one must cut his or her life down (…). In many respects, ethnographic fieldworkers remove themselves from their usual routines' (p.152).

Sharing fieldnotes for researcher development and analytical development

Sharing fieldnotes to develop fieldnote strategies
Writing fieldnotes involves ambivalent and disturbing feelings and it seems to be important to work with them in research groups where a culture of trust exists. In the article 'Making observing protocols strange' (Streck et al., 2013) three doctoral students reflect on their strategies of writing fieldnotes. Their methodological reflections of their writing practices revealed the potential of a shared work with fieldnotes in research groups. As a novice ethnographer I experienced the sharing of fieldnotes in the research project CLASP (Creative Learning and Students' Perspectives) right from the beginning of my ethnographic work. This sharing of fieldnotes was continued in the research project PTICC (Primary Teachers' Identity, Commitment and Career) with Geoff Troman, Bob Jeffrey and Peter Woods.

Bob's fieldnotes appeared to me as little stories. When Bob showed me his notebook with notes taken during his field visit, I realised how much he is writing in his notebook when he is 'out there'. Compared to him I was very reluctant taking notes in the field. Seeing Bob's fieldnotes the first time I realised how much work ethnographers spend on writing and that writing is the major task in my new job. I gradually developed strategies of taking notes in the field and to re-write them as fieldnotes 'out of the field'. The collegial exchange first in the CLASP project and later on in the PTICC project in England was very important for me to gain more security in doing fieldwork.

Discussing my fieldnotes with Geoff Troman on a regular base was very helpful for the research and at the same time helped me to focus more intently.

Making brief notes about more general things and looking at more detailed aspects related to the project became more natural. I attempted to note everything. The collegial exchange was very important to develop my strategies of observing and note taking.

Comparing fieldnotes to those of my colleagues provided a helpful contrast. Analysing Bobs' 'vignettes' years afterwards I would describe them as elaborated texts similar to 'memos' in a Grounded Theory approach. They are rather narratives of the field, lively stories, interesting to read, partly enriched with theoretical assumptions and links being made between different sorts of data. Although it was rather challenging to write fieldnotes after having seen Bob's, as a novice ethnographer, it was also inspiring. I realised that writing fieldnotes was a creative work, a skilful practice.

However, my own fieldnotes are still more 'raw' data (Kouritzin, 2002). Emerson et al. (1995) suggest to write fieldnotes 'loosely and flowingly' (p. 45) – constructing a 'raw' form of fieldnotes. They are the texts written after leaving the field from the notes scribbled in the field; texts I can work with after having brought order into the jotting notes. Sometimes I develop them into a sort of 'vignette' when I share them with students to make them more readable. The next level of textualization would be in my work a 'memo', coming from Grounded Theory, texts already enriched by theoretical thoughts. Fieldnotes are very personal papers and they show a lot of ourselves, as ethnographers and as persons, this shared work with fieldnotes must take place in a community of trust. It can also help to build up trust in the own writing and in conducting research (Dausien, 2007).

By describing fieldnotes as 'secret papers' (Van Maanen, 2011) and arguing that they can 'take on a unique sacredness' (Wolfinger, 2002: 92) a kind of myth around fieldnotes seems to have been constructed. I would ask, why not work with them in a much more practical way? I suggest we see fieldnotes as working papers and sharing them with colleagues enables us to rethink our own perspectives. In our writing we reveal a lot about what we see and what we cannot see and about our tacit beliefs. We translate our experiences in the field into a text and there is no correct way of doing this but through sharing these fieldnotes in a community of trust we can develop strategies in seeing, writing and carrying out research.

Shared analysis – the shared synthesis of ethnographic data
In recent projects I have continued this sharing of fieldnotes, for example, with Christina Huf (Huf & Raggl, 2015, 2017) as well as with other colleagues and research students. When we got to know each other we realized that we both had carried out fieldwork in age-mixed primary classes independently from each other with a very similar focus, interactions between children when

they have been working rather independently on their tasks. The cooperation started after Christina had completed her fieldwork and I was in the middle of mine. We started to select our fieldnotes respectively "ethnographic observing protocols" as Christina would call them for a shared analysis. This process of selecting was itself an interesting issue. Next to selecting it became necessary to 'edit' the observing protocols a bit so that they were easier to understand for the other one who had not written them and who was an outsider to the field. Sitting together and working on these observing protocols of each other evoked a lot of discussions on (1) what was going on in the classes, (2) how the protocols were written and (3) what was left out. I realized that I had still maintained my habit of writing down many 'general' remarks of the situation, however, I had missed a bit the preciseness of the micro-situation. Although I had noted the interactions between the children I realized that Christina was also noting the tasks the children worked on. This helped me to become aware that I had to take more notes on the tasks. Without recording details of the precise task it was hard to understand the problems the children were dealing with in the interactions later on.

We developed two articles of our' shared synthesis' of ethnographic data (Huf & Raggl, 2015, 2017) and concluded: We 'set out to explore how the comparison of data from two different research projects (…) could create a synergy. We aimed at shedding new light on our interpretations of data and challenge preconceived notions' and we 'reflected the implicit selectivity of the respective field' (Huf & Raggl, 2015: 234). Analysing our fieldnotes afterwards showed that two former primary teachers were conducting the fieldwork with a lot of didactical knowledge in their mind. A researcher with a different background, for example a sociologist, would not have taken so many things for granted.

I worked shortly afterwards with another colleague on my fieldnotes who has a background in ethnomethodology and not in teaching. There were many more questions concerning, 'What is actually going on here?' This shared analysis of my fieldnotes showed that working together with ethnographers from different fields is another helpful strategy to 'make the familiar strange'. Sometimes it helps to have a lot of shared ground; sometimes it is necessary to challenge our own perspectives through the lenses of another colleague from a different methodology.

Conclusion
My style of writing fieldnotes has changed over the last 15 years. I came to realise that writing fieldnotes is a craft and that sharing and comparing fieldnotes with others can help to develop this skilful practice. Being so much integrated in a supportive research group at the beginning of my

research career showed that working with fieldnotes can be lived differently. I have continued to share reflections and analysis of fieldnotes in all my later research projects. It is an attempt to overcome the 'lonesome' activity of carrying out fieldwork; seeing it much more as a joint activity. These reflections on writing fieldnotes show that ethnographers have to be creative, inventive and critical when producing fieldnotes and that one must allow a lot of time to write fieldnotes out of the field and to share these 'working papers' with colleagues.

Bibliography

Breidenstein, G., Hirschauer, S., Kalthoff, H. and Nieswand, B. (2015) *Ethnografie. Die Praxis der Feldforschung, Ethnography. Practice of Fieldwork,* 2nd Edition, Konstanz: UVK.

Clifford, J. and Marcus, G. (1986) *Writing culture: The poetics and politics of ethnography,* Berkely: University of California Press.

Dausien, B. (2007) Reflexivität, Vertrauen, Professionalität. Was Studierende in einer gemeinsamen Praxis qualitativer Forschung lernen können, *Forum Qualitative Research,* 8 (1). http://nbn-resolving.de/urn:de:0114-fqs0701D4Da3.

Emerson, R. M., Fretz, R. I., and Shaw, L. L. (1995) *Writing ethnographic fieldnotes,* Chicago: University of Chicago Press.

Huf, C. and Raggl, A. (2017) The normativity of the helping child – meta-ethnographic perspectives on individualised learning in age-mixed classrooms. *Ethnography and Education,* (12)2, 165-177,

Huf, C. and Raggl, A. (2015) Social orders and interactions among children in age-mixed classes in primary schools – new perspectives from a synthesis of ethnographic data, *Ethnography and Education,* 2(2): 230-241.

Jackson, J. (1990) "Deja Entendu": The Liminal Qualities of Anthropological Fieldnotes", *Journal of Contemporary Ethnography,* 19 (1): 8-43.

Kouritzin, S. (2002) The "Half-baked" Concept of "Raw" Data in Ethnographic Observation, *Canadian Journal of Education,* 27(1): 119-138.

Raggl, A. (2015) The international researcher has to 'Make the familiar strange and the strange familiar', in Fritzsche, B. and Huf, C. (ed.). The Benefits, Problems and Issues of Comparative and Cross-Cultural Research. *Ethnographic Perspectives* (pp. 53-67), E&E: Painswick

Rapport, N. (1991) Writing Fieldnotes: The Conventionalities of Note-Taking and Taking Note in the Field, *Anthropology Today,* 7 (1), 10-13.

Streck, R., Unterkofler, U. and Reinecke-Terner, A. (2013) Das „Fremdwerden" eigener Beobachtungsprotokolle – Rekonstruktionen von Schreibpraxen als methodische Reflexion. *Forum Qualitative Research,* 14 (1), http://nbn-resovling.de/urn:nbn:de:0114-fqs1301160. (Accessed 20 March 2018).

Van Maanen, J. (2011) *Tales of the Field. On Writing Ethnography,* second ed., Chicago: University of Chicago Press.

Walford, G. (2009) The practice of writing ethnographic fieldnotes, *Ethnography and Education,* 4(2): 117-130.

Wolfinger, N. (2002): On writing fieldnotes: collection strategies and background expectancies, *Qualitative Research,* 2(1), 85-9.

Author Biographies

Karen Borgnakke, dr.paed., Professor in Education, University of Copenhagen.
She has done research, taught and published in the fields of education and learning research. She has carried out fieldwork, developed case studies, participated in development projects and evaluation research, including projects on strategies for organisational and pedagogical innovation in comprehensive school, upper secondary school and in higher education. She has more than twenty years experience with developing research methodology in education and learning research, including comprehensive experience with research education. Further, she has comprehensive experience with project direction in relation to research program funded by Danish, Nordic and European research councils. Current research project: Ethnographic studies in scholastic, profession-oriented and academic learning contexts.

Angeles Clemente has worked as a professor and researcher University of Oaxaca (Mexico), where she founded the research group in Critical Applied Linguistics. She studied her PhD in Education at the Institute of Education of the University of London. Her main interest is in understanding the dynamics that arise in the interaction between language, culture, agency and identity in Latin American contexts, such as Oaxaca, Mexico. Together with Higgins, she wrote *Performing English with a postcolonial accent: ethnographic narratives from Mexico* (2008); with Milstein, Guerrero, Dantas and Higgins, *Encuentros Etnograficos con niños y adolescentes* (2011), with Marshall and Higgins, *Performing Ethnography in Multilingual and Multicultural Contexts* (2014), and with Guerrero, et al, *Bordes, límites y fronteras : encuentros etnográficos con niños, niñas y adolescentes* (2017) as well as the publication of more than 30 articles in specialized, national and international journals .

Sara Delamont is Reader Emerita in Sociology at Cardiff University. She currently conducts fieldwork on capoeira, the Brazilian dance-fight game, and savate, the French kickboxing martial art. Her most recent book is Sara Delamont, Neil Stephens and Claudio Campos, *Embodying Brazil: An Ethnography of Diasporic Capoiera* (Routledge 2017). Her previous books include: *Feminist Sociology* (Sage 2003); *Key Themes in the Ethnography of Education* (Sage 2014) and *Fieldwork in Education Settings* (Third edition, Routledge 2016). Together with Paul Atkinson she was founding editor of the journal *Qualitative Research* (Sage). She was one of the editors of the *Sage Handbook of Ethnography* (Sage 2001). She is a Fellow of the Academy of Social Sciences and a Fellow of the Learned Society of Wales. She is the recipient of the Lifetime Achievement Awards from the British Sociological Association and the British Research Education.

Alba Lucy Guerrero is an Assistant Professor at the Department of Education at Pontificia Universidad Javeriana in Bogotá, Colombia. She earned her Ph.D. in Education and a Master in Cultural Perspectives in Education at the University of California, Santa Barbara; and MA in Social and Educational Development at CINDE-UPN in Colombia. Her research focuses on anthropology of childhood, particularly on the understanding of the relationship between childhood, education and sociopolitical changes. Another area of interest is research methodology with children. She coordinates the research group Childhood, Culture and Education at Pontificia Universidad Javeriana. She is also a founder member of the International Network of Ethnography with children in educational contexts, RIENN, which aims building a community of researchers that work with children from an ethnographic perspective. Her most recent publication is the book *Bordes, límites y fronteras: Encuentros etnográficos con niños, niñas y adolescentes* (with Clemente, Dantas-Whitney and Milstein, 2017).

Martyn Hammersley is Emeritus Professor of Educational and Social Research at The Open University, UK. He has carried out research in the sociology of education and the sociology of the media. However, much of his work has been concerned with the methodological issues surrounding social enquiry. He has written several books, including (with Paul Atkinson) *Ethnography: Principles in Practice* (Third edition, Routledge 2007), *The Politics of Social Research* (Sage, 1995), *Educational Research, Policymaking and Practice* (London, Paul Chapman/Sage 2002), *Questioning Qualitative Inquiry* (Sage, 2008), *The Myth of Research-Based Policy and Practice* (Sage 2013), *The Limits of Social Science* (Sage, 2014), and *The Radicalism of Ethnomethodology* (Manchester University Press, 2018). Website: http://martynhammersley.wordpress.com/

Bob Jeffrey researched from 1992 the work of primary teachers with Professor Peter Woods and Professor Geoff Troman. They focused on the opportunity for creative teaching and the effects of the reforms of the 1990s in England on this form of pedagogy and teacher identities. In the 2000s they developed this focus to learners and their opportunities for creative learning including a nine nation European study from 2004-2006. He was co-leader of two ESRC studies into Primary Teacher's Careers in Performativity Cultures and into the effects of performative and creative policies on primary schools – 2004-2008 together with Professor Geoff Troman of Roehampton University. Bob is co-founder of the *Ethnography and Education* journal and edited it from

2008-2012 and co-organised an annual ethnography conference in Oxford for ten years. He has also co-edited a book series from 2007-2012 and since then has co-ordinated publications under the imprint of E&E. Since retirement in 2011 he has authored one book, co-edited two and published an article on ethnographic writing in the *Handbook of Ethnography in Education.* www.ethnographyandeducation.org

Diana Milstein has worked as Associated Professor and Researcher at Universidad Nacional del Comahue (Argentina). Currently she is Researcher in the Center of Social Research of National Council of Scientific and Technical Research at Institute of Economic and Social Development (CIS-CONICET-IDES) and Coordinator of the International Network of Etnography with Children and Youth (RIENN). She studied her PhD in Social Anthropology at the Department of Anthropology at Universidade de Brasília. Her fields of interest are ethnography and education, ethnography with children, anthropology of the body and art education. She has published several articles in specialized journals and book chapters. She has written the books *Higiene, autoridad y escuela* (2003) and *La nación en la escuela* (2009), is co-author of *La escuela en el cuerpo* (1999/ 2017) and co-editor of *Encuentros etnográficos con niños y adolescentes* (2011) and *Bordes, límites y fronteras: encuentros etnográficos con niños, niñas y adolescentes* (2017).

Joan Parker Webster is a retired Associate Professor of Education at the University of Alaska Fairbanks (UAF). Specializing in multiliteracies and cross-cultural education, she has worked with Alaska Native storytellers and educators on documenting traditional oral stories, as well as producing heritage language storybooks and bilingual materials for children. Currently she is Affiliated Faculty in the Center for Cross Cultural Studies at UAF. She also works as an educational research consultant, primarily as an evaluator for federally-funded grant programs. Parker Webster continues to conduct ethnographic research with Alaska Native communities and schools and publish in the areas of multiliteracies, multimodal analysis, and Indigenous education.

Andrea Raggl, PhD, is a Prof. for educational research at the Pedagogical University Tyrol since 2017. Before this she was a primary teacher, a research assistant at Innsbruck University and Roehampton University/London and a post-doctorate researcher at the Pedagogical University of Vorarlberg. She has carried out several ethnographic research projects in Austria and England and mixed methods projects together with Swiss partners. Her field of interests are ethnography, primary schools, rural education and comparative research.

Lisa Russell is a Senior Lecturer in Education and Community Studies at the University of Huddersfield. Her research interests focus mainly on issues of social justice and education policy. She has a long standing history of ethnographic work ranging from her ESRC funded PhD exploring pupil resistance in the UK and Australia to her Leverhulme Trust and Joseph Rowntree Foundation ethnographic work with young people not in employment, education and training (NEET).

Pat Thomson is Professor of Education, School of Education, The University of Nottingham. Her primary interest is in socially just pedagogies and educational change: she has been exploring this through ethnographic and action research on the arts in schools and communities. She also has an interest in academic writing and research education: her academic writing and research blog *patter* (patthomson.net) is widely read and used.

Janna Wieland is a cultural anthropologist with a focus on the sociology of space. She studied metropolitan culture and urban design at HafenCity University Hamburg. After graduating from university, she worked in the project 'Wohnbrücke Hamburg' (2015-2017) coordinating the accommodation of migrating people from public housing in private apartments. Since 2016 she has worked as a doctoral student in the research project called 'Transcultural Practices in Postmigrant Theatre and in School' at Leuphana University Lüneburg (funded by BMBF 'Federal Ministry of Education and Research'), focusing on approaches of New Materialism/Material Feminism and Sensory Ethnography. She explores the method mixing (a methodology developed in the project) of three theatre productions with regard to transcultural educational processes. Using ethnographic methods, and in particular material and sonic approaches, she works at the interface of the use of different media and the related modes of thinking.